C. B Butler

Red Cloud, the Solitary Sioux

A Story of the Great Prairie

C. B Butler

Red Cloud, the Solitary Sioux
A Story of the Great Prairie

ISBN/EAN: 9783744677905

Printed in Europe, USA, Canada, Australia, Japan

Cover: Foto ©Thomas Meinert / pixelio.de

More available books at **www.hansebooks.com**

A Story of the Great Prairie.

BY

LIEUT.-COLONEL BUTLER, C.B.

AUTHOR OF "THE GREAT LONE LAND," "THE WILD NORTH LAND," ETC., ETC.

NEW AND CHEAPER EDITION.

"Like a wind, that shrills
All night in a waste land, where no one comes,
Or hath come, since the making of the world."
Tennyson.

LONDON
SAMPSON LOW, MARSTON & COMPANY
LIMITED
St. Dunstan's House
FETTER LANE, FLEET STREET, E.C.
1892

[*All rights reserved*]

Uniform with this Volume.

With numerous Illustrations, 2s. 6d.; gilt edges, 3s. 6d. each.

DICK CHEVELEY. By W. H. G. Kingston.
HEIR OF KILFINNAN. By W. H. G. Kingston.
OFF TO THE WILDS. By G. Manville Fenn.
THE TWO SUPERCARGOES. By W. H. G. Kingston.
THE SILVER CAÑON. By G. Manville Fenn.
UNDER THE METEOR FLAG. By Harry Collingwood.
JACK ARCHER: a Tale of the Crimea. By G. A. Henty.
THE MUTINY ON BOARD THE SHIP "LEANDER." By B. Heldmann.
WITH AXE AND RIFLE; or, The Western Pioneers. By W. H. G. Kingston.
RED CLOUD, THE SOLITARY SIOUX: a Tale of the Great Prairie. By Colonel Sir William Butler, K.C.B.
THE VOYAGE OF THE AURORA. By Harry Collingwood.
ERMONT GRANGE: a Tale of the 17th Century. By J. Percy Groves.
SNOWSHOES AND CANOES. By W. H. G. Kingston.
THE SON OF THE CONSTABLE OF FRANCE. By Louis Rousselet.
CAPTAIN MUGFORD; or, Our Salt and Fresh Water Tutors. Edited by W. H. G. Kingston.
THE CORNET OF HORSE: a Tale of Marlborough's Wars. By G. A. Henty.
THE ADVENTURES OF CAPTAIN MAGO. By Leon Cahun.
NOBLE WORDS AND NOBLE DEEDS.
THE KING OF THE TIGERS. By Rousselet.
HANS BRINKER; or, The Silver Skates. By Mrs. Dodge.
THE DRUMMER-BOY: a Story of the time of Washington. By Rousselet.
ADVENTURES IN NEW GUINEA: The Narrative of Louis Trégance.
THE CRUSOES OF GUIANA. By Boussenard.
THE GOLD-SEEKERS. A Sequel to the above. By Boussenard.
WINNING HIS SPURS: a Tale of the Crusade. By G. A. Henty.
THE BLUE BANNER. By Leon Cahun.
BEN BURTON; or, Born and Bred at Sea. By W. H. G. Kingston.
ADVENTURES ON THE GREAT HUNTING GROUNDS OF THE WORLD. By V. Meunier.

THE THREE DESERTERS; or, Ran Away from the Dutch. By M. T. H. Perelaer.
MY KALULU, PRINCE, KING, AND SLAVE. By H. M. Stanley.
ADVENTURES OF A YOUNG NATURALIST. By Lucien Biart. Edited and adaped by Parker Gillmore (Ubique).
THE STARTLING EXPLOITS OF THE DOCTOR. By Céliere.
THE BROTHERS RANTZAU: a Story of the Vosges. By Erckmann-Chatrian.
THE SERPENT CHARMER. By Louis Rousselet.
STORIES OF THE GORILLA COUNTRY. By Paul Du Chaillu.
THE CONQUEST OF THE MOON. By A. Laurie.
THE MAID OF THE SHIP "GOLDEN AGE." By H. E. Maclean.
THE FROZEN PIRATE. By W. Clark Russell.
THE MARVELLOUS COUNTRY. By S. W. Cozzens.
THE MOUNTAIN KINGDOM. By D. Lawson Johnstone.
A THOUSAND MILES IN THE "ROB ROY" CANOE. By John MacGregor ("Rob Roy").
BLACKS AND BUSHRANGERS; or, Adventures in Queensland. By E. B. Kennedy.
SIR LUDAR: a Tale of Love, War, and Adventure in the days of the great Queen Bess. By Talbot Baines Reed.
WILD LIFE UNDER THE EQUATOR. By Paul Du Chaillu.
MY RAMBLES IN THE NEW WORLD. By Lucien Biart.
NEW YORK TO BREST IN SEVEN HOURS. By A. Laurie.
ROB ROY ON THE BALTIC. By John MacGregor, M.A.
BEVIS. By Richard Jefferies. Edited by G. A. Henty.
THE COBBLER OF CORNIKERANIUM. By Rev. A. N. Malan.
STRANGE STORIES OF ADVENTURE. By Captain Mayne Reid.
THE AZTEC TREASURE-HOUSE. By T. A. Janvier.
HOW MARTIN DRAKE FOUND HIS FATHER. By G. Norway.
ROGER INGLETON, MINOR. By T. B. Reed.

LONDON: SAMPSON LOW, MARSTON & COMPANY, LTD.,
ST. DUNSTAN'S HOUSE, FETTER LANE, FLEET STREET, E.C.

CONTENTS.

CHAPTER I.

Our home in Glencar—A glimpse at the outside world—My parents—My schoolmasters—Donogh—Cooma-sa-harn—The eagle's nest—"The eagle is coming back to the nest"—Alone in the world—I start for the Great Prairie—Good-bye to Glencar 1

CHAPTER II.

Sunset in the wilds—Our first camp—Outlooks—The solitary Sioux—Losses—The Sioux again—A new departure—The *cache* at the Souri—The story of Red Cloud—The red man's offer 28

CHAPTER III.

To the West—Wapiti in sight—A stalk—A grand run—The sand-hills in sight—The finish—A noble beast—A gorgeous sunset—A vast landscape—The Hills of Life and Death 52

CHAPTER IV.

We reach the hills of the Wolverine—Something moves far out upon the plains—The wounded Cree—His story—

Adventure with a grizzly bear—Left alone—A long crawl for life—Hunger, thirst, and travail—A grizzly again—" The Great Spirit, like an eagle, looks down upon the prairie"—Saved—Watched 67

CHAPTER V.

An Assineboine camp—The trader McDermott—The chief " Wolverine "—Fire-water and finesse—The Assineboine war-party—A chance of a Cree scalp—The trader hears a well-known name—A big bid for murder, two hundred skins ! 82

CHAPTER VI.

The Sioux forecasts our course—On the watch—Directions —We separate—Red Cloud is seen far out on the plains —Rival tactics—Scent *versus* sight—A captured scout— The edge of the hills again—The signal fire . . . 97

CHAPTER VII.

The watched one halts—A light to the north-east—The Stonies find their mistake—Distant thunder—A light in the dark—The fire wind—*Sauve qui peut*—How the fire was lighted—We ride across the fire field—Enemies in sight—A dilemma—Between friend and foe—The scout throws in his lot with us—We ride to the rescue . . 111

CHAPTER VIII.

The fight—The Sioux and the swamp—The trader's triumph—Red Cloud fights on foot—The trader finds he has other foes to reckon with—The Assineboine draws a straight arrow—The trader's flight—Our losses and gains —Winter supplies—Our party is completed—" All's well that ends well." 129

CHAPTER IX.

We again go West—Hiding the trail—Red and white for once in harmony—Peace and plenty—An autumn holiday—We select a winter's camp—The Forks—Hut-building—Our food supply—The autumn hunt—The Great Prairie—Home thoughts—Indian instincts—The Lake of the Winds—Buffalo—Good meat—A long stalk—The monarch of the waste—A stampede—Wolves—The red man's tobacco 144

CHAPTER X.

Winter—Wolves—A night's trapping—A retreat—In the teeth of the north wind—The carcajou—A miss and a hit—News of Indians—Danger ahead—A friendly storm—The hut again 177

CHAPTER XI.

Winter comfort—Snowshoe-making—Snow and storm—The moose woods—A night camp—Memories—A midnight visitor—Maskeypeton the Iroquois—Danger—A moose hunt—Indian stalking—The red man's happy hunting-grounds—Plans—Raft-building 191

CHAPTER XII.

The winter draws to an end—A keen look-out—Signs—The break-up of the rivers—An ice block—The evening approaches—A noiseless arrow—The ice still fast—The ice floats—The war-cry of assault—A parley—We embark on the rafts—The hut in flames—On shore again—Freedom—Winter gone 212

CHAPTER XIII.

Horses wanted—New plans—We start south—The Prairie in Spring—No buffalo in sight—Starvation—A last resort—Buffalo at last—We fall in with Blood Indians—The camp—Tashota—A trade—Rumours of war—We depart from the Blood camp 228

CHAPTER XIV.

On the trail—A pursuit—The mark is overshot—A night march—Morning—The curtain rises—We are prisoners—Blackfeet—Penoquam—The Far-Off Dawn—His history—His medicine robe—Interrogations—New arrivals—The trader again 247

CHAPTER XV.

The council of the nation—The wager of battle—Signs of friendship—A private interview—A fair field and no favour—The trader on the scene—I leave the camp—I camp alone—The rock on the hill—The skulking figure—Preparations for the start—The race for life—The snake in the grass—A desperate strait—The odds are made even—Hand to hand—A last chance—Out of range . 260

CHAPTER XVI.

Revulsion—Home again—New plans—We depart for the mountains—The Hand hills—The great range—Home memories—A murderous volley—Donogh sees "the land beyond the grave"—Vain regrets—We enter the mountains—The island—A lonely grave—The Indian's home 279

CHAPTER XVII.

Signs of trouble—Reconnoitring—Precautions—We retire into the island—Daylight—The enemy shows himself—A search—He prepares to attack the island—A midnight storm—The raft—"Aim low, and fire fast"—In the whirl of waters—On the lip of the fall—The end of crime . . 297

CHAPTER XVIII.

The beginning of the end—Deeper into the mountains—The western slope—On the edge of the snow—The golden valley—It is all mine—Night thoughts—Last words—I see him no more 315

LIST OF ILLUSTRATIONS.

	PAGE
"Forbear," I cried, striking up the levelled barrel *Frontispiece*	
The solitary Sioux	33
The Sioux was now almost at the flank of the wapiti	63
Watching an opportunity, the trader addressed the leader of the band	94
Firing the prairie grass	120
We both sprang to our feet, and ran with all speed towards the animals	168
Strange footprints	214
I struck the iron butt heavily down upon the trader's head	277

bed of which was strewn with great boulders of rock, which were bare and dry in summer, but in winter scarcely showed over the surface. Between the big rocks there were pools and shallows, in which trout rose briskly at the midges in the early summer evenings. Whenever I think of that cottage home now, it seems to me to be always sunshine there. There must have been dark days, and wet ones, too, but I can't call them to mind. There was a large flat rock in the middle of the lawn half way down to the stream; one end of this rock was imbedded in the earth, the other leant out from the ground, giving shelter underneath. The only dark thing I can remember about the whole place was that hollow under the big stone. I used to sit in there on the very hot days, looking out across the stream upon the one road that led from the outer world into Glencar. When the weather was not too warm I lay on the top of the rock, looking at the same view. The road came into the glen over a hill that was four miles distant from our cottage; you could see the white streak crossing the crest of ridge, flanked on each side by the dark heather mountain. You caught sight of the road again as it came down the hillside, and here and there at turns, as it wound along the valley to the old five-arched bridge over the Carragh river, and then disappeared around the hill on which our cottage stood. When in the summer days I used to lie on the rock, or beneath its shadows, I was always thinking of the country that lay beyond the boundary ridge, the land to which the white road led when it dipped down behind the hill: that was the outside world to me, the glen was the inside one. As I grew older I came to know more of the outside world; I was able to climb higher up the steep hill behind the house, to get beyond the holly bushes out into the heather, and at last one day I reached the mountain-top itself. That was a great event in my life. It took me a long while to get up; the last bit was very steep; I had to sit down often amid the rocks and heather for want of breath. At last I gained the summit, and sank down quite exhausted on an old weather-beaten flat rock; I was just ten years old that day. Thirty years have gone by since then. I have climbed many a lofty mountain, lain down for weeks alone in forests and on prairies, but never have I felt so proudly conscious of success as I did that day. It was my first view of the outside world. How vast it seemed to me. The glen, my world, lay below, winding away amid the hills. All the streams, all the lakes, were unfolded to my sight, and out beyond the boundary ridge was the great open country. That was on one side—the glen side; but as I turned round to look beyond the mountain I had come up, I saw a sight that filled me with utter astonishment. Below me on that side there lay another glen, smaller than ours; then the hill rose again, but not to the height of the ridge on which I stood; and then, beyond the hill, there spread a great, vast waste of blue water—out—out, until I could see no more, where the sky came down upon it—the end of the world. It was the sea!

It was getting dark when I reached home that day. I went straight to my mother. "Mother," I said, "I have been to the top of Coolrue, and have seen the end of the world." I was fearfully tired; I had fallen over rocks coming down, and was bruised and torn; but what did it matter?

From that day forth the glen seemed a small place to me, and my mind was ever at work shaping plans for the future. About this time I began to read well. There were many old books in our cottage—books of travel and adventure, books of history, and one large old atlas that had maps of every country in the world in it, and in the corner of each map there was a picture of the people of the land, or of some wonderful mountain, or waterfall in it.

I read all these books in the long winter evenings; and many a time I sat poring over the maps, moving my finger up a long waving line of river, and travelling in fancy from island to island in the ocean.

And now I must say something about the inmates of our home. They were few. There was my mother, one old servant woman, and an old man who kept the garden tilled, drove in the cow at nightfall, and took care of everything. In truth there wasn't much to be taken care of. We were very poor, and we were all the poorer because we had once been rich—at least my mother had been. My father had died before I could remember him. His picture hung over the fireplace in our little parlour; and I can almost say that I do remember him, because the picture is confused in my mind with the reality, and I have a dim recollection of a man, tall, pale, and dark haired; but I can't add to it voice or action; it is only a vague kind of shadow. I was four years old when he died.

When I was seven years old my mother began to tell me about him. She used to sit often in the winter evenings looking at his picture; and as I sat at her feet, and she spoke of the old times, and how brave and honourable he was, I remember her voice used to tremble, and sometimes she would stop altogether.

As I grew older I learned more about him. I heard how we had first come to Glencar. It had been a favourite spot with my father in his early days, and whenever he could get leave of absence he used to come to it, for the lakes held plenty of trout, and the mountains had snipe, woodcock, and grouse upon them. After my father's marriage he had built the cottage. My mother was as fond of the glen as he was, and they used to come here for two or three months every year. When they had been three years married my father's regiment was ordered to India. My mother went too. I was only two years old at the time. When we reached India the regiment was ordered up country, for war had broken out. At the battle of Moodkee my father was severely wounded. After a while he was able to be moved down to the coast, where my mother had remained when the regiment went on service. From the coast he was invalided to England. The voyage home was a long one. We arrived in England in the end of summer.

The autumn and winter came. The cold told severely upon my father's weakened state, and when spring arrived it was evident he had but a short time to live. He wished to see Glencar again. With much difficulty he was brought to the cottage, to die.

In the upper end of the glen there was a wild secluded lake called Lough Cluen. A solitary island stood under the shadow of a tall mountain wall which overhangs the lake on one side. The island is little more than a rock, with yew-trees and ivy growing over it. A ruined church, half hidden in the trees, stood on this rock. It was my father's grave. He had wished to be buried in this lonely island, and his wish was carried out.

The little cottage, a few acres of land, the rugged mountain and the stream—now formed, with my mother's scanty pension, all our worldly possessions. Here, then, we took up our residence, and here I grew up, as I have already described—the glen my world; the mountain, lake, and stream my daily playground.

About a mile from our cottage there lived an old pensioner, who, forty years earlier, had followed Wellington from the Tagus to Toulouse. He had served his full term of twenty-one years, and being at the time of his discharge a staff-sergeant, his pension was sufficient to secure him a comfortable home for the rest of his days. He had a few acres of land around his cottage. He was the best angler in the glen. He was my earliest friend and guide with rod and gun on river, lake, and mountain side.

Sergeant MacMahon, formerly of her Majesty's 40th Regiment, was, when I knew him, a man who had passed his sixtieth year. Yet time, despite a score years of fighting and exposure, had dealt lightly with the old soldier, who still stood as straight as the ramrod he had so often driven home upon the bullet of his firelock. From him I got my first lessons in other things besides fishing and shooting. He taught me the "extension motions," the "balance step without gaining ground," the manual and platoon exercises, and the sword exercise. He also showed me the method of attack and defence with the bayonet.

He had the battles of the Peninsula by heart, and day after day did he pour forth his descriptions of how Busaco was won, and how Fuentes d'Onore had been decided, and how Lord Wellington had outmarched "Sowlt," as he used to call him, at Pampeluna, or had out-manœuvred Marmont at Torres Vedras. His personal adventures were told in another style. He had stories of bivouac—" bivoocing" he used to call it—of nights on outlying picquet, of escapes when patrolling, and of incidents in action, that he loved to recount to me as we sat by the river side waiting for a cloud to cross the sun before we tried a cast of flies over some favourite stream.

Once every quarter he set off in his mule-cart for Killarney to draw his pension. On these occasions I used to notice that his voice on his return sounded a little thick, and his face generally appeared flushed. But the next day all would be the same as usual. At the time I fancied that the exertion of the journey had been too much for him, or that the excitement of meeting some old comrades (there were three other Peninsula heroes in the town) had overcome him. He had been a great ally of my poor father's in earlier days, and to my mother he was equally attached. With all his stories of wars and fighting his heart was true and gentle. He was fond of all animals, knew the notes of every bird, and could tell the names of the trees in the wood, or the wild flowers by the river side. He was my outdoor schoolmaster. I learned from him many a pleasant lesson, and many a useful one too.

But I had another schoolmaster at this time. A mile down the glen from our cottage stood the priest's house, next to our own cabin-cottage the most comfortable residence in Glencar. In summer the old man was usually to be found in his garden, in winter in his little parlour, always buried in some old volume from his well-stored shelves.

His had been a curious career. His early student days had been passed in an old French city. In middle age he had been a missionary in the East, and at last he had taken charge of the wild district of Glencar, and settled down to the simple life of parish priest. Here he lived in the memory of his past life. Nearly half a century had gone since last his eyes had rested on the vine-clad slopes of the Loire, but it was ever an easy task to him to fling back his thoughts across that gulf of time, and to recall the great names that had risen in the sunrise of the century, and flashed such a glory over Europe that the lustre of succeeding time has shone faint and dim in contrast. He had seen the great emperor review his guards in the courtyard of the Tuileries, and had looked upon a group of horsemen that had in it Murat, Ney, Soult, Lannes, and Massena. How he used to revel in such memories! and what point such experience lent to the theme! He never tired talking of the great campaigns of the Consulate and Empire. I followed him in these reminiscences with rapt eagerness; the intensity of my interest gave increased ardour to his narrative, and many a winter's night sped rapidly while the old man, seated before his turf fire, rambled on from battle-field to battle-field, now describing to me the wonderful strategy of some early campaign in Italy, now carrying my mind into the snows of Russia, and again taking me back into the plains of France, to that last and most brilliant effort of warlike genius, the campaign of 1814.

At such times, the storm among the mountains would sometimes lend its roar in fitting accompaniment to the old man's story, and then the scene would change to my mind's eye as I listened. The little parlour would fade away, the firelight became a bivouac, and I saw in the grim outside darkness of the glen figures dimly moving; the squadrons charged; the cannon rumbled by; and the pine-tops swaying in the storm, were the bearskin caps of the old Guard, looming above smoke and fire!

Such were my schoolmasters; such the lessons they taught me.

The years passed quickly away. Notwithstanding my strong love of outdoor life, I devoted a good many hours every day to reading and study, and by the time I was fifteen years of age I had contrived to master a curious amount of general knowledge, particularly of history and geography, such as does not usually fall to the lot of boys of that age. I had a slight knowledge of Latin, was tolerably well acquainted with French, knew the habits, customs, and limits of every nation and tribe under the sun, and could travel the globe in fancy with few errors of time, distance, and position.

One companion I had in all these years who has not yet been mentioned—poor Donogh Driscoll, a wild and ragged boy, two years my junior.

In every adventure, in every expedition among the hills, Donogh was my attendant. He it was who used to wade into the reeds of Meelagh river to catch gudgeon for the baits for my night-lines in the Carragh; he carried my bag, later on, when my shooting time came; he marked with clear eye the long flight of the grouse pack down the steep slope of Coolrue; he brought me tidings of wild duck feeding on the pools and ponds amid the hills; he knew the coming of the wild geese to the lonely waste that lay beyond Lough Acoose; he would watch the pools in the Carragh river, and knew to a foot where the salmon lay. Faithful companion through all my boyish sports and pastimes, he shared too with me my dreams of enterprise, my hopes of adventure in the big outside world. Often as we sat on some rock high up on the heather-covered side of Seefin, looking out over the vast waste of ocean, he would wonder what it was like over there "beyant the beyant."

"You wont lave me here alone by myself, when you go away, sir?" he used to say to me. "It's lonely I'd be thin entirely."

"You'd have the fishing and shooting, Donogh," I would reply. "You'd have the hares and the salmon all to yourself when I was gone."

"What good would they be to me, ave you wasn't here with them?" he'd answer. "Sure the duck in November above in Cluen, and the salmon in 'Coose in April, and the grouse here on Seefin in August, would only remember me of the ould days when we hunted thim together."

I used at such times to promise him that whenever I did set out on my travels I would take him with me; and indeed, in all my plans for the future his companionship was always reckoned upon.

At the upper end of the glen, a narrow pass, or gap between two mountains, led out upon a wild and lonely lake, around the sides of which the mountains rose in a gloomy precipice of rock for many hundreds of feet.

Cooma-sa-harn, the name of the tarn that lay thus encompassed by cliffs, was a place that in my earliest wanderings filled me with feelings of awe and wonder. Strange echoes haunted it. Stones loosened from the impending cliffs rolled down into the lake with reverberating thunder, and their sullen splash into the dark water was heard repeated for many seconds around the encircling walls. On one side only was the margin of the lake approachable on level ground. Here loose stones and shingle, strewn together, formed a little beach, upon which the sullen waters broke in mimic waves; and here, too, the outflow of the lake escaped to descend the mountain side, and finally add its tribute to the many feeders of the Carragh river.

I was about twelve years of age when I first extended my wanderings to this lonely spot. Later on, Donogh and I made frequent expeditions to it. Its waters held no fish, and its shores rose too steep and high for game. But for all these deficiencies, Cooma-sa-harn held one wonder that sufficed to atone for every other shortcoming, and to make it a place of unceasing interest to us. It had an eagle's nest. There, 600 feet over the lake, in a smooth piece of solid rock, was a shelf or crevice, and in that hollow a golden eagle had built his nest year after year. From the little beach already mentioned we could see the birds at their work. From the top of the encircling cliffs we could look down and across at them too; but the distance in either case was great, and do what we would to obtain a closer view, we were always baffled by the precipitous nature of the mountain. We tried the mountain immediately above the nest, but could see nothing whatever of the smooth rock. We worked our way along the edge of the water, by the foot of the precipice, but were again baffled in the attempt. Projecting rocks hid the whole side of the cliff. We were fairly puzzled.

Many an hour we spent looking up from the shore at the coveted shelf, which it seemed we were never likely to learn more about. The eagles seemed to know our thoughts, for they frequently soared and screamed high above our heads, as though they rejoiced in our discomfiture. It was not alone in the spring and summer that we were reminded of our enemies thus perched on their inaccessible fortress. In the last hour of daylight of winter evenings a solitary speck over the valley would often be seen sailing downwards through space. It was the golden eagle going home to his ledge at Cooma-sa-harn.

It would be idle to deny that we both felt keenly our inability to get to this eagle's nest. During four years we had looked across the dark waters, had watched the old birds flying in and out, had seen the young ones sitting on the ledge, and had listened to their screams as their mother came down to them with a prey from the surrounding hills. There was in our cottage an old telescope that had belonged to my father in his early days. This I brought out one day, and looking through it, with elbows resting upon knees, and glass directed upon the shelf of rock, I could discern plainly enough the inmates of the rough nest; but all this only made more tantalizing our helplessness to scale the rock, or to descend from above to the projecting ledge. The day on which I brought out the telescope to make a closer survey of the spot, was bright with sunshine. As the hours grew later the sun moving towards the west, cast its light full upon the face of the nest, which had before been in shadow. The inequalities of the surface, and the formation of the cliffs around the large flat rock, became much more apparent than they had ever been before to me. Among other things, I observed that the ledge in which the nest was made was continued in a shallowed state along the face of the cliff until it touched the end at one side. I noticed also that on the top of the smooth-faced rock there was a ridge, or kind of natural parapet, and that this ridge was connected with a deep perpendicular cleft, or chimney, which opened at top upon the accessible part of the mountain. Scanning with the utmost attentiveness all these places, I began to see what I thought might prove a practicable line of approach to the much-desired nest. That it was possible to reach the top of the smooth-faced rock by means of the chimney shaft appeared tolerably clear, but this top ridge or parapet already mentioned, was fully forty feet above the ledge on which the nest stood.

By the time I had fully investigated all these details, so far as they could be examined by means of the telescope, the face of the cliff had become again involved in shadow, and it was time to turn our faces homewards for the evening; but enough had been discovered to give us food for conversation that night, and to raise high hopes that our efforts to reach the nest might yet prove successful.

We started early next morning for the top of the mountain ridge which looked down upon Cooma-sa-harn. On the previous evening I had taken the precaution of fixing the position of the top of the chimney, by getting it in line with two large boulders—one on the beach by the lake, the other some distance back from the shore. Arrived at the upper edge of the encircling basin I had no difficulty in bringing the two boulders, now at the further side from us, in line with each other, and then at the edge of the rocky rim we found a break in the rock, as though water in time of heavy rain had flowed down through it to the lake.

We entered this break, and descending cautiously soon found ourselves on the top of the flat rock. Below us lay the black pool of Cooma-sa-harn; on each side the flat parapet ended in steep mountain side; above us was the mountain top, accessible only by the hollow shaft through which we had descended. So far all had gone as the survey through the telescope had led us to hope—we had reached the top of the smoothed-faced rock; but the nest lay thirty or forty feet below us, still, apparently beyond our reach. We sat down on the top of the rock, reluctant to quit a spot so near to the long-coveted prize. The rock on which we rested was flanked on one side by a broken slant of mountain, down which a descent seemed possible if there was anything at hand to hold fast by; it was, however, bare of vegetation. It occurred to me now that a descent could be made down this slant by means of a rope, held by a second person standing on the ridge where we stood. The ledge which held the nest was situated so perpendicularly underneath as to be hidden altogether from our standpoint; but if my survey through the telescope had been correct, a person descending the slant should be able to reach that end of the ledge which I had seen in the sunlight extending on one side to the extremity of the rock. All that was required to put this theory to the test of practice was a strong rope some fifty feet long, which, held by one at the top, would act as a support to one of us while going down the slanting rock, and would afterwards afford help for a side movement along the narrow ledge to the nest itself. As I sat thinking out this plan one of the birds came soaring on moveless pinion from the mountain downwards towards the nest. He saw us long before he reached the ledge, and his loud and angry screams rang around the steep rock-walls, making strange echoes over the gloomy water.

We went home that evening full of the thought that we had at last discovered a means of getting to the eagle's nest. It would take a few days to obtain a rope of the length and strength necessary for the undertaking, and then a final effort would be made to solve the long-considered problem. It took me some days to procure the rope. I had consulted Sergeant MacMahon vaguely on the subject, but finding that he was opposed to it as being too dangerous, I had fallen back upon my own resources and those of Donogh. At length all preparations were completed; we had tested the rope by fastening one end of it to the fork of a tree and swinging out on the other end; we had also got an iron stake to fix in a crevice of the rock by which to attach the rope; with these and a few other necessary articles we set out early one morning for Cooma-sa-harn. We struck across the shoulders of Meelagh mountain, dipped into Glentahassig, and breasting up the steep side of Seefin came out on the edge of the cliff which looked down upon the dark lake. Descending the chimney, we were soon in our old position on the parapet rim of the large flat rock. We now set to work to fix the iron stake firmly between two detached rocks we fastened the rope securely to the stake, letting the loose end fall down the mountain by the edge of the perpendicular cliff. Now came the anxious moment; holding on by the rope, I began to descend the steep slanting face of the mountain. During the first twelve feet of the descent the work was easy enough. I was in sight of Donogh, whom I had directed to remain at the stake to see that all was right there. After a bit the hill side became steeper, a piece; of smooth rock occurred, and then there was a drop of about six feet, that hid Donogh from my view. When I had passed this drop the slant became again easier, and without much difficulty I gained the end of the ledge or groove upon which, but still distant from me, stood the nest. The real difficulty of the undertaking was now before me. I had to move along the ledge, a narrow shelf on the face of a perpendicular rock many hundred feet above the lake. It was now Donogh's work to unfasten the rope from the iron stake, and to move along the top, keeping pace with my progress on the ledge beneath. Every-thing depended upon his steadiness; but I had full faith in his strength and skill. . Up to this time all had been perfectly quiet at the nest; there was no sign of the old bird, nor could we hear the young ones screaming. I began very cautiously to move along the narrow ledge; step by step I went along As I proceeded forward the ledge became wider, and I found sufficient room for both my feet to stand together upon it. I could not yet see the nest, as the rock curved out towards its centre cutting off the view beyond. Arrived at the bend of the rock, I leant round the projection and peered anxiously forward. There, on the bare shelf of the ledge, lay the eagle's nest; two young eaglets sat dozing on the rock; around lay fragments of bones, tufts of fur torn from rabbits, feathers, and the dry stems of heather.

Another step and I was round the bend and at the nest. At this spot the shelf deepened considerably into the rock, leaving space sufficient to give standing-room without need of assistance. Intent only upon securing the young birds, I let go my hold of the rope, and seized the nearest eaglet before he was fully awake; the second one, hearing his companion scream, retreated further into the hole. Then it was that, looking outward, I saw the rope hanging, dangling loosely in mid-air. It was beyond my reach. For a moment the fearful position in which I so suddenly found myself caused me to sink upon the shelf. All the reality of my situation rushed full upon my mind. The rope hung fully five or six feet out over the abyss, for the rock above the ledge was formed like the roof of a cavern, projecting outward between me and Donogh's standpoint, and when I had let go my hold of the line it had swung out to its level fall. That I could get back over the space I had come, and ascend again to the parapet where Donogh stood, I knew to be impossible. To reach the line from the nest seemed quite hopeless. In Donogh lay my sole chance of relief. If by any means he could convey the rope to me, all would be well. If not, there seemed nothing save the awful alternative of death by starvation or the precipice before me. I shouted to Donogh what had happened. I told him that I could not reach the rope by fully three feet—that my sole chance of escape lay in his being able to follow my line of descent and bring the rope to me, leaving it fixed at the other end, in some part of the parapet above which would allow the line to pass from the nest to the end of the ledge.

 - The minutes now passed in terrible suspense. Donogh shouted to me that he was looking for a secure place to fasten the upper end of the rope to. I remained seated in the hollow, scarcely daring to think what the next few minutes might bring forth. Suddenly Donogh shouted to me, "The eagle is coming back to the nest." The news roused me from my stupor—the eagle was coming back! I crouched into the inmost recesses of the hollow. I still held one of the young birds in the bag round my waist, the other bird kept on the ledge at the further side from that by which I had approached. I had not much fear as to what the bird could do; I had a knife in my belt, and while an arm was free I knew I was more than a match for any bird. From the spot where I sat I could see out over the lake into the blue and golden sunshine.

All at once a large dark object crossed the line of light —soon recrossing it again as another wheel brought the huge bird nearer to its nest. Loud screams were now audible as the eagle became aware of something being wrong in the nest. Then there was the fierce beating of wings close outside the aperture, and the bird was perched on the edge of the rock, fiercely defiant, and making the echoes wild with her tumult. But amid all these surroundings I was only conscious of one fact. The eagle had struck the rope as it hung down in front of the opening; it had caught in the large outstretched pinion, and it was again within my reach, passing under the flapping wing of the bird as she stood clasping the rock ledge in her talons. There was not a moment to be lost; I thrust the young eagle at full arm's length towards the mother; she fluttered forward as I did so—the rope was again within my grasp. In an instant the eagle had relaxed her hold upon the rock, and clutching her young in her talons she went soaring downward to a lower ledge amid the cliffs. I thought I could never get away fast enough now. A complete change had come over my mind. I had learnt a lesson never to be forgotten; and my life, forfeited in a vain and foolhardy attempt to gain the eagle's nest at Cooma-sa-harn, was given back to me by the wild bird whose young I had come to rob from her. I now called out to Donogh that all was again right, and that he was to reverse his former practice to enable me to rejoin him. I passed safely back along the ledge, reascended the slant, and gained once more the parapet.

"Come, Donogh," I said when I was again with my companion, "let us leave this spot. Whatever happens, we will never again rob the nest or kill the young of birds or beasts. There is sport enough in the world for us without that."

On the edge of the mountain side we paused for a moment to look down upon Cooma-sa-harn, and the scene that lay beyond it. One eagle was screaming loudly from the nest, the other was sweeping down on outspread pinion from the purple wastes of Seefin.

I have dwelt long upon this episode in my early career, not so much from its importance, but because it did more to bring home to my mind certain truths that are often realized later on in life than anything that had happened to me up to my sixteenth year. I had soon to learn another, and a more bitter lesson.

The summer passed away; autumn came; the smell of dying leaves was in the woods of Carragh, the wind sighed amid the sedgy grass of Lough Cluen, the pine-trees by the priest's house moaned in the breeze. Things looked sad in the glen, but they wore even a sadder aspect in our little cottage. My mother was leaving me for ever.

One evening in October I was sitting with her in our little parlour; the flush was bright upon her cheek, her wasted hand was resting upon mine; she spoke to me in a low voice.

"You will soon be alone in the world," she said. "My life has only a little while to run. It is better that I should go. I could have been of little use to you in life, and I might have held you back in the world. In any case we must have parted soon, for your days could not have been spent here in this distant glen. The mountains and the lakes have been good friends to you, but it is time for you to leave them, and go forth to take your place in the work of the world. I should have wished you in your father's profession, but that could not be; we are too poor for that. Of one thing I am satisfied, no matter what the future may have in store for you, I feel you will be true to your father's name and to my memory. When I am gone you will have the world all before you to choose from. Bear well your part in life whatever it may be. Never be ashamed of your God, or of your country. And when the day is over and you kneel down in prayer, do not forget the two graves that lie far away in the little island of Lough Cluen."

About a week after this she passed quietly away, her hand clasped in mine, its pressure still speaking her affection long after the power of utterance had ceased.

When all was over I left the chamber of death, and moved out mechanically into the open air. Night had fallen; the moon was high over the glen. I walked onward, scarcely knowing whither I was going. I saw all things around as though in a dream. I passed through the wood behind the cottage; the moonlight shone bright upon the silver stems of the birch-trees; streaks of vapour lay in the hollows where the trees ended. I saw all these things, and yet my brain seemed unable to move.

I turned back from the end of the wood, passed the garden gate, and entered the little plot of ground in which my mother had been wont to tend flowers. It was now wild and desolate; grass grew on the walks; weeds and dead leaves lay around; only a few chrysanthemums were still in blossom—she had planted them in the past summer, and now their short life had lasted longer than her own—their pale flowers in the moonlight gave forth a sweet fragrance on the night air.

Death had chilled my heart; my eyes had been dry; my

brain seemed to have stopped its working; but here the scent of the flowers she had planted seemed all at once to touch some secret sympathy, and bursting into a flood of grief I bowed my head to the cold damp earth, and prayed long and earnestly to God.

A footstep on the walk roused me. The old priest had sought me out. "Weep not, my poor boy," he said, as he took my arm in his own and led me to the cottage. "You pray for your mother on earth. She is praying for you in heaven."

My boyhood was over. I was alone in the world. The winter deepened and passed, the spring dawned, and with its returning freshness and sense of life my old dreams of distant travel came again upon me. I determined to seek my fortune abroad, to go forth into the waste wilds of the earth. Glencar had but trained my mind and body to further flights. I must go forth to the struggle. It did not take long to arrange matters for this great change. My worldly possessions were easily realized; the cottage and little farm soon found a purchaser; the few mementoes of my father's life, the keepsakes which my mother had left me, were put carefully away in charge of the old priest; and I found myself the possessor of a few hundred pounds in money, a gun, my father's sword, a small case containing miniature portraits of my parents—with which to face the new life that lay before me. What was that life?

It was to be a life of wandering in the great wilderness of Western America. I had formed from books a pretty accurate idea of the great divisions of the Northern Continent of America which yet remained in the domain of untamed nature. I knew that far beyond the last settler's hut there lay a vast region of meadow, which finally gave place to a still vaster realm of forest, which in time yielded dominion to a wild waste of rock and water, until the verge of the Polar Sea. I knew too that these great divisions held roving and scattered tribes of Indians, sometimes at war with each other, always engaged in the pursuit of the wild beasts and birds whose homes were in those untamed wastes. More I did not need to know. I had trust, firm trust, in this great Nature, her lonely hill-tops, her wild lakes. The sigh of winds across November moors had had for me no sense of dreariness, no kinship with sorrow. Why should I dread to meet this world, whose aspects I loved so well, in the still wilder and grander scenes of an empire where civilized man was a total stranger?

Nor was I to be altogether alone in my travels. Donogh was to continue in his old sphere of companion and attendant. Together we had roamed the hill sides of Glencar; together we would tread the vast prairies, pine forests, and mountains of the American wilderness.

The day of our departure came.

It was a bright morning in early summer. We put our small baggage on Sergeant MacMahon's mule-cart, said good-bye to all our friends, and set out upon our road. The old sergeant insisted upon accompanying me as far as Killarney, from which place the train would take us to Cork, where the steamer for New York called. As we approached the priest's house, the old man stood at his gate waiting for us. His voice trembled as he said good-bye, and gave us his blessing. "God is everywhere, my boy," he said, as he wrung my hand. "Remember Him, and He will not forget you."

At the crest of the hill where the road left the valley, we stopped a moment to take a last look at the old glen. It lay deep in sunshine, every peak clear and cloudless in the summer heaven.

CHAPTER II.

Sunset in the wilds—Our first camp—Outlooks—The solitary Sioux—Losses—The Sioux again—A new departure—The cache at the Souri—The story of Red Cloud—The red man's offer.

A YEAR passed away.

It was summer again—summer hurrying towards autumn —and the day drawing near the evening.

The scene had changed.

Far away into the west stretched a vast green plain. No hills rose on either side; sky and earth met at the horizon in a line almost as level as though land had been water. Upon one side some scattered clumps of aspens and poplars were visible; save these nothing broke the even surface of the immense circle to the farthest verge of vision.

I stood with Donogh in the centre of this great circle, realizing for the first time the grandeur of space of land. We had travelled all day, and now the evening found us far advanced upon our way into the great plains. It was our first day's real journey. Early on that morning we had left behind us the last sign of civilized settlement, and now, as evening was approaching, it was time to make our first camp in the silent wilds. The trail which we followed towards the west approached some of those aspen thickets already mentioned. The ground, which at a little distance appeared to be a uniform level, was in reality broken into gentle undulations, and as we gained the summit of a slight ascent we saw that a small sheet of blue water lay between the thickets, offering on its margin a good camping-place for the night.

The sun had now touched the western edge of the prairie; for a moment the straight line of the distant horizon seemed to hold the great ball of crimson fire poised upon its rim; then the black line was drawn across the flaming disc; and then, as though melting into the earth, the last fragment of fire disappeared from sight, leaving the great plain to sink into a blue grey twilight, rapidly darkening into night.

We stood on the ridge watching this glorious going down of day until the last spark of sun had vanished beneath the horizon; then we turned our horses' heads towards the lake, still shining bright in the after-glow, and made our first camp in the wilds. It was easy work. We unloaded the pack-horse, unsaddled the riding-horses, hobbled the fore-legs, and turned them adrift into the sedgy grass that bordered the lakelet. Donogh had a fire soon going from the aspen branches, the lake gave water for the kettle, and ere darkness had wholly wrapt the scene we were seated before the fire, whose light, circled by the mighty solitude, grew ever brighter in the deepening gloom.

While here we sit before our first camp fire, it will be well that I should say something about our plans and prospects for the future.

Without adventure of any kind, and with only those difficulties to overcome that lie in all undertakings of life where real effort has to be made, we had reached the confines of civilization; a kind of frontier settlement, half wigwam half village, had sprung up to meet the wants of those traders in furs and peltries who form the connecting link between the red man of the wilds and his white brothers in civilization. This settlement marked, as it were, the limits of the two regions—on one side of it lay judge and jury, sheriff, policemen, court-house, and fenced divisions; on the other, the wild justice of revenge held empire, and the earth was all man's heritage.

I had only delayed long enough in this frontier settlement to procure the necessary means of travel in the wilds. I had purchased four good ponies, two for saddle use and two to act as pack animals for our baggage—arms we already possessed—ammunition, blankets, knives, a couple of copper kettles, a supply of tea, sugar, salt, pepper, flour, and matches, a few awls, and axes. These I had obtained at one of the Indian trading stores, and, keeping all our plans as much as possible to ourselves, we had on this very morning set our faces for the solitude, intent upon holding on steadily into the west during the months of summer that yet remained. By winter time I counted upon having reached the vicinity of those great herds of buffaloes which kept far out from the range of man, in the most remote recesses of the wilderness, and there we would build a winter hut in some sheltered valley, or dwell with any Indian tribe whose chief would bid us a welcome to his lodges.

Of the country that lay before us, or of the people who roved over it, I knew only what I had pictured from books in the old glen at home, or from the chance acquaintances I had made during our stay in the frontier settlement; but when one has a simple plan of life to follow, it usually matters little whether the knowledge of a new land which can be derived from books or men has been obtained or not; time is the truest teacher, and we had time before us and to spare.

We ate our supper that night with but few words spoken. The scene was too strange—the outlook too mysterious, to allow thoughts to find spoken expression.

Had I been asked that night by Donogh to define for him the precise objects I had in view in thus going out into the wilds, I do not think that I could have given a tangible reason. I did not go as a gold-seeker, or a trapper of furs, or a hunter of wild animals. We would follow the chase, trap the wild animals of the streams or marshes, look for gold too; but it was not to do all or any of these things that I had left civilization behind me. This great untamed wilderness, this home of distance and solitude, this vast unbroken dominion of nature—where no fence crossed the surface of the earth, where plough had never turned, where lakes lay lapped amid shores tenanted only by the moose and the rein-deer—all this endless realm of prairie, forest, rock, and rapid, which yet remains the grandest domain of savage nature in the world, had had for me a charm, not the less seductive because it could not then find expression in words, or give explanation for its fancy. Enough that we went forth with no sinister object in view against man or beast, tree or plain; we went not to annex, to conquer, nor to destroy; we went to roam and rove the world, and to pitch our camps wheresoever the evening sun might find us.

Before turning in for the night I left the light of the fire, and wandered out into the surrounding darkness. It was a wonderful sight. The prairie lay wrapt in darkness, but above, in the sky, countless stars looked down upon the vast plain; far away to the south, the red glow of a distant fire was visible; our own camp fire flamed and flickered, sheding a circle of light around it, and lighting up the nearer half of the lakelet and the aspen clumps on the shore. At times there passed over the vast plain the low sound of wind among grasses—a sound that seemed to bring

The Solitary Sioux.

[*Page* 33.

to the ear a sense of immense distance and of great loneliness. For a moment I felt oppressed by this vague lonely waste; but I thought of the old priest's words, and looking up again from the dark earth to the starlit heavens, I saw all the old stars shining that I used to know so well in the far-away glen at home. Then I knelt down on the prairie, and prayed for help and guidance in the life that lay before me.

Daylight had broken some time when I awoke, and rose from my blanket bed for a survey of the morning. How vast seemed the plain! Far away it spread on all sides; all its loneliness had vanished; it lay before me fresh, fair, and dew-sparkled—our trail leading off over distant ridges, until it lay like a faint thread vanishing into the western space.

As my eye followed this western path, I noticed a mounted figure moving along it about a mile distant, approaching our camping-place at an easy pace. I called to Donogh to get the fire going and make ready our breakfast, and we had barely got the kettle on the flames when the stranger had reached our camp.

He rode right up to the spot where we stood, alighted from his horse, and throwing the reins loose on the animal's neck, came forward to meet me. I advanced towards him and held out my hand in welcome. A large shaggy hound, half deer half wolf-dog, followed closely at his heels. We

D

shook hands; the stranger seated himself near the fire, and silence reigned for a few minutes. My experience in the settlement had taught me the few rules of Indian etiquette, and I busied myself in helping Donogh to complete the arrangement for breakfast before questioning the new comer upon his journey or intentions.

Our breakfast was soon ready. I handed a cup of tea and a plate of pemmican to the Indian, and sat down myself to the same fare. When we had eaten a little, I addressed our guest, asking him his length of journey and its destination.

He had come many days from the west, he said in reply. His destination was the west again, when he had visited the settlement.

Then it was my turn to tell our movements. I said exactly what they were. I told him that we had come from a land across the sea, and that we were going as far as the land would take us into the north-west, that we were strangers on the prairie, but hoped soon to learn its secrets and its people.

While the meal proceeded I had opportunity of studying the appearance, dress, and accoutrements of our guest. They were remarkable, and quite unlike anything I had before seen.

He was a man in the very prime of life; his dress of deer-skin had been made with unusual neatness; the sleeves fully interwoven with locks of long black hair, were covered with embroidered porcupine-quill work, which was also plentifully scattered over the breast and back; the tight-fitting leggings and sharp-pointed moccasins were also embroidered.

He carried across his saddle-bow a double-barrelled English rifle; but the ancient weapons of his race had not been abandoned by him, for a quiverful of beautifully shaped Indian arrows, and a short stout bow, along the back of which the sinews of the buffalo had been stretched to give it strength and elasticity, showed that he was perfectly independent, for war or the chase, of modern weapons and ammunition.

As head covering he wore nothing, save what nature had given him,—long jet-black hair, drawn back from the forehead and flowing thickly over the shoulders. A single feather from an eagle's tail formed its sole ornament. The end of the feather, turned slightly back, was tied with the mystic "totem" of chieftainship. His horse, a stout mustang of fourteen hands high, carried the simple trappings of the plains—the saddle of Indian workmanship, the bridle, a single rein and small snaffle with a long larêt attached, and from the neck was suspended the leather band by means of which the rider could lay his length along the horse's flank farthest from his enemy while he launched his arrows beneath the animal's neck, as he galloped furiously in lessening circles around his foe.

He spoke English with an accent that showed he had been taught in western schools; but though the language was English the manner of its utterance was wholly Indian; it was Indian thought put into English words, and accompanied by the slow and dignified action of Indian gesture. He took the tobacco pouch which I offered him when our meal was finished, filled his greenstone pipe, drew a lighted stick from the fire, and began to smoke quietly, while his dark eye seemed to rest upon the ashes and embers of the fire before him. But the keen sharp eye was not idle; and one by one the articles of our little kit, and the horses which Donogh had now driven in preparatory to saddling for the day's journey, had been conned over in his mind.

After smoking for some time he spoke. "Does my brother know what he will meet on the path he is following?" he asked. I told him that I had only a very shadowy idea of what was before us; that I intended going on from day to day, and that when the winter season came I hoped to build a tent, and live in it until the snow went, and I could wander on again. I told him, too, that I was not going to seek for gold, or to trade for furs and peltries, but only to live on the prairies—to meet the red men, to breathe the open air of the wilderness, and roam the world. Then I asked some more questions about his own intentions. I asked him how it was that he was all alone on this long journey; for I knew that the Indians were in the habit of moving in parties, and that it was most unusual for them to be seen travelling alone. He replied that he travelled by himself partly from choice and partly from necessity.

"I am the last of my people," he said, "the last of the Mandan branch of the Sioux race. It is true that I might find companions among the Ogahalla or Minatarree branches of my nation, but then I would have to dwell with them and live their lives. The work I have to do can only be done by myself; until it is finished I must follow a single trail. I have for companion this dog, an old and oft-tried friend."

I then asked him if he had seen much of the prairie.

He replied that he knew it all; that from the Stony Mountains to the waters of the Lake Winnipeg, from the pine forest of the north to the sage-bush deserts of the Platte, he had travelled all the land. Shortly after this he rose to depart. We shook hands again; he sprang lightly into his saddle and rode off towards the east. When he was gone we rolled up our blankets and traps and departed on our western way. It was the morning after the second night from this time that we found ourselves camped at break of day in the valley of a small stream which flowed south toward the Souri river. So far, all had gone well with us. We had met with no difficulty, and had begun to think that our western course would continue to be marked by unchanging success. On this morning, however, we awoke to other thoughts.

Two of our horses had disappeared. At first we thought that they had strayed farther away than the others, but after searching far and near over the prairie we came to the conclusion that they had been stolen. It was a cruel blow. At first I felt stunned, but bit by bit I thought the matter out and determined to face the difficulty. After all it might have been worse, we had still two horses left; we would put all our supplies on one animal, and ride by turns on the other. We would camp early, let the horses feed while it was yet daylight, and keep them picketted by our camp at night. So, putting a good face upon the matter, we got our things together, and set out about mid-day on our western road. Donogh was on foot leading the pack-horse; I rode slowly on in front. It still wanted two full hours of sunset when we halted for the evening. We turned out the horses to graze. I took my gun and sat down on a ridge to watch them as they fed. It was then that the loss we had suffered seemed to come heaviest to me. As I sat there I thought over the length of time we must now take to reach the distant prairies of the west, and my heart sank at the prospect of slow and weary travel, with the chances of further losses that would leave us helpless upon the vast plains.

As I sat thus brooding upon our misfortunes I noticed one of the horses raise his head from feeding and gaze steadily back upon our trail. Looking in that direction I saw a solitary figure approaching upon horseback. A glance sufficed to tell me that it was the same man who had visited our camp two mornings earlier. For a moment I involuntarily connected his presence with our loss; but then it occurred to me that he would not seek our camp again if he had stolen our horses, and I remembered too that he had told me he was going west when he had visited the frontier settlement.

He came up to where I was, and shook hands with me without dismounting, his dog keeping close by his horse's flank. I told him of our loss, and spoke freely of its serious nature to us. I said we were now reduced to only two horses, and asked him frankly if he could do anything to help me. He listened quietly, and when I had done speaking he said,—

"The prairie without horses is like a bird without wings. When I left you two days ago, I thought you would soon learn that life in the wilderness was not all so easy. Your horses have been taken by some Salteaux Indians. I saw their trail at mid-day to day as I came hither. They are far away from here by this time. I am sorry for you," he went on, " for you are the first white man I have ever met who came out to this land of ours with the right spirit. You do not come to make money out of us Indians: you do not come to sell or to buy, to cheat and to lie to us. White men think there is but one work in life, to get money. When you told me your story a couple of mornings since I thought it was my own life you were telling me of. Now you ask me if I can help you to get back the horses which have been taken from you. I could get them back, but it would take time and long travel. I can do better for you, my brother; I can get you new horses in place of the old ones."

I scarcely believed the words I listened to, so good was the news they told me.

"If you like," he went on, "to learn the life of the prairie, I will teach it to you. Do not sorrow any more for your loss; we will camp here to-night, and to-morrow we will see what can be done."

So saying he unsaddled his horse, and throwing saddle, bridle, and blanket on the ground, sat down by the fire and began to smoke. When supper was ready I gave him a share of our meal, and he camped with us that night.

We were astir very early on the next morning. In order to travel with greater speed the Indian divided our baggage into three portions, which he placed equally on the three horses, adjusting the loads in front and behind the saddles. This enabled Donogh to ride; and although it put a heavy load on all the horses, it would only be for one day. What plan the Indian had formed I had at this time no idea of, but I already looked upon him in the light of a true benefactor, and I was prepared to follow implicitly his guidance.

The sun had just risen when we quitted our camping-place and took the old trail to the west; but an hour or so after starting, the Indian, who led the way, quitted the trail and bent his course across the plain in a south-westerly direction. During some hours he held his way in this direction; there was no trail, but every hill and hollow seemed to be familiar to our guide, and he kept his course in a line which might have appeared to me to be accidental, had I not observed that when we struck streams and water-courses the banks afforded easy means of crossing. About mid-day we quitted the open prairie, and entered upon a country broken into clumps of wood and small copses of aspen; many lakelets were visible amid the thickets; and the prairie grouse frequently rose from the grass before our horses' feet, and went whirring away amid the green and golden thickets of cotton-wood and poplars.

It was drawing towards evening when our little party emerged upon the edge of a deep depression which suddenly opened before us. The bottom of this deep valley was some two or three miles wide; it was filled with patches of bright green meadow, and dotted with groups of trees placed as though they had been planted by the hand of man. Amidst the meadows and the trees ran a many-curved stream of clear silvery water, now glancing over pebble-lined shallows, now flowing still and soft in glassy unrippled lengths.

Drawing rein at the edge of this beautiful valley, the

Indian pointed his hand down towards a small meadow lying at the farther side of the river. "There is the Souri river," he said, "and those specks in the meadow at the far side are my horses. Our halting-place is in the wood where you see the pine-tops rise above the cotton-trees." So saying he led the way down the ridge. We soon became lost in the maze of thickets in the lower valley; but half an hour's ride brought us to the meadows bordering upon the river, and soon we gained the Souri itself. The Indian led the way into the stream, and heading for a shelving bank on the other side ascended the opposite shore. On the very edge of the stream at the farther side stood the grove of pines which we had seen from the upper level half an hour before.

Into this grove we rode, pushing through some poplar brushwood that fringed its outer edges. Once inside this brushwood, the ground beneath the pine-trees was clear. Almost in the centre of the "bluff" an Indian lodge was pitched. It stood quite hidden from view until we were close upon it. I soon saw that the pine bluff occupied a "point" on the river; that is to say, the stream formed almost a complete curve around it, encircling the bluff upon three sides. From the doorway of the lodge a view could be obtained of the ground within and beyond the narrow neck formed by the river's bend as they approached each other.

Immediately on arrival the Indian had dismounted.

"Here," he said, "is my home for the present, and whenever I wander into these regions. To-night we will rest here, and to-morrow continue our way towards the west. This morning you gave me food from your small store; to-night you will eat with me."

So saying he set about his preparations for evening.

From a branch overhead he let down a bag of dry meat and flour; from a pile of wood close by he got fuel for a fire in the centre of the lodge; from a cache in the hollow trunk of one of the trees he took a kettle and other articles of camp use; and before many minutes had passed our evening meal was ready in the lodge, while the horses were adrift in the meadow beyond the "neck," with the others already grazing there.

Before our meal was finished evening had closed over the scene, and in the shadow of the spruce pines it was quite dark. An ample supply of dry fuel was piled near the tent door, and the fire in the centre of the lodge was kept well supplied. It burned bright and clear, lighting up the features of the Indian as he sat before it cross-legged upon the ground. He seemed to be buried in deep thought for some time. Looking across the clear flame I observed his face with greater attention than I had before bestowed upon it. It was a handsome countenance, but the lines of care and travail showed deeply upon it, and the expression was one of great and lasting sadness. In the moments of action in the work of the prairie this sad look had been less observable ; but now, as he sat in repose, looking intently into the fire, the features had relapsed into their set expression of gloom.

At last he raised his head and spoke.

"You must know my story. When you have heard it, you can decide for yourself and your friend what course you will follow. I will tell you how it has happened that I am here, and why I am going west so soon. Listen to me well."

Then, as we sat around the fire in the centre of the lodge, he thus began:—

"Among men I am called 'Red Cloud.' It is now more than ten years since I joined my people, the Mandan Sioux, on the shores of Minnie Wakan. They had just been driven back by the soldiers of the United States. My tribe had dwelt on the coteau by the edge of the great Pipe Stone quarry. The buffalo were numerous over all the surrounding prairies. We were then at peace with the Americans. They had purchased from our chiefs the valley of the Bois des Sioux, the Red River, and the land of the Otter Tail. We had given up all that fair region of lake and meadow, hill and copse, which still carries the name we gave it, "Minnesota," or the Land of Sky-coloured Water. The white waves were coming on faster and faster from the east, and we, the red waves, were drifting before them farther and farther into the west. I dwelt with my people at the Minnie Wakan, or the Lake of the Evil Spirit. It is a salt and bitter water which lies far out in the great prairie; but it was a favourite haunt of the buffalo, and the wapiti were many in the clumps of aspen and poplar along its deep-indented shores.

"For a time after the surrender of Minnesota peace reigned between our people and the white man; but it was a hollow peace; we soon saw it could not last. Many of our old chiefs had said, 'Take what the white man offers you. Let us fix the boundaries of our lands far out towards the setting sun, and then we will be safe from the white man, who ever comes from the rising sun. We will then live at peace with him.'

"Well, we went far out into the prairie; but the white man soon followed us. The buffalo began to leave us; the wapiti became scarce around the shores of Minnie Wakan. We were very poor. At the time when I joined my people an army had taken the field with the avowed intention of driving the remnants of our once strong race across the great Missouri river. I could not remain an idle spectator of a struggle in which my people were fighting for home and for existence.

"It is true I had been brought up a Christian, educated in a school far away in Canada with white people, and taught the uselessness of contending with civilization; but what of that?

"Blood is stronger than what you call civilization; and when I got back again into the prairie, and to the sky-bound plain—when I felt beneath me the horse bound lightly over the measureless meadow—and when I knew that my people were about to make a last fight for the right to live on the land that had been theirs since a time the longest memory could not reach—then I cast aside every other thought, and turned my face for ever towards the wilderness and my home.

"The Mandans received me with joy. As a boy I had left them; as a man I returned. My father was still a chief in the tribe, and from his horses I had soon the best and fastest for my own.

"I had forgotten but few of the exercises which an Indian learns from earliest childhood. I could ride and run with the best of them, and in addition to the craft and skill of the wilderness, I had learned the use of the weapons of civilization, and the rifle had become as familiar to hand and eye as the bow had been in the days of my boyhood.

"Soon we heard that the Americans were advancing towards the coteau. We struck our lodges by the Minnie Wakan, fired the prairie, and set out for the south. By the edge of the coteau our scouts first fell in with the white men. We did not fire, for the chief had decided that we would not be the first to fight, but would seek a parley when we met.

It was my work to meet the white people and hear what they had to say. I was able to speak to them.

"I approached their scouts with a few of my men, and made signs that we wished to talk. Some of the white people rode forward in answer, and we met them midway. I began by asking what they wanted in our land; that they were now in our country, and that our chief had sent me to know the meaning of their visit.

"One of them replied that they had come by order of the Great Father at Washington; that the land belonged to him from sea to sea; and that they could ride through it where they willed.

"While we spoke, one of my braves had approached a large, strongly-built man who rode a fine black horse. All at once I heard the click of a gun-lock. In token of peace we had left our guns in the camp; we carried only our bows. The gun thus cocked was in the hands of the white man riding the black horse. It has been said since that he did the act fearing that the Indian who stood near meant harm; if so, his belief was wrong, and it cost him his life. The Indian heard the noise of the hammer. With a single bound he was at the horse's shoulders, had seized the barrel of the gun and twisted it from the white man's hands. As he did so, one barrel exploded in the air. An instant later the other was discharged full into the white man's breast, and before a word could be uttered, the brave was in his saddle, driving the black horse furiously over the plain. There was nothing for it but to gallop too; we were well mounted, and the shots they sent after us only made our horses fly the faster. We reached our people. The war had begun.

"I will not tell you of that war now. In the end we were beaten, as we always must be. Two men will beat one man, twenty will do it faster.

"Many of us were killed; many more fled north into English territory. My father was among the latter number. I remained with a few others in the fastnesses of the Black Hills.

"Now listen to me.

"My father, the old chief, went, I have said, north into British land. I never saw him again. A year later I also sought refuge in this region, and this is the story I gathered from the few scattered people of our tribe.

"My father, 'The Black Eagle,' had been invited to a trader's house on the banks of the Red River, not fifty miles from where we now are. This trader had given him spirit to drink. In the spirit he had put laudanum. My father drank unsuspectingly, and was soon plunged into deep unconscious sleep. From that sleep he woke to find himself in the hands of the Americans.

"It was the depth of winter. His betrayers had bound him while asleep upon a sledge drawn by a fast horse. In the dead of night they had carried him to the American lines at Pembina, and there sold him to the Yankee officer, bound and helpless.

"The price paid was 500 dollars. A week later the old chief, my father, was hanged as a traitor in sight of the very river by whose banks he had been born.

"You wonder what has brought me to these northern lands? My father's spirit has brought me. Five times since that day I have sought my father's murderer, and each time my search has been fruitless. Yes, through all these years, through many changes, and from far distant places, I have come here to seek revenge. Again I have been baffled. The man for whom I look has gone far out on the plains, trading with the Crees and Blackfeet. I learned this two days ago, in the settlement, and at once turned my horse's head towards the west, determined to seek this spot, get my horses, pack up, and follow the trail of my father's murderer into the great prairie.

"By chance I saw you again this morning. You are different from all the white men I have ever met. You seem to love the wilderness for its wildness, as a bird loves the air for its freedom. Well, it is for that that I love it too. In our old times, when the Sioux were strong and powerful, the young men of the tribe, the best and bravest, used to swear an oath of brotherhood and lasting friendship to the young braves of other tribes. That oath meant, that if they met in battle, or in danger, the life of one was sacred to the other.

"To you I will give that promise and that oath. I have no friends but my horse and dog. My people are scattered far and wide over the wilderness. Most of those who were with me ten years ago are now dead. I am an outcast on the earth; but I am free, and fear no man. We will together roam the wilderness; at any time if you desire it, you are free to part. I do not ask your assistance to revenge the wrongs I have suffered. That shall be my own work. For the rest I have quarrel with no man. Ever since that war with the Americans I have fired no hostile shot at a red man of any race or tribe. When attacked I have defended myself; but I have joined no tribe to fight another tribe. If I fall into the hands of my enemies I know that my father's death will be my death—that as his bones were left to bleach in sight of the land in which he was born, so mine would be also gibbetted, as a warning to the wretched remnants of my race who yet live, spectral shadows, on the land that once had owned the dominion of the Sioux." Red Cloud has spoken."

The Indian ceased speaking. The fire still burned bright and clear.

As the light of the evening grew fainter, and darkness closed over the scene, the sounds of the wilderness fell distinctly upon our ears—the ripple of the river, the lonely cry of grey owls, the far-off echo of some prowling wolf.

For some minutes the silence of the lodge remained unbroken. I was too much affected by the story I had listened to to speak, but I held out my hand to the Sioux and shook his, in silent token that henceforth we were brothers.

CHAPTER III.

To the West—Wapiti in sight—A stalk—A grand run—The sand-hills in sight—The finish—A noble beast—A gorgeous sunset—A vast landscape—The Hills of Life and Death.

At dawn on the following morning we departed from the camp on the Souri, holding our way towards the west.

It was a fair fresh morning; the summer, verging towards autumn, held already in its nights and first hours of day the faint breathings of the northern chill of frost; the dew lay upon the ground in silvery sheen and glitter; all was yet green in meadow and willow copse; the current of the river ran with fresh and sparkling eagerness, and from its mimic rapids on the shallows little streaks of vapour rose—an indication that the air of the morning was cooler than the water of the river. Over all the scene, over the hill and the valley, on wood and stream and meadow, there lay a sense of the perfect rest and ceaseless quiet of the wilderness.

The path which the Indian took led for awhile along the valley of the Souri. At times it climbed the higher ridges that bordered on the north and south the alluvial meadows which fringed the river, and at times it dived into the patches of poplar thicket and oak-wood copse that dotted alike both hill and valley.

The Sioux was mounted on the same horse which he had ridden on the previous day, but a change had fallen on the fortunes of Donogh and myself. We now bestrode two close-knit wiry horses, whose sleek coats and rounded flanks showed that the early summer had been to them a season of rest, and that they had profited by the quiet of the last few days to inprove the "shining hours" on the fertile meadows of the Souri. We went along now at an easy pace, half walk, half trot—a pace which got over the ground with little fatigue to man and horse, and yet made a long day's journey out of the travel hours of daylight.

As the morning wore towards mid-day, and the trail led at times over places which commanded a wider view of river and valley, the Indian riding in front watched with keen glance each open space, and often cantered his horse to the upper level for a better survey of the higher plateau. All at once he stopped, and lay low upon his horse. He was some distance ahead of us, but near enough to be seen by me. I at once pulled up. Presently the Sioux came back to where we were standing. There were wapiti in sight, he said; I could go forward with him on foot and see them. We left our horses with Donogh, and went forward very carefully to the spot from whence the Sioux had seen the game. It was at the end of a willow copse. From here, looking partly through and partly over the leaves of some small aspens, I now saw at the farther side of an open space which was more than a mile across, a herd of large dun-coloured animals, and high above all stood one stag, erect and stately, looking in our direction, as though the echo of our approach had apparently reached him.

These were the wapiti, the giant red-deer of North America. The monarch of the group was evidently a gigantic specimen of his race, who, with the true kingship of nature, kept watch and ward over his weaker subjects, and did not, as in modern society, delegate that chiefest function of leadership to other less favoured mortals. And now how was this noble animal to be reached? The forest of antlers fixed and rigid showed that his gaze was fixed too upon the spot from whence an attack might be expected.

The Indian, surveying the ground for a moment, whispered to me, "We cannot approach him from this side; his suspicions are already aroused. And yet he is a noble prize, and well worth the trouble of the chase. There is only one way it can be done. Where the ground rises to the north, on the right of where we now stand, there is a large open expanse of prairie, once on that level plain it would rest with our horses to reach him: the few scattered clumps of trees growing upon it cannot hide him from our view; he must be ours. So far, he has neither seen nor winded us; he has simply heard a sound; he is watchful, not alarmed. Let us see what can be done."

Having said this, he drew back a little, plucked the heads of a few long grasses growing near, and flung the dry light seeds into the air. They floated towards the east; the wind was from the west. "Now," he said, having noted this, "we must retrace our steps along the path we have come for some distance, then it will be possible to get round yonder beast. We shall see."

So saying, we fell back with easy and quiet footsteps, and, followed by Donogh, were soon a long way from the open glade and its denizens. Having gained the required distance, the Sioux stopped again to detail to us the further plan of attack; it was simply this. We were to make a long détour to the south; when the right position had been attained, we would advance in the direction of the herd, emerging upon the clearing full in view of the stag, whose course, the Indian said, would when alarmed at once lead up the wind, or towards the west. This, however, was not the direction in which the Indian wanted him to go. How then was it to be done? We shall presently see.

Striking from the trail towards the south, we pursued our way through mixed open and thicket country until the required distance had been gained, then bending round to the west we gradually drew nearer to the open ground on which the wapiti had last been seen.

When the neighbourhood of the open space was reached the Indian again stopped, and spoke his last directions to us. "Wait here until you hear a wolf cry twice; at the second call ride straight to the north at an easy pace. When you emerge upon the open you will be in sight of the big stag, but a long way from him; after looking at you for a moment he will trot away to your left; then you must ride straight up the hill until you gain the level plain on the summit; you will then see the stag not very far from you. I will be there too. Let the pack-horses follow quietly to the upper ground." Having said this, the Indian turned his horse to the west, and was soon lost to sight in the thickets and undulations of the ground.

About a quarter of an hour passed; at length we heard the cry of a wolf sounding a long way off to north and west. We listened anxiously for the second signal. It soon came, and as it died away in the silence of space we put our horses into a trot and rode straightforward. Two minutes' riding brought us to the edge of the prairie, on the other side of which, but now some miles distant, we had first looked upon the wapiti. As we entered upon the open ground we caught sight of the herd, still in the same spot. The chief had apparently ceased to reconnoitre, for his huge antlers no longer towered aloft; he was quietly feeding like the others. We now rode at a walk straight for the herd. Our presence in their area of vision was almost instantly detected, and all heads were lifted from the ground to examine the enemy; then the leader led the way, and the band, following his steps, filed off quietly towards the wind.

I was sorely disposed to follow, but, remembering the directions of the Indian I put my horse into a sharp canter, and held straight for the high ground, the edge of which was visible in our front. As we crossed the centre of the open space, a shot rang out some distance to our left, and then there came a faint Halloo! borne down the west wind. Still we held on our course, and climbing the steep ridge, gained the open prairie land above. As our heads topped the ridge, we beheld a sight that made our hearts beat fast with excitement. There, not half a mile distant, going full across the plain, was the herd of wapiti, still close grouped together; behind them, and not more than three hundred yards distant from them, rode the Indian, his horse held full within his pace but going at a free gallop across a level plain, on which the grass grew short and crisp under a horse's hoof. I did not need the waving arm of the Indian to tell me what was to be done. My horse seemed to realize the work too; I shook free his rein, and was soon in fast pursuit of the flying stag.

There are many moments in wild life, the minute sensations

of which are worth the oft-indulged recollections of after time—moments when every nerve is strained to action, when eye and ear and nostril are filled with the sound, the sight and the scent of nature's freshness—and when the animate or inanimate thing that bears us, the horse or the canoe, become sharers in the keenness of our progress, and seem to quiver with the excitement of our impetuous onset; there are such moments in the wild life of the wilderness, amply sufficient to outweigh the hardships and privations of travel and exposure in a land where the sky is the roof, and the ground the bed, the table and the chair of the wayfarer.

Much toil and trouble had befallen us since that distant day when we had quitted the little roof of our far-away home; the goal aimed at had often seemed a long way off, and many had been the obstacles that had forced in between us and the wild life I had sought to reach; but now it was ours—fully, entirely ours; and as my horse, entering at once into the spirit of the chase, launched himself gamely along the level sward I could not repress a ringing cheer, the natural voice of freedom found, and of wild life fully realized.

I was now in wild pursuit. I directed my horse towards a spot far in advance of the flying herd; the wapiti in turn, not slow to perceive the advance of a fresh enemy from the flank, bent away in the opposite direction, giving the Indian the advantages of a similar advance upon an oblique line to cut them off, and so cause them to again alter their course in my favour.

It is a singular fact in the hunting of wild game, that if a particular animal of a herd be selected for pursuit, even though he may at the time be in the midst of a number of other animals all flying from the hunter, nevertheless, the one marked out as the special quarry will quickly realize that he alone is the object of the hunter's aim, and he will soon become the solitary one, deserted by his companions, who seem to understand his position. Such was now the case. One by one the meaner ones in the little herd had dropped off to the right or to left, and ere two miles had been ridden the monarch stag pursued alone his wild career.

His pace was still the long rapid stride or trot peculiar to his breed. To the inexperienced eye it looked a rate of speed which could be easily overtaken by a horse; but, nevertheless, although a good horse will always outrun a wapiti, it takes both time and open country to enable him to do so. The long swinging trot is really the wapiti's best pace. When he is forced to change it for a gallop, his end is near—his course is almost run.

Right on over the level prairie held the stag, and at full speed we followed his flying steps. The prairie lay an almost unbroken level for six or seven miles, then a succession of sand-ridges appeared in view, and farther still rose the blue outlines of more distant hills. It was toward this refuge that the stag now held his way.

When the last of his little band had fallen from him, and he was alone with his pursuers, it seemed that his energies only reached their fullest power; for, more than half way across the plain he not only kept his distance in the race, but increased it by many lengths; nor did he appear to labour in his stride, as with head thrown forward, and antlers lying back almost upon his haunches, he spurned behind him the light soil of the plains.

With rapid survey the Indian scanned the hills towards which his quarry was now leading, and his practised eye soon caught the features of the land, while he still maintained the same headlong speed. We knew that if the stag once gained those ridges of light brown sand his chances of final escape would be great. The yielding surface would give the spreading cloven hoof the support which it would refuse to the more solid pressure of the horse.

In all these things nature never fails to instruct her creatures in the means of escape she provides for them in their hours of trouble. The hare seeks the hill when coursed by the grey-hound, because the great length of her hind legs gives her an increased power to traverse with rapidity rising ground.

When the falcon is abroad, the birds know that their

wings are their weakest refuge, lying close hid on moorland or in cover.

The moose makes his place of rest for the day to the leeward of his track during the night, so that he may have the wind of every hunter who follows in his trail.

It is in that acute knowledge of all these various resources, instincts, and habits, possessed by the wild game which they pursue, that the Indian hunter surpasses all other hunters of the earth.

It is not too much to say that a good Indian hunter can anticipate every instinct of the animal he is in quest of.

We have seen in the present instance how completely the Sioux had forced the herd of wapiti to take the upper level. This he had achieved by knowing exactly where they would run upon being first disturbed, and then placing himself in such a position that they were enabled to scent his presence before they could see that he meant to follow them. By this means he caused them to abandon the partly wooded country before they had become thoroughly frightened by a closer attack.

Under the different conditions of suspicion, fear, and absolute danger, wild animals, like human creatures, show widely different tactics. It is these finer distinctions of habit and emotion that the red man has so thoroughly mastered, and it is this knowledge that enables him almost invariably to outwit the keenest sense of animal cunning.

In most of the wisdom of civilized man he is only a child. His perceptions of things relating to social or political life are bounded by narrow limits. But in the work of the wilderness, in all things that relate to the conquest of savage nature, be it grizzly bear, foaming rapid, or long stretch of icy solitude, he is all unmatched in skill, in daring, and in knowledge.

But while we have been speaking thus of Indian skill in the chase, our stag has been nearing with rapid strides the sand-hills of his refuge.

We had now drawn closer to each other in the pursuit, and it seemed that hunters and hunted were straining their every nerve, the one to attain, the other to prevent, the gaining of this refuge.

I had thought that the horse ridden by the Sioux had been going at its utmost speed. But in this I was mistaken, as the next instant proved.

All at once he shot forward, laying himself out over the prairie as I had never before seen any horse do.

He was soon close upon the flying foosteps of the stag, which now, finding himself almost outpaced, broke from his long-held steady trot into a short and laboured gallop, while his great antlers moved from side to side, as he watched over his flanks the progress of his pursuer.

The sand-hills were but a short half-mile distant. Another minute would decide the contest. Just when I thought the stag must win, I saw the Sioux urge his horse to a still faster effort. He was now almost at the flank of the wapiti. Then I saw him with the quickness of lightning unsling his short bow, and place an arrow on the string. One sharp draw, apparently without any aim, and the shaft sped upon its way, piercing the heart of the giant stag, which, with one great leap forward into space, rolled dead upon the prairie.

He was a noble specimen of those gigantic animals now growing scarce on the American prairies.

From fore hoof to tip of shoulders he stood seventeen hands high. His antlers were the finest I ever saw. They branched from his frontlet in perfect symmetry and regularity, each tier was the exact counterpart of the opposite one From brow to tip they measured more than five feet, and their ribbed sides shone like roughened bronze, while the strong tips were polished ivory. Standing breathless beside my breathless horse, I looked on the dead animal in mute admiration, while the Sioux set to at the more practical work of getting some meat for dinner.

"You may well look at him," he said to me; "he is the finest of his tribe I have yet seen."

"It is almost a pity we have killed such a noble beast," I replied; "to lay such a proud head low."

"Yes," answered the Indian. "But it is in such things that we learn the great work of war. To ride a chase to the end; to shoot an arrow fast and true after a six-mile gallop; to watch every turn of the game enemy, and to note every stride of the steed; to avoid the deadly charge of the buffalo, and to wheel upon his flank as he blindly pursues his impetuous onset; to stand steady before the advance of the savage grizzly bear, and to track the wary moose with silent footfall into the willow thickets,—these are the works by which, in times of peace, the Indian learns his toil in the deeper game of war.

"And then, the health, the strength, the freshness of these things; the pleasure they give us in after-time when by the camp fire in the evening we run back in memory some day of bygone chase. Well, now we have other work to do. This run has taken us far from our trail. The sun gets low upon the plain. We must away."

So taking with us a few tit-bits of the wapiti, we retraced our steps to where the pack-horses had been left with Donogh when I joined the pursuit, and then rode briskly towards the now declining sun.

By sunset we came in sight of a small creek, on the banks of which grew a few dark pine-trees. Beneath one of these pines we made our camp; the horses found good pasturage along the edge of the creek, and from a high sand dune which rose behind the camp the Sioux pointed out to us our course for the morrow.

As we stood together on the summit of the sand ridge,

the scene that lay to the west was enough to make even the oldest voyageur pause in wonder as he beheld it. Many a long mile away, over a vast stretch of prairie, the western sky blazed in untold hues of gold, saffron, orange, green, and purple. Down to the distant rim of the prairie, the light shone clear and distinct. No fog, no smoke blurred the vast circle of the sky-line. Never before had we realized at a single glance the vastness of earthly space. The lustrous sky made dim the intervening distance, and added tenfold to the sense of immensity.

The Indian pointed his finger full towards the spot where the sun had gone down.

"There lies our course," he said. "Would that, like yon sunset, the prairie land circled the world, then we might for ever travel into the west."

"Well, master, we're in the big wilderness, surely," said Donogh, as he stood by my side watching intently this vast ocean of grass, slowly sinking into night beneath the many-hued splendours of the western skies. "When we used to sit together on the top of Seefin, talking of the lands beyond the seas, I didn't think that one short year would carry us so far."

"How do you like it, Donogh?" I asked him.

"Like it, sir! I like it as long as it holds you in it. And I like it for all the fine wild birds and beasts it has. But I'd like it better if it had a few more hills, just to remind

F

me of Coolrue, and the rest of the old mountains about Glencar!"

"We'll come to the hills all in good time," I replied. "There, beyond where you see the sun has gone down, twenty long days' riding from here you will see hills that will make Seefin and Coolrue seem only hillocks in comparison—mountains where the snow never melts."

"What name do the Indians call the Rocky Mountains?" I asked Red Cloud, who was listening to our conversation.

"The Blackfeet call them the Ridge of the World," he answered. My people named them the Mountains of the Setting Sun; and the Assineboines, who dwell at their feet, call them the Hills of Life and Death, because they say that the spirits of the dead climb them to look back on life, and forward on the happy hunting-grounds."

"Do you hear, Donogh?" I said.

He laughed as he answered,—

"Who knows but we'll see Glencar from there, sir?"

CHAPTER IV.

We reach the hills of the Wolverine—Something moves far out upon the plains—The wounded Cree—His story—Adventure with a grizzly bear—Left alone—A long crawl for life—Hunger, thirst, and travail—A grizzly again—" The Great Spirit, like an eagle, looks down upon the prairie "—Saved—Watched.

IN five days' easy travel, riding each day at a kind of amble, half trot half walk, we reached the hills of the Wolverine, a low range of ridges surrounded upon all sides by a vast plain. We pitched camp close beside a small lake which was situated nigh the western extremity of the group of hills, and from the top of a ridge behind the lodge the eye ranged over an expanse the greater part of which was destitute of trees.

It was the Indian's wont every evening, after camp had been made, to make a long circuit around the camping-place armed with his fowling-piece. From these excursions he usually returned at dusk, bringing with him a brace of wild ducks or a few prairie grouse for the morning meal.

On the evening of our arrival at the Touchwood Hills he

and I set out as usual upon this evening ramble, leaving Donogh to look after the camp. Ascending the ridge I have spoken of, we surveyed intently the plain which stretched from the base of the hill on which we stood until it was lost to sight in the western horizon. It was so vast a prospect that the eye wandered over it for a length of time ere it could note even the nearer portion that lay well within the range of vision. The Sioux took a long survey of the scene. Shading his eyes with his hands, he slowly traversed the great circle of the horizon; then his gaze sought the nearer landscape, passing along it in a manner that left no portion of the field of sight unscanned. As thus he looked, his slow-moving eyes all at once became steadily fixed upon one object set within the mid-distance of the scene. To an ordinary eye it appeared a speck, a rock, or a bush, or perhaps some stray wolf roving the plain in search of food; to the quick eye of the Sioux it was none of these things. It moved very slowly in the landscape; it appeared to stop at times and then to go on again, keeping generally the same direction. It was slowly approaching the Wolverine Hills. At last the Sioux seemed to satisfy himself as to the nature of this slow-moving object. Quitting the summit, he descended with rapid steps to the camp, caught his horse, told me to secure mine, passed a piece of leather into his mouth as bridle, and springing upon his bare back and calling upon me to follow, set off at a gallop into the plain in the direction of the strange object.

It yet wanted about half an hour of sunset, and by riding hard we would reach the spot ere night had closed in ; for darkness comes quickly on the heels of the day in the prairie, and though a lustrous after-glow lives sometimes in the western sky, the great plain instantly grows dim when the sun has gone beneath the horizon. From the lower level of the plain at the foot of the hills no sign was visible of the object which he had seen from the summit ; but this mattered little to the Sioux, whose practised eye had taken in the line of direction by other objects, and his course was now held straight upon his mark.

When we reached the neighbourhood of the spot in which he had last seen the moving object, he pulled up his horse and looked around him on every side. There was nothing to be seen. The plain lay around us motionless and silent, already beginning to grow dark in the decreasing light. A man gifted with less acute sight would have rested satisfied that the moving object which he had looked upon was a wild animal—a wolf or a wolverine, whose sharp sense of sound alarmed at the approach of man, had caused it to seek concealment ; but the Indian had noticed certain peculiarities in the object that led him to form other conclusions regarding its nature. In a loud, clear voice he called out in an Indian language that he was a friend, and that whoever was near need have no fear to discover himself.

"It is the Red Cloud who speaks," he said. "No Indian need fear to meet him." Scarcely had he thus spoken when from a dry watercourse near at hand there rose up a figure which seemed in the twilight to be that of a man who was unable to lift himself fully upon his feet. He was distant about one hundred yards from us, and it was evident from the manner in which he drew himself out of the depression in which he had lain concealed from sight, that he had difficulty in making any movement. As the figure emerged from the hollow, it resumed the crouching attitude which had been first noticed. We were soon beside this strange apparition. It proved to be a young Indian of the Cree nation, a man so spent and worn, so thin in face and figure, and so tattered in dress, that he scarcely resembled a human being. He was utterly unable to rise from a kneeling position. One arm hung at his side, broken below the elbow; one leg was painfully dragged after him along the ground; his leather dress hanging in tatters upon his back showed many cuts and bruises upon his body. The Sioux spoke a few words to this wretched object; but the man answered in such a broken voice and rambling manner that little could be gleaned from what he said.

The Sioux having dismounted for a better examination of this maimed creature, now lifted him without difficulty on to his own horse; then mounting himself, we set off at an easy pace for the camp. The man now appeared quite senseless, his head and feet hanging down the horse's sides like that of a dead body. The night had quite closed in when we rounded the base of the outer line of hills and came full into the firelight of the camp. Donogh was astonished to see us bearing back to camp an apparently lifeless body, which was immediately taken from the horse and laid on the ground before the fire.

The warmth of the fire, and a drink of hot tea which was soon given him, brought consciousness back again to the poor creature. For a while he looked wildly and vacantly around, seemed slowly to take in the new state of existence that had so quickly come to him, then he seized the vessel of tea that Donogh was holding near his lips and drained it to the dregs. Some time elapsed, however, ere he could answer in a collected manner the questions put to him by the Sioux, but by degrees the following story was elicited. It ran thus :—

"More than forty days ago I quitted a camp of Crees near the Lone Mountain prairie to go south on the war-trail, there were fourteen of us in all; our horses were fat, and we travelled fast. On the fifth day we reached the woody hills. There were no Indians near, and we began to hunt buffalo, which were numerous over all the prairies south of the Qu'appelle river.

"It was about the tenth day that one of our party, who had gone out with the horses in the morning, came back to camp saying that he had struck the trail of a large grizzly bear some little distance from where we lay. Four of us started out with him to hunt the bear; I was one of them. We soon struck the trail. The bear had crossed a ravine and ascended a steep bank beyond; the side of this bank was covered with cotton-wood thicket. We followed the trail right into the thicket; we were all on foot. All at once we heard, as we walked in file along the trail, a heavy tread sounding close at hand, and a loud breaking of branches and dry sticks. Then appeared in front the object of our chase. He was a very large grizzly, and so wicked that he did not wait for us to attack him, but came all at once full upon us.

"I stood second in the line. The foremost brave sprang aside to enable me to fire, and also to get clear of our line himself. I levelled my gun and fired full upon the huge beast; one or two other shots sounded about me, but I saw through the smoke that the bear had not been killed by them—he was advancing right upon me. I stepped back on one side, with the intention of running until I could again load my gun, but at that instant the upraised root of a tree caught my foot, and I fell full upon the ground almost at the feet of the advancing animal, now doubly maddened by the wounds he had received. I had only time to draw my knife from my belt when he was full upon me. I struck blindly at him, but it was no use, his claws and his teeth were fastened in my flesh; I was bruised, wounded and torn ere I could repeat the blow with my knife. Then I heard two or three shots above my head, a heavy crushing weight fell upon me, and I knew no more.

"When next I knew what was passing around me everything was changed. I was a helpless cripple; my leg and my arm had both been broken; I was torn all over my body. My companions had carried me back to camp, but what could they do with me? They were all braves whose work is war and the chase; our women and old men lay far away, six long days' riding, ten easy days' travel. Besides we were on the war-path. At any moment the Blackfeet might appear. I would be worse than useless to my friends, I would be a burden to them. I read their thoughts in their faces, and my mind was made up.

"'Dry plenty of buffalo meat,' I said to them; 'put it where my hand can reach it; lay me by the edge of the stream of water; then go away and leave me to die here. Destroy the trail as you go away, so that no one will ever find the spot, and my scalp will not hang in the lodge of a Blackfoot.'

"They did as I told them; they put beside me a pile of dry buffalo meat; they loaded my gun and left it at my right hand, so that I could defend myself against a wild beast while my life lasted; and they laid my blanket by the edge of a stream of water, so that I could get drink without moving; then one by one they wished me good-bye, and I saw them depart for ever.

"It was the middle of the day when they thus left me. When they were all gone and I could no more hear the sound of man or horse, I felt very lonely, and wished to die. I saw the daylight growing dim and the night coming down through the trees. Then I felt hungry, and taking some meat from the pile beside me, I ate it, drank some water, and slept.

"When I awoke next morning I felt better. My leg and arm were both useless, but my flesh-wounds were beginning to heal, and I did not seem so weak as I had been. That day passed, and another, and another. I began to get accustomed to the solitude, and to watch everything around me. Two whiskey jacks came and sat looking at me on a branch close to my head. I threw small bits of meat to them, and at last they came so close that they took the food from my hand and hopped over my body. I was glad to have them, they were company to me during the long daylight hours. About ten days passed, and I was still alive—alive, and gaining strength day by day. What was to be done? I looked at my store of meat, and saw that it could not last more than ten days; after that time I would starve to death. I began to think very anxiously on what

I could do to save myself from this death. To stay where I was, meant to die a lingering death after ten days. I thought I would try to move and practise myself in moving even on my hands and knees. Each day I crept more and more about the thicket in which I had been. I crept to the edge of it and looked out over the plains. They lay around me to the north and west far as my eye could reach. They never seemed so large to me before. I saw buffalo feeding a long way off towards the north; that was the way we had come. My camp lay away in that direction—but so far. I thought over the direction in my mind; I remembered all the streams we had crossed, the places where we had camped, the hills and the valleys we had passed: it seemed as long as a dream at night.

"For four days I kept moving to and fro, crawling on hands and knees about the thicket. I began to go farther and farther away from it, and each day I found I could move faster. I had the use of one leg and one arm quite strong; the other arm was sound to the elbow, but the hand was helpless; my left leg had been broken below the knee. I felt much pain when I moved, but that did not matter; anything was better than lying in the trees waiting for death. On the sixth day after this I put together all that remained of my dry meat store, and with nothing but my knife in my belt (I never could have carried my gun), I crawled forth from the camp in which I had lain during so many days. I held my slow way towards the north almost along the same line we had travelled but a month earlier, when we swept so swiftly along over the prairie.

"For many hours I plodded on. It seemed as though I could never get out of sight of the thicket; often I looked back, and there it was still close to me; at last the night hid it from sight, and I stretched my aching limbs upon the ground.

"All next day I went on. About noon I came to a stream, drank deeply, and washed my wounds in the cool water; again I crawled on towards the north, and slept again in the middle of the plain.

"By the fifth day I had finished the last scrap of my meat. I now looked about anxiously for the bodies of buffalo that had been killed. On our journey down we had killed many buffaloes, and I was now passing over ground where we had hunted twenty days before; but it is one thing to look for buffalo on horseback, and another thing to seek for it lying level upon the ground. I could not see far before or around me; sometimes I crawled to the top of a hillock for a wider survey of the plain. The night came, I lay down without food or water. Next morning I began to move as soon as it was light enough to see. I made for a small hill that stood a little to one side of my line; from its top I saw, a long distance away from my course, a small black speck. I knew it to be a dead buffalo. I made for it, but it was noon when I had reached it. I ate a little, then cut with my knife as much as I could carry, and set out to find water, for I was very thirsty. I held on in the direction of a valley I had noticed from the top of a hill. It was sunset when I got to it, and to my great joy I found water; then I ate a great deal of my meat and drank plentifully of the water, and lay down to sleep, happy.

"The next morning I ate and drank again, and then set out once more. Day by day I went on; sometimes I dragged myself all day along, starving and thirsty; sometimes I had to lie down at night with burning throat; sometimes I came to a buffalo, so long killed that of his flesh the wolves had left nothing except the skin and muscle of the head and hide. At night when I had got no food during the day I used to dream of old times, when the camp had feasted upon freshly-killed buffalo, when the squaws had dressed the tongues; and at other times I thought I had some moose noses before me, and was seated in my lodge while the briskets were being boiled over the fire in the centre; and then my lips would open and close, and I heard my teeth strike together as though I had been eating, and I woke to find I was weak and hungry, and that only the great dark prairie lay around me.

"At last I lost all count of the days. I only thought of three things—food, drink, and the course I had to travel. My pain had become so much my life that I had ceased to think about it. One day I was as usual dragging myself along when I noticed right in front of me an object that filled my heart with terror. Before me, over the ridge of an incline which I was ascending, appeared two small pointed objects. They were sharply seen against the sky over the rim of the ridge. I knew instantly what they were. I knew that under these two small pointed objects there were the head and body of a grizzly bear. He was lying there right in my onward path, watching for buffalo. I knew that he had seen me while afar, and that he now awaited my approach, thinking that I was some wild animal of whose capture he was certain.

"I laid myself flat upon the ground, and then I drew away to the left, and when I had gained what I had deemed sufficient distance I again tried to ascend the incline; but again, full in my front, I saw the dreaded pointed tips over the prairie ridge. The bear had seen me as I moved to the left, and he too had gone in that direction to intercept me on the brow of the hill. Again I laid myself flat upon the prairie and crawled away to one side, this time taking care not to attempt to cross the ridge until I had gone a long way to the flank. Creeping very cautiously up the hill, I looked over the ridge. The bear was nowhere to be seen. I made all haste to leave behind the spot so nearly fatal to me, and continuing to crawl long after night had fallen, I at length lay down to sleep, feeling more tired, and hungry, and exhausted, than I had yet been since I set out first upon my long journey. That was only a few days since. Three days ago I came in sight of these hills, they filled my heart with hope; but only last night I had again to lie exposed to a great danger—a band of Indians passed me making for these hills. I could hear them speaking to one another as they went by; they were Assineboine Indians on the war-path; they were so close that some of their horses scented me, for I heard one say, 'Fool, it is only a wolf you start from.'

"This morning I almost gave up hope of ever reaching succour. I knew my people must have left these hills, or else the Stonies could not have been there. Then I thought that some of their scouts would be sure to see me on the plain, and that it would be better to lie down in some watercourse and die there, than to die at the hands of my enemies and have my scalp hung at the mane of an Assineboine's horse; but when I thought of all that I had gone through—of how, when I had been dying of thirst, water had lain in my track—of how I had found food when starving,—I took hope again, and said to myself, 'The Great Spirit sees me. Like an eagle in the mid-day, His eye is cast down upon the prairie; He has put food and water on the plain; He has shielded me from the grizzly, and wrapt the night around me when my enemies passed near me. I will not lie down and die; I will go on still, in hope.'

"Well, I went on, and it grew dark once more. I was determined to drag on until I reached these hills, for I knew that there was plenty of water here. Then all at once I heard the noise of a horse's hoofs, and I hid myself, thinking it was an Assineboine scout; and then I heard your voice, and I knew that I was safe."

Such was the story.

The poor fellow spoke in his native tongue, which the Sioux understood, and as to him many Indian dialects were familiar, interpreted to me as we sat at the camp fire. The Red Cloud, familiar as his life had made him with every phase of hardship of Indian existence on the great prairie, had never before met with such a singular instance of Indian fortitude and perseverance as this was; but the concluding portion of the Cree's narrative had roused other thoughts in his mind, and to these he directed his questions.

"The Assineboines that passed by you last night," he said, "how many might they have numbered?"

"They were but few," answered the Cree; "about fifteen men."

"What part of the hills were they making for?"

"They were on a line that would lead them north of where we now are."

The Sioux remained silent for some time. He was thinking deeply upon the presence of this war-party. It boded trouble in the future. It was true he had quarrel with no Indian tribe; but a small war-party of fifteen braves is not particular on the score of cause of enmity, and if horses are to be captured or scalps taken, it usually matters little whether actual war has been declared beforehand; and the adage that those who are not with me are against me, holds good on such wild raids as that upon which the party seen by the Cree were now bound. Thinking out many different courses, and weighing well their various probabilities of success or failure, the Sioux at length wrapped himself in his blanket and lay down to rest. We had spread a blanket for the Cree, and had done all we could to make him comfortable. At first the poor creature seemed scarcely to understand the meaning of so much kindness and attention from a stranger. Under the influence of a good supper he soon forgot the fearful hardships which he had so lately passed through, and the full realization of his immediate safety seemed to obliterate all anxiety for the future. And yet, as he now lay by the camp fire of his preserver there was as much danger hanging over him as ever had threatened him in the darkest moment of his terrible journey.

Over the brow of a hill close by, a pair of watchful eyes were looking into the camp, intently noting every movement in and around it.

CHAPTER V.

An Assineboine camp—The trader McDermott—The chief "Wolverine"—Fire-water and finesse—The Assineboine war-party—A chance of a Cree scalp—The trader hears a well-known name—A big bid for murder, two hundred skins!

THE events that now began to unfold themselves in my life and in those of my companions, took shape and context only after long lapse of time had passed by.

It was frequently when months had vanished that I learned the various threads of action which had led to incidents of more or less importance to me. Hitherto I had been only a boy-actor in the drama of existence. I was now about to become a sharer in a larger sphere of action, and to participate in scenes of adventure the springs of which were involved in the lives and actions of other men. Writing now as I do from a standpoint of life which looks back across many years to those early adventures, I am able to set down the record with its various parts complete. I can see the lines of life upon which other men moved, and can trace the impulses upon which they acted—can fill in, as it were, the gaps between their action and mine own, and give to the story of my life at that period an insight into events which then lay veiled from me by distance. It will therefore be necessary, in order that my readers may comprehend clearly the thread of the events I am about to relate, that I should at times carry them away to scenes in which personally I was not an actor, and that they should occasionally o'erleap the boundaries of the moment to look upon a far wider theatre of events than I myself had at the time beheld.

We will therefore leave the scene at the camp-fire in the Wolverine hills, and travel in imagination a hundred miles to the south-west, where, on one of the sources of the Qu'appelle river, a large camp of Assineboines, or Stone Indians, is pitched.

The camp is a large one, for the buffalo have been numerous all the summer long on the prairies south of the Qu'appelle, and many scattered bands of the tribe have come together to hunt and feast upon the mighty herd. A brisk trade is being carried on too in skins and robes; for a rich trader has arrived in the camp, with goodly store of guns, blankets, trinkets, powder and ball, and beads; and chief and brave, and squaw and boy, are busy at the work of barter and exchange.

On the evening we speak of, the chief of the Assineboines was seated smoking in his lodge, when the leather door was raised and the figure of a white man entered. It was McDermott, the trader from the Red River.

The Wolverine extended his hand to the new comer, the trader shook it, seated himself on the opposite side of the small, clear wood fire that burned in the centre of the lodge, and began to smoke in silence. The Indian scarcely moved a muscle, but sat smoking too, his eyes fixed upon the flame. At last the trader broke silence. "Has any news come of the young men who are on the war-path?" he asked.

"No," answered the Wolverine, "they will carry their own news; when they have something to tell and to show, then they will return."

McDermott had his own reasons for asking; he wanted horses, and he knew that if the war-party was successful he would obtain them for a trifle. Horses lightly got upon the war-path, are lightly parted with by their captors. A trading gun and some ball and powder would purchase a good horse in the camp; ten guns' value would not buy him in the English settlement on the Red river.

The Wolverine knew well that the trader did not ask these questions without good reason; and although he had that day received news of the war-party, both of their whereabouts and future movements, he was not going to give the smallest item of that news to his questioner without receiving some substantial return for it.

On his part McDermott was also aware that a messenger had come in during the day from the war-party, but of the purport of the news, or the movements of the party, he could not glean any tidings; but he had brought with him to the lodge of the Wolverine a potent key to unlock the secret store of that chief's mind, and as he now produced from his pocket a bottle of the strongest fire-water, there came a look into the impassive eye of the old Indian opposite that told the trader at once that the information he sought for would soon be his.

Taking a small tin vessel, he poured out into it some of the fiery poison, and handed the cup across the fire to the chief. As his hand passed over the flame he shook a few drops of the spirit on the fire; a bright blue flame shot quickly up, illuminating all the interior of the lodge and lighting up the dusky features of the Wolverine, whose arm was already outstretched to receive the drink he so deeply thirsted for.

"It is good fire-water," he said as he saw the blaze, "so it will light up the heart of the red man as it does this red stick."

McDermott cautiously refrained for some moments from asking any more questions of the whereabouts of the war-party. A perfect adept in the ways of Indian trade, he knew the fire-water would soon do its work on the brain of the Wolverine.

The Indian drank, and returned the empty cup to his visitor.

"I wished to learn the movements of your young men," said McDermott after a long pause, during which his sharp eye had noted the Indian's face as he sat glowering over the fire, "because I am about to quit this camp, and I am afraid they may come upon my horses at night and mistake them for those of an enemy."

"What direction do you travel?" asked the chief.

"Towards the settlement," replied the trader. "My supplies are nearly exhausted, and it is time to return home."

This was a lie. He had no intention whatever of leaving the plains, and the best portion of his goods he had kept concealed from the Assineboines in a cache on the Qu'appelle river. For the third time he filled the cup, and already the eye, glistening in the firelight like that of a serpent, told the effect the fiery liquor was having upon the Wolverine's brain. "I want you," went on the trader, "to send with me the Indian who came to-day from the war-party. He will protect my horses from being taken, in case I should fall in with your young men."

"There will be no danger to your horses," said the Indian. "My young men are far away from the trail that leads to the settlement; but you want to get the horses they have taken, not to protect your own. Well, give me the rest of that bottle, and you may take with you the young man who 'o-day has come from the party. He will lead you where you will find them."

The bargain was soon struck, and as the trader quitted the lodge the Wolverine was clutching in his bony fingers the fatal fire-water, which, more than war, hunger, or exposure, has destroyed the red man's race over the wide continent of North America.

McDermott having obtained the chief's consent to his taking the brave lately arrived from the war-party away with him, without which permission it would have been fatal to his future interests in trade to have moved him, lost no time in setting out on his road. He put together the greater portion of his goods, and leaving a half-breed servant to continue the exchange of those things that it was impossible for him to take away, he departed from the camp at midnight, and by daybreak was far away from the last trace of the Assineboines.

He had with him the Assineboine scout as guide, and two retainers, a French half-breed and a Salteaux Indian. The party rode rapidly; they had a large band of horses, and packs and saddles were frequently changed. By the evening of the first day they drew near the last mountain range of hills. The scout led the way. When night fell upon the plain they were on the edge of the hills; presently a small lake was reached. It was now dark, but the guide knew the track, and he pushed on into the hills.

A long ride further through rough and broken ground, on which they had carefully to pick their way, brought them suddenly face to face with a small fire burning in a glen between abrupt hills. Around the fire were seated several figures. It was the camp of the war-party. The braves sat late around their fires, but there was reason for their doing so. A scout had only lately returned with news of importance. The story he had to tell was to this effect. At sunset he had been looking from a hill over the prairie to the west; he had suddenly observed two horsemen riding from a point in the line of hills farther to the south, out into the plain. Judging from the lateness of the hour, that a camp must be in the neighbourhood of the place from whence those horsemen had gone, the scout had ridden cautiously forward towards that portion of the hills. He had soon discovered a fire, beside which a solitary white man sat. Concealing himself effectually from sight, he had watched and waited.

Soon there had come an Indian and another white man, bearing with them what seemed the dead body of another Indian. But this man was not dead; he shortly began to speak, to eat, to drink. He was a Cree, who told a story of having crawled a long way over the prairies from the south. The scout knew only a little of the Cree language, and he had been able only to follow roughly what the wounded man had said. As for the other men—the white men he had never seen before, but the red man was the Red Cloud, the famous wandering Sioux.

Now the principal item of this story that had interest for the Assineboines, who sat eager listeners around the fire, was that which had reference to the wounded Cree Indian : the Crees were enemies ; the war-party had as yet taken no Cree scalps. How could they return to their camp with no trophy to show? The women and children would laugh at them; the old men would say, "Ah! it was different in our time; we did not come in from the war-trail without horses or scalps." Here then was a great chance of supplying this most pressing want.

It was true that the Red Cloud was well known over all the northern prairies. It would be no easy matter to carry off the Cree from his protection ; nor would it be safe to molest the white men who were with him, for the noise of harm done to white men travelled sometimes far over the prairies, and reached even the ears of the Great Mother who dwelt beyond the big sea in the land where the sun rose.

These things considered made it wiser to attempt the capture of the Cree while both the Indian and his white friends were absent from their camp. If this could be effected, then indeed the party might return in triumph to their friends and justly receive the rewards of bravery.

It will be seen from the foregoing summary of the conversation which had been held over the fire by the Assineboines now grouped around it, that the bravery of the party individually or collectively was not of the highest order ; but in truth the thing we call courage is much the same among red men as among white all the world over. Confined to no class or to no people, its examples will be found often mixed with strange evidences of cowardice; and side by side with the man who dares for the sake of daring, will be found the man in whose heart a bit of cheap courage is only less cherished than his life.

It was while thus the party of Assineboines debated their future action that the voice of the scout who had left them some days previously was heard saluting from the darkness. The new arrivals came forward into the circle of light. McDermott was an old acquaintance, and he and his Salteaux were soon seated around the fire. The presence of the trader did little to interrupt the flow of conversation between the Assineboines. Too much engrossed by the prospect of such an easy prey, they soon resumed the thread of their discussion, and after some questions asked and answered the new comer was left to smoke in silence.

But as the Assineboines debated their plans, and mention had been made once or twice of the two men in the other camp against whom the braves had no quarrel, there came into the trader's face an expression of rapt attention, and he listened eagerly to every word that fell from his companions. He might well start at the utterance of one name—the name of the Red Cloud, the son of the man he had foully betrayed to his doom.

Face to face he had never met the Sioux chief, but a vague undefined fear had oppressed him whenever his name had been mentioned. He well knew that the vengeance of the Sioux is deep and lasting; he knew too that if any act merited revenge it was the act which he had committed upon the father of this man with whom he had had no cause of quarrel, with whom he had been on terms of long and deep intimacy, in whose tent he had eaten in former times, when the Sioux had held their lands up to the shores of the Otter Tail and to the sources of the Mississippi.

Nine years had passed since that foul deed had been wrought. In the wild life of the prairies, and amid a society whose deeds of violence were of too frequent occurrence, the memory of any particular act of bloodshed is soon forgotten; but time had never blotted out the recollection of the treachery of the trader McDermott. There was not a Sioux on the most southern tributary stream of the great Missouri who had not heard of that dark night's work, when, drugged at the feast to which he had gone in the confidence of old friendship, the chief Black Eagle was carried through the snow of the winter night and yielded a prisoner at the frontier post on the Red river.

Since that time the trader had grown rich. He had many

successful ventures on the plains; for the quarrels of the Sioux were not the quarrels of the Crees, the Assineboines, and the Blackfeet, the Sircees or the Salteaux; but through all these years he lived as it were in the shadow of his own crime, and he felt that while a Sioux was left to roam the prairie, the dead body of the man whose life he had sold was still unburied. Many a time when the shadows darkened upon the great landscape had he heard in his heart the mysterious voice of conscience, upbraiding him with the deed of blood; but more than all had he conceived, with the intuitive faculty of fear, a dread of the Red Cloud.

Whether there came tidings of a battle or a skirmish, fought between the remnants of the Sioux, the Mandans, the Minatarre, or the Ogahalla branches of that once mighty nation with the troops of the United States, McDermott longed to learn that this wandering chief, whose presence ever haunted his imagination, had at last met his end. But he ever seemed to bear a charmed life.

At one time he was heard of in a raid upon the American post on the great bend of the Missouri; again came tidings that he had led a small band of the Ogahalla against a detachment of soldiers in the fort hills of Montana, and that not one living soul had escaped to tell the fate of the American soldiers; and again there came news that a solitary Indian had been seen by the Touchwood hills, or in the broken ridges of the Mauvais Bois, and that this roving red man was the Red Cloud.

That curious instinct which danger frequently gives to the mind long before any actual symptom of its approach is visible, had warned the trader McDermott that while the Sioux lived he had reason to dread at his hands a fate as cruel as the one to which he had consigned the old chief.

Now all at once, sitting here at this camp fire, he heard the dreaded name of his enemy, and gathering from the conversation that only a few miles away from where he sat lay camped the man he feared more than anything on earth, it is little wonder that his heart beat loudly within his breast, and his face showed unmistakable traces of the conflict of passion that raged within him. For with the news of this proximity of his hated enemy there was also a chance not to be lightly lost. Here was the Sioux in company with a wounded Cree, close to a war-party of Assineboines hungry for trophies and for plunder. His course was plain. Could he succeed in inducing the Assineboines to attack the Sioux camp, and end for ever his hated enemy? It would go hard with him if he could not.

Listening to the conversation of the braves, and at the same time endeavouring to frame his plans for the destruction of the Sioux, he sat silent for some time. The presence of white men in the camp of the Sioux alone disquieted him; it prevented his openly proposing to the

Indians who were with him to attack the camp, and joining them himself in doing so.

The death on the prairies of two Indians would have mattered little, but the murder of two white men was an event that might give rise to unpleasant questions being asked in the Red River; and when next he visited his home there, it might be to find himself charged with complicity or actual share in the crime.

He pretended therefore not to have heard much of what the Assineboines had been speaking among themselves, but to approach his object from an outside point altogether.

Watching an opportunity, and addressing himself to the leader of the band, he began.

"I see no trace of war," he said, "and I hear of no horses having been captured. Are the Crees too strong, that your braves have feared to encounter them? or do they watch their horses so closely that you cannot get near them?"

The taunt struck the mark it had been aimed at. "We have not taken scalps," replied the leader, "because the Crees keep together and shun our presence. The horses of the Crees are fleet to run away; but it may not be long," he added, "before we have horses, and scalps too."

"I want some good horses," went on the trader, "and I will give a large price for them; but they must be of the right kind—not small, starved ponies, but mustangs of size and power, fit for a chief to ride."

Watching an opportunity, the trader addressed the leader of the band.
[*Page* 94.

He well knew the horses which the Red Cloud usually rode and used, and in mentioning the style of horse he now required he painted exactly those of his enemy.

"And what would you give for such a horse?" asked the Assineboine leader.

The trader thought for a moment. Here was his opportunity. Now or never he would name a price dazzling to the Indian—cheap to him, since it might for ever rid him of the man he feared and hated.

"I would give for such a horse," he slowly replied, "two hundred skins."

Two hundred skins! Never had horse fetched such a price since the mustang breed had reached these northern prairies from the great plateau of New Mexico and the Spanish frontier, two hundred years ago. The Indian was dumb with astonishment—for three such horses he and his band would get 750 skins. Why they would be rich for evermore. They would be the envy of every young Assineboine in the tribe. The fairest squaws would be their wives, for they could lay such a pile of presents at the lodge doors of the parents that it would be impossible to deny their suit. What guns, too, they could buy, and fancy rifles, and store of beads and gaudy dress, with porcupine quills, and blankets of brightest hue!

All these things flashed through the minds of the war-party as they listened to the trader's offer. The bid was too high; the last doubt about attempting to kill the Cree and carry off the horses of the Sioux vanished, and already they began to speculate upon their future disposal of so much wealth and so much finery. So far as they were concerned the doom of the Cree, and for that matter of the Sioux, and his associates if resistance was offered, was settled.

The trader saw with suppressed joy this realization of his fondest hopes. He well knew the Sioux would fight to the bitter end sooner than lose friend or horse. He had only one fear, and that was that the murder of the Cree and the capture of the horses might be effected while the Sioux was absent from his camp, and that thus the life of his enemy might be saved.

As he wrapt himself in his robe a little later on in the night, and lay down to sleep by the still smouldering embers of the camp fire, he felt at last that his long fear was wearing to an end, and that the fate of his enemy was sealed.

CHAPTER VI.

The Sioux forecasts our course—On the watch—Directions—We separate—Red Cloud is seen far out on the plains—Rival tactics—Scent *versus* sight—A captured scout—The edge of the hills again—The signal fire.

AND now the reader must come back to our own camp, where we have all this time been comfortably settled for the night. The concluding portion of the Cree's story had thoroughly alarmed the Sioux. From the few words in which the Cree had described the passing of the war-party, he had easily been able to put together all that was needful for thoroughly understanding the situation. His knowledge of the prairies, and his complete mastery of every detail of Indian thought and habit, made easy to him the task of tracking the further progress of the party, and guessing their whereabouts almost to exactness.

They were camped, he thought, only some seven or eight miles distant, in the same range of hills, and not far from where the level prairie bordered on the west the broken ground.

Of course he knew nothing of the arrival, in the camp of

the war-party, of his deadly enemy, the trader; but he had long surmised the whereabouts of that individual to be not very remote, and from the information which he had gained when in the neighbourhood of the settlement, he was led to conjecture that the first large Indian camp he came to would have the trader as one of its inmates.

But as to the probable movements of the party, he formed a very correct anticipation. Their scouts would be sure to discover our camp at furthest on the morrow, even if they had not already done so; the Cree would prove to them too strong a temptation to be resisted, and the near presence of such good horses would be sure to give rise to some attempt at robbery. He did not communicate any of these thoughts to us, his companions, now. He determined to wait quietly until we were asleep, then to drive in the steeds, and to remain on watch until daybreak. With these precautions there would be little danger.

Departing quietly from the camp when our easy and regular respiration told him that we were asleep, he drove in the hobbled horses to the fire; then hobbling them so that the neck and forelegs were fastened together in addition to the fastening of the two forelegs, he withdrew to the shelter of a small thicket which commanded a view of the camp and its neighbourhood, and wrapping himself in his robe sat down, with his rifle between his knees and his dog beside him, to pass the night on guard.

How weary such a night to a white man! How slowly the long dark hours would roll by! How anxiously the first gleam of light would be looked for in the east! Not so with the red man; night after night will he thus sit, watching with eyes that never close, with ears that never deaden in their keen sense of sound. Sometimes in his lodge, sometimes as here in the thicket on the plain, thus will he sit hour after hour until the grey light steals into the east, grows broader over the sky, and the night is done.

At the first gleam of daylight Red Cloud moved gently back to camp, threw wood upon the fire, roused me from my slumbers, and got breakfast ready.

The meal over, he took me aside and unfolded to me his plan of action.

"To-day," he said, "we are sure to be found out by the war-party of Assineboines. They will not venture openly to attack us during the day, but they will reconnoitre our camp, and probably to-night they will attempt to run off the horses and kill this Cree. We cannot wait here, they are too many for us; neither can we move out into the plain, they would instantly see us and give chase; and though you and your companion might make a good stand with me by ourselves, yet with this Cree we could not do it. What I propose doing is this: the Cree is able to sit a horse; you three will start at once, taking the hound with you, heading straight into the hills. The Cree will know the line to follow, and how to keep the bottom of the valley. Until one hour before noon you must hold your course deep into the hills due east, then you will turn to the north and ride fast for three hours until the sun is half-way to the prairie. Then turning quickly to the west, you will continue your way until you come again to the edge of three hills; by this course you will have followed three sides of a square. Within that square lies the camp of the Assineboines. This evening, if you do all I say, you will be as far to the north of that camp as we are to the south of it now. Look how the grass falls."

So saying, he threw some dry grass into the air. It fell towards the south, the wind was blowing from the north.

"To-night," he said, "that wind will blow in the direction I want. You will reach the edge of the hills before the sun has set. When it is quite dark make a small fire on the slope of one of the hills facing towards the plain; let it be in such a position that while visible to a person out on the prairie, it will be concealed from the sight of any one in the hills to the south. Keep the fire burning for half an hour after dark; then extinguish it, and make your camp near the spot, but within the shelter of the hills. Soon after that time I will be with you. For the rest, fire no shot during the day unless you should happen to be attacked, and move silently in your course through the hills."

The preparations for moving were soon made; there was no time to be lost. We took three horses and set off into the hills. The Sioux spoke a word to the dog, ordering him to go with us; the dog reluctantly obeyed, but his training was perfect and he trotted on after the Cree. Having seen us out of the camp and behind the first intervening rise of ground, he turned his horse's head full for the plains, and taking the lariat of a loose pack-horse carrying only a few light articles, he set off at a sharp pace into the great prairie.

He had kept his own plans to himself, but they will unfold themselves to view as we follow his steps.

Keeping for some time along the base of the hills, he had at length begun to edge farther and farther out into the plain, until after a couple of hours' riding he was many miles in a diagonal line from his starting-point. Then he began to direct his horse more to the west, making a wide curve the base of which was the range of hills, then turning towards the north he continued for some time to hold a course in that direction. He was now fully ten miles out in the plain, a distance which made him and his horse appear mere specks in the immense range of vision.

Small as these specks of life were, they did not escape, however, the watchful glance of a scout, who from the neighbourhood of the Assineboine camp scanned the plains; but not even Indian sight could resolve at that distance these objects. Horsemen or horseman certainly—but what horsemen? No human eye could tell.

The scout's report brought quickly to the standpoint some more of the braves, but no additional light could be gleaned from their opinions as to who the distant specks might be, or where their course was laid for: At break of day that morning the trusty scout who had first discovered the camp, and had brought tidings of the Cree to his companions, had started to again reconnoitre the place and its occupants.

While Red Cloud is thus slowly making his way across the plain, under the distant range of vision of the Assineboines, we will follow for a time the fortunes of this single scout, whose work it was to watch during the day the camp, the attack of which had been fixed for the following night.

In his survey of the previous evening, the Assineboine scout had observed that at the farther side of the camp to the one on which he had approached it, there stood a hill partly covered with brushwood, which would afford him, if he could gain its shelter, a better position for watching the movements and hearing the conversation of the occupants of the camp. His only means of reaching the cover of this hill was to make a long détour through the broken ground lying towards the east, and by coming out south of the camp approach it from its most distant side: this he determined to attempt.

Estimating the two camps to be ten miles from each other, the course the Assineboine proposed to travel would take him about fifteen or twenty miles. He pushed rapidly along, keeping to the hollows between the ridges, and at times leading his horse through thickets and copsewood, and ever and anon in wet and boggy ground, stopping to listen, or ascending some ridge higher than others for a wide view around.

Thus it happened that about the same time of the morning the Assineboine scout and our little party were pursuing two circular courses, the lines of which must intersect each other at one point. Whoever came to that point last would be made aware of the passage of the others. No eye could fail to see a trail in the soft turf of the valleys.

Leaving the scout to pursue his way, we will now follow our own fortunes along our path. Without incidents of any kind, we had continued our course through the hills towards the east. It was almost time for that change of direction which the Sioux had enjoined upon us.

I led the way, closely followed by Donogh; the Cree was in the rear with the dog. Between them ran two pack-horses. The Cree was mounted on the other pack-horse whose load was now light, inasmuch as the supplies of meat had been considerably lessened by the consumption of the past three days, no large game having fallen since the death of the wapiti; the wild ducks and prairie grouse so plentiful in this part of the plains having amply sufficed to keep our party in food.

As we now journeyed on, the Cree, who was in rear of all, saw by the attitude of the dog that it suddenly betokened the presence of some animal to the left. He called my attention to the fact.

The dog showed unmistakable signs of having either seen or smelt some living thing. He stood with head turned towards the left, and ears pointed forwards, as though he partly expected an advance from that quarter, of man or beast. At times a low growl escaped his half-closed mouth.

Determined to discover what it could mean, I spoke a few words to the dog. Instantly he bounded forward full into a thicket, which stood only some sixty paces distant. There was a loud noise and breaking of branches in the thicket; a succession of fierce barks were succeeded by a sharp howl of pain, and there broke forth from one side of the thicket the figure of an Indian on horseback closely followed by the hound. Ere the horseman had got quite clear of the wood the dog was upon him, upon the side nearest to us. With a terrific spring he fastened upon the right leg of the Indian. In vain the man struck him with a short bow and a handful of arrows which he held in his right hand. In an instant the dog had dragged him from his pony, and both dog and man were rolling together upon the ground.

At this moment we rode in upon the struggle. Ere the Indian could rise and shake himself loose from his savage assailant I had struck him a violent blow upon the head with the butt of my gun, which effectually put a stop to all power of resistance; then ordering the dog to loose his hold, we had time to take note of both dog and captive. The first-named was bleeding profusely from an arrow, which the Indian had shot at him at the moment he had entered the thicket. The shaft had struck full upon his breast between his fore legs, but the direction of the arrow fired from on horseback was downwards, and the point had penetrated the flesh and muscle of his chest, coming out again beneath his ribs. Still it was an ugly wound, one half-inch higher, or fired even from the level of a man on foot instead of on horseback, and the poor dog must have been a dead animal.

But it is these half-inches that make all the difference between a dead dog and a captured Assineboine; for, as the reader must be aware, the Indian was no other than the scout on his way to reconnoitre from the south the camp we had so lately quitted.

And now the question presented itself to our minds what was to be done with the captive. The Cree's solution was perfectly simple—it was to instantly despatch him as he lay, and with his scalp and his horse in our possession (for the steed had in true Indian fashion stopped when his rider fell) resume our way; but I could not hear of this proposal. First tying the Assineboine, so that no attempt at escape could become possible even if he were sufficiently recovered from the vigorous application of the butt of the gun, I next examined carefully the dog's wound, and having extracted the arrow by breaking the shaft outside the wound and drawing the head fully out, we saw that it was not dangerous. Then we caught the Assineboine's pony, and bringing the steed to its fallen rider—who by this time had sufficiently recovered consciousness to be fully aware of all that had passed and was passing around him—we made him mount his horse, his arms still remaining tied; then passing a leather line tightly round his legs, we strapped our prisoner to the horse's girth, and passing a double line through the animal's mouth, remounted our own horses, and set out on our road—first having given the Assineboine a pretty intelligible hint that any attempt to escape would quickly cause the revolver in my holster to speak its mind.

The course was now to the north, and for some hours we held our way in silence, through the small hills and deep valleys in which thickets of alders and cotton-wood trees abounded. In many places the grass rose above our horses' knees thick and dry, the hot sun of the summer, now nearly over, had made it as sere and yellow as straw, and it sounded against the horses' legs like stalks of corn, as our file of horsemen came along at a good pace through hill and dale.

I now realized as I rode through this tangled mass of dry vegetation what a prairie fire must be when it has such a material to feed on in its rapid flight across the plains in autumn. For the first time, too, as I rode along this day, the idea of my being the leader of a separate movement of the character of a branch expedition became present to my mind. I felt elated to think that in such a very short space of time I had reached the real home of adventure, and was bearing my part in the wild work of the wilderness. I had each day learned something of that life I had so often longed for, and as my experience had widened out, it seemed that each item of knowledge gained had also lengthened out the time, and distance.

I could scarcely believe that it was but a week since we had started on this journey with only the hope of toiling on day by day into the prairie. Already we had become actors in a real adventure, and were engaged in the performance of those things the mere recital of which at home had so often given me the keenest pleasure.

While thinking these pleasant thoughts now as we rode along, I nevertheless watched with jealous eye the security of our prisoner. I was especially anxious to take the Assineboine alive into camp; the Cree's method would on no account have suited me. I desired to be able to hand over the prisoner to Red Cloud, and to say, "Here is an Assineboine brave taken by your dog. The Cree wanted to kill him. Dead men tell no tales; but neither can they give any information. From this man you will hear all news—the Assineboine plans will be laid bare to you."

Thus ruminating within myself we held our way, until the time had come for changing the course towards the west.

Taking advantage of a valley running through the hills in that direction, we turned abruptly to our left, and riding for about two hours began to draw nigh the edge of the broken ground.

The sun, now low upon the horizon, poured along the little valley the full flood of his evening splendour. Soft and still the landscape lay, tinged in many a colour of green and gold; for the first shades of autumn on the cotton-wood trees gave back the salute of the sunset from their bronzed and yellow leaves, and the green of longer-lived foliage lay still intermixed among them, as fresh as though spring had but lately left these quiet hillsides.

At last we reached the edge of the hills; before us the great plain lay in the glory of the sunset, stretching into what seemed an endless west: it was an ocean of green shored by a sky of gold.

But I had other things to think of, and leaving the prisoner in a hollow in Donogh's charge, I rode to the summit of one of the hills and began anxiously to scan the plain beneath. No trace of life met my eye; the great ocean of grass held upon its bosom no sign of existence. Then I set myself to do all that Red Cloud had told me. The camp was made some little distance in rear amid the shelter of the hills. Donogh with gun in hand sat sentry over the prisoner, and the dog lay alternately licking his wounded chest and gazing ominously at his enemy, as though the very smallest provocation would induce him to repeat his onslaught of the mid-day.

By the time camp was made night had fallen. I had already selected my ground for the signal fire; it was a saddle-back depression between two ridges, it was fully open to the plain west and south-west, but a higher ridge hid it from the direct south. Here I made a small bright fire, continuing to feed the flames with dry wood, which cast up a bright clear light about three feet in height. For half an hour I kept the flame steadily burning; then quenching it, I returned to our camp to find supper nearly ready.

We could as yet only communicate with the Cree by signs, but Donogh was quickly becoming an adept in the sign language of the wilds, and he and the Cree had exchanged much information. The prisoner evidently regarded me as his sole guarantee for safety, and his face brightened considerably when I returned to camp.

Another half-hour passed; supper had been ready some time, and the Cree and the Assineboine had already fallen to upon their portions of dry meat. I began to look anxiously towards the western darkness for the arrival of the Sioux.

CHAPTER VII.

The watched one halts—A light to the north-east—The Stonies find their mistake—Distant thunder—A light in the dark—The fire wind—*Sauve qui peut*—How the fire was lighted—We ride across the fire field—Enemies in sight—A dilemma—Between friend and foe—The scout throws in his lot with us—We ride to the rescue.

I MUST leave our little group round the camp fire, anxiously awaiting the arrival of the absent one, and carry my readers away to follow the fortunes of Red Cloud, whom we left far out upon the plains, under the vision, at a long distance, of the watchful eyes of many Assineboine enemies.

About the mid-day hour he halted by the edge of a small pool of brackish water, let his horses crop the short grass, and lay down himself as though he fully intended to camp upon the spot for the remainder of the day and the ensuing night. He well knew that all his movements were now under the closest observation from the distant line of hills, and each move he made was the result of much forethought; bit by bit the entire line he was pursuing, had been thought out during the previous night as he sat watching our camp in the aspen thicket. And this curious course which he had held to-day, as well as the lines upon which he had directed us to travel, were alike the result of careful plans long considered in every detail.

The Assineboines who watched his progress had, in fact, planned an expedition to intercept his further course, when suddenly they observed him halt, and camp upon the open plain. His capture now appeared to them to be certain; they had only to wait for nightfall, and then make a dash from the hills upon him, carry off the horses, and, if he was an enemy, take his scalp.

They therefore, watched with impatience the decline of day, and as soon as the first shades of twilight were thrown across the prairie they were riding hard for the spot where the last gleam of light had shown them the solitary traveller camped in fancied security.

But no sooner had these first shades fallen, than the seemingly unsuspecting traveller had sprung to his feet and made a rapid movement towards departure. As he jumped into his saddle a faint speck of light began to glow far off towards the north-east; soon it was seen to burn into a steady flame. Full upon the beacon Red Cloud held his way. It was his object to make as much distance as possible while the little ray of light still burned, so he galloped hard over the level ground. All at once it disappeared as suddenly as it had arisen, but the line it had given him he had marked by a star in the north-east heavens, and he kept on with unfaltering pace.

Anticipating every move of his enemies, he felt assured they would leave the hills as soon as twilight promised cover to their approach.

If he had allowed the fire to be continued in our camp, the Assineboines could not fail to see it when they reached the neighbourhood of his resting-place in the plains; but he had calculated all things exactly, and when about an hour after nightfall they sought in vain for trace of man or horse upon the very ground where, during the daylight, they had, as they thought, marked their prey, nothing save the dim blank of the prairie wrapped in darkness met their eyes, and no sound came to their listening ears save the long sigh of the night-wind through the dry grass of the plains.

Then all at once it flashed upon them. It was Red Cloud, the Sioux, whom they had watched all day upon the prairie; he had placed himself thus as a decoy to distract their attention from the camp where lay the sick Cree and the horses. While they had been watching this solitary Indian, doubtless the others had slipped away to some distant place of meeting, and the much-coveted prize of horses and scalp were lost to them for ever.

But men who have set their hearts upon gaining something which they eagerly long to obtain do not easily relinquish all hope of success. After a short consultation the

Assineboines determined to return to their camp, and early on the morrow to set out on a vigorous pursuit of the fugitives, who, they reasoned, encumbered by stores and a wounded comrade, would be able only to move slowly along. At the Sioux camp it would be easy to strike the trail, and a couple of days' riding would place them upon the skirts of the party again.

Arguing thus amongst themselves, and feeling that the much-coveted prize might still be theirs, the Assineboines returned to their camp. The rage of the trader McDermott knew no bounds when he heard the result of the stratagem by which the Sioux had eluded his enemies. Never had such a chance been given him of freeing himself for ever from the terror of his life—never had chance been so utterly and foolishly thrown away. Bitterly he reviled the Assineboines for their want of sagacity in thus letting slip a prize almost within their grasp.

"I gave ye," he said, "a chance of becoming at one stroke chiefs among your tribe. Ye have lost that chance; but your enemies can't be far away. To-morrow, if ye set out at daybreak, and do not rest until ye have overtaken them, ye will yet return to your people as big Indians."

But meantime a fresh cause for anxiety arose amongst the Assineboines. Their comrade who had gone out in the morning to spy the camp had not returned. Some mishap must surely have befallen him ; and yet it seemed difficult to imagine how he could have suffered harm at the hands of a wounded Cree and a couple of young white men. The morning would, perhaps, bring him forth safe and sound.

While thus around the camp-fire of the Assineboine war-party various surmises were afloat, and different plans were being formed for reversing on the morrow the mishaps of the day just passed, there was heard a low, distant noise—a sound seemingly far away in the night—that caused the Indians to spring suddenly to their feet, and gaze anxiously out into the darkness. And then they beheld a sight which the glare of their own fire had hitherto concealed from them. It was a lurid glow which overspread the entire northern heaven. Against this red light the trees and thickets of the nearer hills showed black and distinct. A fresh breeze was blowing from the north, and on its wings came the low roar of flame—that terrible noise which, when echoed in the full volume of a prairie fire, is one of the most awful sounds the human ear can listen to. And now, as the Assineboines looked and listened, the roar grew each moment louder, the glare spread into broader sheets of light across the north. For behind the fire there was rising the well known fire-wind, which came to fan into furnace flame the devouring element, and to hurl it in more furious bounds along the quivering earth.

Borne on this hot blast, the roar of the many-tongued

flame came louder than the waves against the rocks in winter tempest. Within the vast volume of sound could be distinguished the sharper crackle of the dry trees as the tide of fire reached some thickets, and at a single bound swept through them, from end to end, shooting out great tongues of flame high into the heavens, and sending others to leap madly on towards the south in strides that mocked the speed even of wild birds to escape before them.

A glance had been sufficient to tell the Assineboines of their danger. Wildly they rushed for their horses, and strove to get together their arms. Many of the horses had been only lately turned adrift, and these were easily caught; but the animals belonging to the trader were further away, and his pack-saddles, containing his provisions and several articles of trade—gunpowder, lead, flour, tea, sugar, and a small bale of blankets—lay on the ground near the camp. Amidst the dire confusion of the scene, while the Indians ran hither and thither, and the horses, already frightened at the roar of the approaching fire, began to snort in terror, the wretched trader might have been seen rushing frantically amid his packs, shouting orders that were unheeded, and vainly trying to get his goods together.

His Indian and half-breed attendants meantime rushed to the spot where the horses had been left, and managing to secure the five, came riding back in all haste with them to the camp. But the confusion and terror of all concerned had now reached the wildest pitch. In the great glare of the approaching fire faces and figures were plainly visible. Each man seemed only to think about his own safety, and all were so busy at their own work that they had no time to think of another's. One by one they began to get away from the scene, all taking the direction of the plains, and soon only the trader and his two attendants remained in the camp. By dint of great exertions the saddles were placed upon three of the horses; but it was impossible to get the heavier packs on to the animals.

The near approach of the fire, and the multitude of sparks that already filled the air around where they stood, caused the horses to kick and plunge violently, and it soon became apparent that a longer delay would only engulf the entire party in ruin. A last hope seemed to seize McDermott. There was a small pond of water near the camp; into this he would put his goods. Much would be hopelessly spoiled; but many of the articles would sustain but little damage, and he would return again to succour them. Hastily acting upon this idea he carried the packs into the pond, and laid them in about two feet of water, not far from the shore. The half-breed helped him with the work. The Salteaux stood ready with the horses. Then the trader sprang into the saddle, and all three rode wildly from the scene. It was a close shave.

As they cleared the hills the tongues of flame were licking the air above their heads. The fragments of fire were falling in showers around them. Once out in the plain they were safe; the grass was short and crisp, and the flames could make only a slow progress upon it.

When the trader and his two companions were safe beyond the range of the fire, they looked around on every side for their late friends; but no trace could be seen of man or beast. The great mass of flame made visible a wide circle of prairie; beyond that circle all was profound darkness.

They rode on farther into the gloom. The circle of light began to decrease in area as they got farther away from the blazing hills. Still there was no sign of life. Their companions had evidently deserted them.

McDermott determined to encamp where he was, and to trust to daylight to show him his friends or restore to him at least some portion of his lost goods. The Assineboines had indeed acted in a cowardly manner. They had ridden straight away into the plains to a spot many miles distant. A sudden panic appeared to have possessed them. Abandoning the trader to his fate, they had retired to concoct amongst themselves fresh plans for the future.

Leaving McDermott, gloomily watching from his bleak bivouac the raging fire as it flew along its course to the south, we must come back to our camp, where sat the Cree,

Donogh, the Assineboine prisoner, and his capturers, by the fire in the Wolverine hills.

The Cree and his prisoner had just finished their meal of dry meat and tea—the latter a luxury which Donogh gave them as a great treat, making no distinction between his ally the Cree and his captive the Assineboine—when from the hill close by there sounded the low plaintive cry of a wolf.

I recognized instantly my friend's signal, and made answer in the fashion the Sioux had taught me. Then Red Cloud came riding up into the circle of light which surrounded the camp-fire, and safe after a long and adventurous day our little prairie party stood once more united.

The Sioux did not lose time, however, in asking questions or in listening to the recital of the day's work. There was still much to be done ere it was time to sit down and eat or rest. The questions and answers would keep.

Bidding me follow him, and telling Donogh and the Cree to keep watch, with his gun at the "ready," over the prisoner, whose legs were still firmly fastened together, he walked straight from the camp into the dark hills towards the south.

Walking close behind him in his [footsteps, I waited anxiously to know what this new movement portended. I had not long, however, to wait. Some little distance to the south of the camp a chain of lakelets, partly joined together by swamps, ran through the hills from east to west. Passing over one of the causeways of hard, dry ground which lay at intervals through this chain, and going round a small lake until he had reached the farther side of the water, the Sioux stopped and turned to me.

"Now," he said, "I am going to fire the grass along the edge of this water. The wind blows strongly from the north —it will blow stronger when this grass is on fire. Standing in the wet reeds you will be perfectly safe from the flames; they will quickly burn away from you. I will fire the grass in many places along this line. I want you to do the same to the east while I do it to the west. The flames will not burn back towards the north in the face of this wind, and across these wet swamps, but to the south! Ah! there you will see such a blaze as you never before saw in your life!"

So saying, he struck a match and applied it to the dry and withered grass. For an instant it flickered low amid the blades and stems; then it caught fully. A sudden gust of north wind smote it and drove it down amid the roots of the grass, and then it rushed wildly away up the inclined plane which rose from the water and spread out to either side in widening circles of vivid fire.

The Sioux tore some dry grass from the ground, held it in the blaze, and then ran quickly along, touching the grass as he went, and leaving behind him a trail of fire. On the

Firing the prairie grass.

[*Page* 120.

other side I did the same. Wider grew the void—faster down the wind sped the rushing flame. In a very short time an immense band of fire lay across the hills—a band that moved to the south with a pace that momentarily grew more rapid—a roar that increased in volume every instant, until, in a great surge of flame, fanned by the full strength of the fire-wind, the torrent fled southward over hill and valley towards the camp of the Assineboines.

Half an hour later we met again in the camp, and as the roar of the fire grew fainter in the hills we sat together over our supper, and had full time to talk of the adventures of the day.

Before daybreak next morning a thick rain began to fall. The Sioux roused me, and told me that he intended to reconnoitre the site of the Assinboine camp, to which he would make the prisoner lead the way. He explained to the captive that his people had of necessity fled from the fire; that he did not desire to be brought into contact with them, but that he wished to see the line of their retreat. He also explained to the prisoner, that while he had no intention of taking his life in cold blood, yet that nevertheless any attempt at escape, or any appearance of treachery, would at once lead to his (the prisoner's) being shot. Donogh and the Cree were left in the camp, and as they were fully armed there was no danger to apprehend from attack.

The ground lying south of the chain of marshes was now one vast black waste. It would have been impossible to have ridden over it if the rain had not extinguished the glowing ashes at the roots of the burnt grass and cooled the surface of the ground. Here and there a thicket still smoked, or the trunk of a fallen tree smouldered in the morning air; but the rain had blotted out all signs of fire save the blackened earth, which, under the influence of the damp, made the entire landscape appear as if it had been overspread with ink.

Guided by the Assineboine, who was securely tied in his saddle, and whose left arm was firmly fastened to his side, we drew nigh to the site of the abandoned camp. As we gained the summit of a hill which commanded a view of the place from the north side, the Sioux, who led the way with the prisoner at his side, pulled in his horse abruptly, and motioned me to hold back; for there, by the edge of a small pond at the foot of the hill were three dark figures, and some spare horses on the darker ground. A glance had sufficed to show the Sioux that one of these figures was a white man; making a significant gesture to the prisoner, he whispered for a moment into his ear. A dark shadow crossed the face of the Sioux as he listened to his captive's reply. Here, within four hundred yards of him, stood his hated enemy, the man whose life he sought, the murderer of his father. And yet it was not thus he had longed to meet him. For the two men who were with his enemy he cared little. A sudden attack upon the three he would not have shrunk from, even though the odds would have been desperate; but how could he involve another in such a struggle? and what should he do with the Assineboine prisoner, who at the first symptom of attack would turn against his captors?

Rapidly he had taken in all these things; but for a moment he was unable to frame his course amid so many conflicting thoughts. Soon, however, his mind appeared made up, and he began to retrace his steps in the direction from which we had come. When we had gained a sufficient distance from the scene he again halted, and spoke to me. "There are some people in front whom it will be better that I should examine alone. Return with the prisoner to our camp; if I fail to rejoin you there before sunset, you may know that I have ceased to live. My horses and all I possess will then be yours. I am sorry that I should be forced to leave you thus; but you will not be worse off than when we met one week ago."

Then taking my hand, he shook it in silence, and turned back towards the ridge from whence he had seen the strange figures.

I was dumb with astonishment. What was the meaning of this strange conduct on his part? I tried in vain for an explanation. I remembered that the Assineboine had spoken to the Sioux, and that it was the information he had given which had first caused the change in my friend's plan. Instinctively I now looked towards my prisoner in the hope of finding an explanation of the mystery. The prisoner met my look with an expression of face that seemed to say, "I know what you are thinking of; but I cannot speak your tongue."

The Indian is, however, an adept in the art of communicating his thoughts by sign and gesture. There are few incidents of life on the plains that he cannot portray by the motion of his hands, the attitudes of his body, or the expression of his features. There is in fact a universal sign language common to all the various tribes over the vast wilderness, and when Sioux meets in peace Arrapahoe, or Crow and Blackfoot come together, they are able by means of their sign language, to exchange with each other all news of war, chase, or adventure, though no spoken word will have passed between them.

As the Assineboine now looked me full in the face, he began by instinct to express his meaning by signs. He placed his head resting on one side with his eyes closed, to indicate a camp or resting-place; then he pointed to himself, and held up the fingers of one hand twice, to show that it was the camp of his friends the Assineboines that he meant; then he touched me on the cheek and held up one finger, at the same time pointing in the direction of the ridge which they had just quitted, and moving his hand in the form of a circle, to show that he wished to carry his companion in thought beyond the circle of that ridge. Again he pointed to my face and repeatedly held up one finger. This was easily understood, it meant a white man; and following this clue I arrived at the fact that in the camp of the Assineboines there had been a white man. That was enough for me; my friend guessed, and guessed quickly, the rest. The white man was the trader McDermott. One of the three men seen by the Sioux from the ridge-top was the enemy he had so long sought for, and now he had gone back to risk his life in a desperate and unequal struggle with this inveterate foe.

I looked towards the ridge, and noticed that the figure of the Sioux was no longer visible upon its black surface. He was evidently following the valley, to gain some point from which he might make a closer onslaught upon the party.

I had small time left for reflection; but when a man keeps one great object steadily in view, it is ever an easy matter to decide upon the general outline of the course he has to follow; that great object in this case was to help my friend—to save him, if possible, in the desperate venture in which he was about to engage. I could not accept quietly the part which in this instance the Sioux would have assigned to me. Friendship is no limited liability, and in the peril of the work we had undertaken it should be all and all alike.

The presence of the Assineboine was, however, a fact not to be overlooked in the affair. It would have been an easy matter to have rid myself of this prisoner, and then galloped direct to the assistance of my friend; but I could not entertain such a thought for a second. Life taken in fair fight had little terror for me; but not even the safety of my friend's life, or of my own, could induce me to slay in cold blood a fellow-creature.

One sign I made to the Assineboine. Holding up two fingers, I pointed to the Assineboine and then motioned with my hand across the ridge. The question was understood, and the prisoner shook his head in reply—the other two men whom we had seen were not Assineboines. That was all I wanted to know. In an instant I had severed the cords which bound the prisoner in his saddle, and had cut free his left arm from its binding; then I motioned with my hand that he was free to go whither he pleased. Since the prisoner's capture many things had caused him unutterable astonishment. His life had been spared, he had been well fed; his leg, which had sustained only a trifling injury from his encounter with the dog, had been carefully looked after by the man who had taken him prisoner; and here now, when he could fully read in that white man's face the reasons why he (that white man) might have taken his life in order to be free to assist his comrade, liberty was given to him, and he was told to go which way he might select.

He was a bold and adventurous Indian, this Assineboine—perhaps of his party the best and bravest. Still he would not have scrupled at any moment, had occasion offered, to make an effort for his freedom at the expense of the lives of those around him; but now, the generous act of the white man struck him in a totally new light, and he sat on his horse unable to shape a distinct line of action amidst the many conflicting thoughts that thronged his brain.

There had existed, in days when his people, the Assineboines, were one of the most formidable tribes on the northern prairies—when Teltacka, or the Left-handed, ruled from the Souri to the South Saskatchewan—there had been, he knew, a custom in the tribe for young men to show unexpected clemency to a vanquished foe; but never had he heard, amid the stories told over the camp fire of deeds of bygone battle or of ancient prowess, such an example of generosity and courage as that now before him. As a boy he had heard his father tell how once, in a battle with the Gros Ventres near the Knife river, he had spared the life of a young man whose horse had plunged into a snow-drift, leaving its rider completely at his mercy, and how years after the same Gros Ventre had repaid the gift by saving his former benefactor from the fury of the victors, when the might of the Assineboines was crushed by the same band on the banks of the Missouri. These things now all flashed through the mind of the Assineboine, in a tenth of the time it has taken me to put into words the scene in which he found himself suddenly set at liberty, and free to follow what course he pleased.

I did not wait to see what my late prisoner would decide upon, but turning my horse quickly from the spot I rode in the direction of the place where the Sioux had been last seen. I had not gone very far before I was aware that my late prisoner was following in my wake. An idea of treachery at once crossed my mind; but looking back I saw the Assineboine making signs of friendship. I pulled up and awaited his approach. As he came up he pointed to his defenceless state; then to the bow and arrows which I had taken on the previous day, and which I still carried slung over my shoulder; then the Assineboine's arm was directed towards the ridge, and placing his hands in the attitude of those of a man drawing an arrow to full stretch at the moment of firing, he indicated plainly enough his meaning. He would help in the coming struggle if he had arms to do so. I handed him his bow and quiver, and then we two, so lately captor and captive, rode forward as comrades to the fight.

CHAPTER VIII.

The fight—The Sioux and the swamp—The trader's triumph—Red Cloud fights on foot—The trader finds he has other foes to reckon with—The Assineboine draws a straight arrow—The trader's flight—Our losses and gains—Winter supplies—Our party is completed—"All's well that ends well."

THERE was no time now for reconnoitring the ground before the attack began. There was in fact nothing for it but to ride straight over the ridge, and lunge at once into the struggle, for, as we rode briskly up the black incline towards the top of the hill the sharp report of a shot already echoed through the hills, a signal that the fray had begun. It was even so.

The Sioux, following the valley round the foot of the ridge, had debouched close to his foe, and had put his horse straight for the spot where the trader was still engaged, on the edge of the pool, in loading the stores which he had just carried from the water, upon the backs of his pack animals.

The presence of the Sioux became instantly known to his enemy. Relinquishing his work, the trader seized his gun from the ground where it was lying, and dropping upon

K

one knee he took deliberate aim at the advancing horseman. The Sioux bent low upon his horse's neck as the white smoke flashed from the muzzle, and the bullet whistled over his lowered head, burying itself in the hill-side,

Meanwhile the trader's two attendants had sprung to their saddles, apparently more ready for flight than for fight. The onslaught of the Sioux was so sudden and so unexpected that these men had no time to realize the fact that there was only one assailant; more than this, they had engaged with their master to trade, not to fight; and, though neither of them was thoroughly deficient in courage, the first impulse of both on this occasion, was to fly; and had the Sioux been permitted to continue his onward career full upon McDermott he would have found himself alone face to face with his hated foe; but such was not to be.

Between the Sioux and the trader there lay a small swampy spot, half stagnant water, half morass, not more than six paces across; it ran inland from the pool for some distance. The blackened ground lying on every side had completely hidden from the keen eye of the Indian the dangerous nature of the spot. All at once he saw before his horse, now at full gallop, this fatal obstacle. To have checked his horse would have been no easy matter, so impetuous was his rate of motion; but had it been possible to have stayed his own charger, he would have presented such a sure mark for the keen eyes of the men on the further side of the pond as to ensure the destruction of both horse and rider. There was nothing for it then but to go full at the dangerous spot, and trust to strength of horse and skill of rider to come through.

Raising the horse a little in his pace, the Sioux held straight upon his course; the soft ground broke beneath the horse's feet, but so rapid were the movements of his legs, and so strong were his efforts to draw himself clear of the spongy soil, that for a second or two it seemed as though he would pull through and win the other side. At the far edge, however, a softer and deeper spot opened beneath the vigorous hoof, and, despite all efforts, the brave little animal sank helpless to his girths.

The Sioux sprang to his feet, and in another second he had gained the dry, firm ground at the farther side; but the water of the swamp had for a moment covered his gun, the priming had become hopelessly clogged, and the weapon utterly useless to him. The mishap had given his adversary time for reflection and preparation; and the two retainers, realizing the fact that they were attacked by only one assailant, and that even that one was already half engulfed amid a swamp, took heart and came down to the assistance of their employer; while the trader himself had profitted by the delay to jump into his saddle and to fall back out of reach of the Sioux in order to reload his gun.

Long practice in following the herds of buffalo over the

prairies at headlong speed, had made him an expert hand at rapid loading and firing on horseback. To throw from his powder-horn a charge of powder loosely into the gun; to spit from his mouth a ball down the muzzle, so that the action caused at the same instant the powder to press out into the priming-pan and the bullet to fit against the powder—these motions of the buffalo-hunter took him but a few seconds, and wheeling his horse at the charge, he now came thundering down full at the Sioux. But though little time had been lost in these movements of loading, enough had passed to enable Red Cloud to change his tactics and to secure himself from the first furious onslaught which he saw impending. Springing across the treacherous morass, he gained the side on which he had first entered it, and with his bow at the "ready" he calmly awaited the charge of his enemy.

While yet fully one hundred yards distant, McDermott saw and realized the change on the part of the Sioux, and knowing the fatal nature of the ground, he forbore not only to risk his horse across the swamp, but to approach within fifty yards of its nearer side—a distance which would have brought him within range of his enemy's fire; he however looked upon the fate of the Sioux as certain; and well it might appear so to him.

All chance of escape was now cut off; the horse still lay helpless in the morass, buried to the girths; his rider, active and expert though he was on foot, could only hope to delay his fate when pitted in fight against three horsemen, and with nothing but a bow and arrow to oppose to their firearms. If the position could not be forced in front, there was ample room to turn its flank and move round it on the hill side. Thus menaced in front and attacked in rear, the position of the Sioux might well seem desperate.

Fully did Red Cloud in these few seconds of time realize the dangers that encompassed him; nevertheless, he thought far less of his own peril than of his inability to meet his deadly foe. Bitterly he repented of his rash onslaught, and still more bitter were his regrets that he should have left his trusty double-barrelled rifle—which he usually carried slung upon his back—in the camp that morning, and that he had no more effective weapon now than the bow and arrows, which he could so dexterously handle, but which were only of use at fifty or sixty yards, while his rifle would have enabled him to cover his enemies at four times that distance. McDermott was, as we have said, no novice in the art of prairie war or chase. He quickly saw the strength or weakness of his adversary's position.

Calling to his attendants to watch the side of the small swamp nearest to where he stood, and thus prevent the Sioux from again executing a movement across it, he wheeled his horse rapidly to one side, and rode furiously towards the base of the hill, so as to pass round upon the dry ground at the end of the swamp, and bear down upon his foe from behind. As he passed his retainers, he shouted to them to ride up and fire upon the Sioux, promising that the horse and all that belonged to its rider should be the reward of him who would bring the foe to the ground.

The French half-breed showed little inclination, however, to render the already long odds against the Sioux still more desperate; but the Salteaux belonged to a tribe long at deadly enmity with the Sioux nation, and he also inherited much of the cowardly ferocity of his own tribe, who, unable to cope in the open country with their enemies, never scrupled to obtain trophies which they could not win in war, by the aid of treacherous surprise or dastardly night attacks. The present was a kind of warfare peculiarly suited to his instincts, and he now rode forward to fire upon the Sioux across the swamp, at the moment when he would be engaged with a more formidable enemy on his own side.

These movements, quickly as they passed, were all noted by the watchful eye of the Sioux. He cast one quick look at his horse, in the hope that it might be possible to extricate him from the swamp ere the trader had yet got round the northern side; but a glance was enough to tell him that all hope in that quarter was gone, for the ooze had risen higher upon the poor animal, and nothing but the united labour of two or three hands, could now draw him from the quicksand. His head was still free, however, and Red Cloud had time to notice in his own moment of peril how the eye of his faithful friend and long-tried servant turned upon him what seemed a look of sympathy in his great extremity. But now the trader had gained the end of the swamp and was already beginning to wheel his horse towards where the Sioux stood. A natural impulse bid the latter move forward to meet his foe. Short as was the space that separated the two men; rapid as was the pace at which one was momentarily lessening that distance, Red Cloud rushed forward to meet the advancing horseman. The trader's plan was to keep just out of the range of the Sioux' arrows, and to manœuvre his horse so that he could get frequent shots at his enemy without exposing himself to the slightest danger. He knew too well with what terrible accuracy the red man can use his bow at any object within fifty yards of his standpoint. McDermott was a true shot, whether on horseback or on foot; he knew, too, all those shifts of body by which the Indian manages to partially cover himself by his horse at moments of attack; but on the present occasion he intended simply to continue hovering round the Sioux, who was just in the angle formed by the swamp and the lake, and to take his time in every shot he would fire. Pulling up his horse at about eighty yards' distance, he placed his gun to his shoulder and laid his head low upon the stock, aiming right over the ears of his horse upon the advancing figure of the Sioux. But while yet his finger paused ere pressing the trigger, the sharp ring of a bullet smote his ear; his horse gave a convulsive spring upwards, and the trader, retaining his seat with difficulty, fired wildly and harmlessly into the air. Then, ere he could sufficiently recover his suddenly startled senses, there came loud shouts of advancing men from the ridge upon his left. Turning his head in that direction, he beheld two horsemen riding at a furious gallop down upon him. His life was dearer to him than the hope of destroying his enemy. Fortunate at finding that his horse had only received a flesh wound, and that he was still able to carry a rider, McDermott wheeled quickly to the rear, to retire the way he had come. As he did so, an arrow grazed his shoulder, and whistled past into the ground; then, from the ridge another shot rang out, this time fired in the direction of the Salteaux, who had advanced to within sixty paces of the Sioux on the opposite side of the swamp. The ball went sufficiently near its mark to cause that worthy to abandon his attempt at murder, and to execute a rapid retrograde movement; indeed, so thoroughly did he appear convinced that the battle was irrevocably lost, that he ceased not to continue his flight, quite unmindful of any fate which might overtake either his master or fellow-servant.

McDermott seeing that the game was up, now made a final effort to save his pack animals from capture; but my blood was now thoroughly roused—the fever of fight was on me, and no power on earth could stay my onward career.

Followed closely by the Assineboine, I swept round by the head of the swamp, and made straight for the spot where the trader was endeavouring to get his pack animals into motion. As I rode along at full gallop, I passed the French half-breed at some distance; the latter dropped his gun across his bridle arm and fired in front of my horse. The ball struck the animal in the neck, and plunging forward, horse and rider were instantly stretched upon the ground in one confused mass. But the Assineboine was riding close in my wake.

Seeing the action of the half-breed, he turned his horse slightly to the right, and with an arrow drawn to the fullest stretch of his stout Indian bow, he bore full upon the flank of this new enemy.

Too late the half-breed saw his danger, and turned to fly. At thirty paces' distance the Assineboine let fly his shaft, with so true an aim that the arrow pierced the half-breed's leg and buried itself deeply in his horse's side. He did not await another shot; drawing a pistol, he fired wildly at the Assineboine, and followed the Salteaux in his flight.

Meantime the Sioux had crossed the swamp, and was approaching swiftly on foot to this new scene of combat. The trader beheld with rage the sudden turn which the fight had taken. His horse had suffered little from his flesh wound, and now that the only two steeds whose pace and mettle were matches for his own were disposed of, he could still easily distance any attempt at pursuit; but to delay longer in endeavouring to save his goods would soon have cost him his life. Red Cloud was drawing rapidly near—the Salteaux and the half-breed had fled. For a moment he thought of falling back to continue the fight at longer range, using his horse to carry him from ridge to ridge; but now another rider suddenly appeared upon the sky-line on the side from which the first attack had been delivered. It was Donogh riding down to the rescue. This fresh accession to the strength of his enemies decided him.

Utterly beaten at all points, and flinging an impotent malediction towards his enemies, McDermott hastened from the scene of the disaster, leaving two pack-horses and all his stores in the hands of the victors.

Donogh now joined us. He was wild with excitement, and his joy at finding me safe knew no bounds. For some time after our departure from camp he had sat quiet, but the Cree had told him by signs that a fight was probable, and then he could stand inaction no longer. He had followed our trail; as he neared the scene of action, the report of fire-arms had told him the struggle had already begun; and then he had galloped straight to the rescue. Seeing me on the ground, his first idea was to charge the trader, and it was this new and impetuous onset that finally decided McDermott's flight.

The Sioux made it his first care to ascertain what damage had befallen his friend. I had half risen from the ground; but the violence of the shock had been so great that it was some little time before I fully understood what was passing around. As soon as Red Cloud had ascertained that I had sustained no greater injury than the concussion the fall had given me, he turned his attention to the Assineboine, whose aid, at the most critical moment, had completely turned the fortunes of the day. It was in his own noble nature to comprehend the change which had worked upon our late prisoner and made him a staunch and firm friend; he took the hand of the Assineboine, and shook it warmly. "I owe you much for this day," he said; "I shall begin to repay it from this moment. Help me to draw my horse from yonder swamp, and then we shall see to our prizes."

So saying, but first securing the pack animals, and giving the lariat which held them into my hands, the Sioux, Donogh, and the Assineboine turned to rescue the horse from the swamp where he had lain, sinking gradually deeper, since that disastrous moment when first breaking through the spongy soil he had so nearly ended for ever the career of his rider.

By dint of great exertions, working with leather lines

passed around the neck and quarters of the horse, they at length succeeded in drawing him from the morass. The Sioux was overjoyed at once more recovering his long-tried horse; for a moment he half forgot the bitterness of having lost his enemy, in the pleasure of finding himself still the owner of this faithful friend.

But the full importance of the victory just gained only burst upon our little party when we came to examine the goods that had fallen to us as victors. The two pack-horses had only been partly loaded, and many of the parcels and bags still lay in loose heaps upon the ground; they were all dripping with water, having been only recently brought from out of the lake, where they had lain since the alarm of fire on the previous night; but a careful examination showed that they had sustained little damage from the water. It is well known that flour lying closely packed in a sack resists for a great time the action of damp, the portion nearest to the sack becomes a soft sort of cement, which prevents the water from penetrating more than a couple of inches further in. Thus, the three sacks of fine Red River flour formed a most precious treasure to men whose winter hut was to be built still farther among the vast solitudes than the spot they were now on. A small barrel of gunpowder, coppered on the inside, was of course perfectly water-tight; a case of knives, with some axe-heads and saws, only required to be dried and cleaned to be again in perfect order;

a few hours' exposure to sun and wind would suffice to dry the blankets and flour; the tea, most precious article, was to a great extent saved by being made up in tin canisters—only that portion of it which was in lead paper had suffered injury; and the sugar, though the wet had quite penetrated through the bag, could still be run down by the action of fire to the consistency of hard cakes, which would be quite serviceable for use in that state. Two bags of salt, though wet, were also serviceable.

Of course such things as shot, bullets, and a few hardware articles, had suffered no injury whatever.

Thus as, one by one, all these things were unpacked and laid out upon the ground, we realized how fortunate had been the chance that had thrown so many valuable essentials of prairie life into the possession of our party.

"We are now," said the Sioux, "quite independent of every one. We have here supplies which will last us for the entire winter and far into next year. You, my friend," he said to the Assineboine, "will continue with us, and share all these things; they are as much yours as they are ours. If you decide to join us, even for a while, you will live as we do. We are on our way far west, to hunt and roam the plains; we will winter many days' journey from here. If it should be your wish to go and rejoin your people, one of these horses and a third of these things shall be yours to take away with you; but if you remain with us, you will share our camp, our fire, our food."

The Assineboine did not ponder long upon his decision; to return to his people would have been to open many causes of quarrel with them or with the trader or his agents. The new life offered everything that an Indian could covet. Red Cloud was a chief of the Sioux—a people who had ever been as cousins to his people—whose language closely resembled his own. "Yes he would go west with these men, even to where the sun set."

The Assineboine—who in future shall bear the name by which he was first known to us, of the scout—had possessed himself of the half-breed's gun, which that worthy had dropped at the moment he received the arrow wound. His steed, a thoroughly serviceable Indian pony, had both speed and endurance, and was therefore suited for any emergency which war or the chase might call forth. My horse had been the only loss in the affair; but in his place there had been a gain of two good steeds, and there were spare goods in the packs sufficient to purchase a dozen horses from any Indian camp the party might reach.

While the Sioux and the scout were busily engaged in looking through the trader's captured stores, I sat revolving in my mind every incident of the recent struggle. On the whole I felt well-pleased; it was my first brush with an enemy, and I had not flinched from fire or charge.

From the moment of my first shot from the ridge top—a shot fired at two hundred yards' range—to my last onslaught upon the retreating trader, I had never lost my head; eye, hand, and brain had worked together, and I had unconsciously timed every move to the demand of the passing moment.

I fully realized the reasons why Red Cloud had decided not to involve me in his struggle with the trader, but I could not help saying to my friend when we were about to leave the spot, "We were to have been brothers in war, as well as in peace. You have not kept your word fairly with me."

"All's well that ends well," said the Sioux. "Henceforth our fights shall be shared evenly between us."

Having stripped the dead horse of his saddle and trappings, I mounted one of the captured animals, and his load divided between the other animals, the whole party set out at a rapid pace for our camp.

CHAPTER IX.

We again go west—Hiding the trail—Red and white for once in harmony—Peace and plenty—An autumn holiday—We select a winter's camp—The Forks—Hut-building—Our food supply—The autumn hunt—The Great Prairie—Home thoughts—Indian instincts—The Lake of the Winds—Buffalo—Good meat—A long stalk—The monarch of the waste—A stampede—Wolves—The red man's tobacco.

As we rode back to camp, the Sioux learned from the scout all that had happened in the camp of the Assineboines, from the time that he had himself brought news of the presence in the hills of the disabled Cree and his protectors, until the moment when he had been captured by the united efforts of the dog and his masters.

The Sioux listened eagerly to the story of the trader's having literally set a price upon his head; and when he reflected that all the precautions which he, Red Cloud, had taken had been done in complete ignorance of the machinations of his enemy, and only from casually learning from the Cree that a party of hostile Indians had passed him on the previous night, he felt how true is that lesson in war which enjoins never neglecting in times of danger to guard against the worst even though the least may only be threatened.

But Red Cloud learned from the story of the scout information for future guidance, as well as confirmation of the course he had already followed. He realized the fact that though the fire had already freed him from the presence of the Assineboines, yet, that it could only be a short respite; the bribe offered by the trader was too high to allow these men to relinquish all hope of taking prizes which were to make them great Indians for the rest of their lives. The necessity of quickly shifting his ground, and of leaving altogether that part of the country, became so fully apparent to him that he lost no time in communicating to us his plan of action.

It was, to march that evening about ten miles towards the north, and then to strike from the hills due west into the great plain. Being heavily loaded with stores, we could not hope by dint of hard marching to outstrip our enemies; but by taking unusual precautions to hide our trail, we might succeed in successfully eluding the watchful eyes of the Assineboines.

A hasty dinner followed the return of the party to camp, and then preparations for departure were at once made. The Cree had made, in the rest and care of the last two days, more progress to recovery than in the whole period

L

of his former convalescence, and he was now well able to take his share in the work of striking camp.

When men bivouac in the open it takes but little time to make a camp or to quit it, and ere the sun had set the whole party had got in motion, and, led by the Sioux, were threading their course through the hills farther towards the north.

The rain had ceased, but the grass was still too wet to burn, so that the simple expedient of setting fire to the prairie in order to hide a trail, was in this instance impossible. As, however, the point of departure from the hills for the west was the point most essential to obliterate, the Sioux did not so much care that our trail while in the hills could easily be followed.

Not until midnight did he give the word to camp, and the first streak of dawn found us again in motion. While the morning was still young we arrived at a small river which flowed out from the hills into the plain, and pursued, far as the eye could determine to the west, a course sunken in a narrow valley deep beneath the level of the prairie. Here was the point of departure. The stream was shallow, and the current ran over a bed of sand and pebbles. The Sioux, Donogh, and I, led the pack-horses along the centre of this river channel, while the scout and the Cree were directed to ride many times to and fro up the farther bank, and then to continue their course towards the north for some miles.

It was Red Cloud's intention to camp about fifteen miles lower down the stream; he would only keep his horses in the bed of the channel for one hour, by that time he would have gained a considerable distance down stream; then selecting a dry or rocky place, we would have left the channel and continued our course along the meadows on one side.

When the scout and the Cree had put some miles between them and the stream they were to turn sharp to their left hand; first one, and later on the other, and then rejoin us some time during the following day. By these plans the Sioux hoped to foil any pursuers who might be on his trail, and he would certainly succeed in delaying a pursuit until the fine weather would again make the grass dry enough to allow it to burn.

Down the centre of the stream we led the pack-horses in file, and away to the north went the scout and the Cree. It was toilsome work wading along the channel of the river, which in some places held rocks and large loose stones; but by little and little progress was made, and ere sunset the dry ground was once more under foot, and our party was pursuing a rapid course along the meadows to the west.

Red Cloud had told the scout that he would await him at the Minitchinas, or Solitary Hill, a conical elevation in the plains some twenty miles away to the west. At the north side of this hill our whole party came again together about the middle of the following day, and after a hearty meal we turned our faces towards that great plain which stretches from the base of this solitary mound into what seemed an endless west.

Everybody was in high spirits; even the dog had quite recovered from the effects of his arrow-wound, and the scout and he had become firm friends.

It was a curious group this, that now held its course into the western wilds.

There were representatives of three of those strange families of the aboriginal race of North America—that race now rapidly vanishing from the earth, and soon only to be known by those wild names of soft sound and poetic meaning which, in the days of their glory, they gave to ridge, lake, and river, over the wild wilderness of their vast dominions; and two white men from a far-distant land, alien in race, strange in language, but bound to them by a sympathy of thought, by a soldier instinct which was strong enough to bridge the wide gulf between caste and colour, and make red and white unite in a real brotherhood—a friendship often pictured in the early dreams of the red race when the white man first sought the wilds, but never fully realized in all these long centuries of war and strife, save when the pale-faced stranger whom they called the Black Robe, came to dwell amongst them and to tell them of a world beyond the grave, more blissful than their fabled happy hunting-grounds, where red men and white were to dwell, the servants of One Great Master.

And now days began to pass of quiet travel over the autumn prairies—days of real enjoyment to me, who hour by hour read deeper into the great book which nature ever holds open to those who care to be her students—that book whose pages are sunsets and sunrises, twilights darkening over interminable space, dawns breaking along distant horizons, shadows of inverted hill-top lying mirrored in lonely lakes, sigh of west wind across measureless meadow, long reach of silent river, stars, space, and solitude.

Ten days of such travel carried our little party far into the west. We had reached that part of the northern plains which forms the second of those sandy ridges or plateaux which mount in successive steps from the basin of the great lake Winnipeg, to the plains lying at the base of the Rocky Mountains.

In this great waste game was numerous. Buffalo roamed in small bodies hither and thither; cabri could be seen dotting the brown grass, or galloping in light bounds to some vantage hill, from whence a better survey of the travellers could be had; wolves and foxes kept skulking in the prairie depressions, and dodged along the edges of ridges to scent or sight their prey. The days were still fine and bright; but the nightly increasing cold told that winter was slowly but surely coming on.

It was now the middle of September, early enough still for summer travel, but it would soon be necessary to look out for some wintering-ground, where wood for a hut and fuel could be easily obtained, and where the grass promised food for the horses during the long months of snow.

Almost every part of this vast ocean of grass had become thoroughly known to Red Cloud. Land once crossed by a red man is ever after a living memory to him. He can tell, years after he has passed along a trail, some of the most trifling landmarks along it; a bush, a rock, a sharply marked hill, will be all treasured in his memory; and though years may have elapsed since his eye last rested upon this particular portion of the great prairie, he will know all its separate features, all the little hills, courses, or creeks which lie hidden amid the immense spaces of this motionless ocean.

For some days the Sioux had been conning over in his mind the country, seeking some spot lying within easy reach of where he was now moving which yielded what our party required—timber, fuel, and grass. A few years earlier he had camped at the point of junction of two rivers, the Red Deer and the Medicine, not more than four days' journey to the north-west of where he now was. He remembered that amid a deep thicket of birch, poplar, and cotton-wood, there stood a large group of pine-trees. If fire had spared that part of the prairie, he knew that the alluvial meadows along the converging rivers, would yield rich store of winter food for the horses. He knew, too, that in other respects the spot had many recommendations in its favour; it lay almost in the centre of that neutral zone between the Cree country and the sandy wastes of the Blackfeet nation, and that it was therefore safe in winter from the roving bands of these wild tribes, whose warfare is only carried on during the months of spring, summer, and autumn. All these things combined made him fix upon this spot for the winter camping-ground, and he began to shape the course of the party more to the north, to see if the place held still in its sheltered ridges all the advantages it had possessed when he had seen it for the first and last time.

Riding along one sunny mid-day, he explained to me the prospect before us.

"It is getting late in the season," he said; "all the grass is yellow; the wind has begun to rustle in the dry seeds and withered prairie flowers; the frost of night gets harder and colder. At any moment we may see a great change; that far off sky-line, now so clear cut against the prairie, would become hidden; dense clouds would sweep across the sky, and all the prairie would be wrapped in snow-drift.

"The winter in this north land is long and severe; the snow lies for months upon the plains, in many feet in thickness it will rest upon yon creek, now so full of bird-life. The cold will then be intense; all the birds, save the prairie-grouse, the magpie, and the whisky jack, will seek southern lands; the buffalo will not, however, desert us, they may move farther north into the Saskatchewan, and wolves, foxes, and coyotes will follow in their wake. Neither horse nor man can then brave for any time the treeless plains.

"We must prepare for the winter," he went on, "and my plan is this: some days' march from this is a spot which, when I last saw it, had around it all that we shall require for our winter comfort. Where two rivers come together there stands, sheltered among hills, a clump of pine-trees. The points of the rivers are well wooded, and the marshes along the banks hold wild vetch, and the pea plant of the prairie grows through the under-bush, high above the snow, giving food to horses in the worst seasons of the year.

"I don't know any fitter place for winter camp in all the hundreds of miles that are around us. We are now bound for that spot, and if things are as I last saw them, we shall make our hut in the pine wood and settle into our winter-quarters ere the cold has come. We have still much to do, and it is time we set to work."

I heard with joy these plans for the winter. The life was still so new to me—the sense of breathing this fresh bright atmosphere, and of moving day by day through this great ocean of grass, was in itself such pleasure, that I had latterly ceased almost altogether to think much about the future, feeling unbounded confidence in my Indian friend's skill and forethought.

Donogh and I had in fact been enjoying the utmost bliss of perfect freedom—that only true freedom in life, the freedom of fording streams, crossing prairies, galloping over breezy hill-tops, watching wild herds in their daily habits of distance, seeing them trail along slowly into golden sunsets, or file in long procession to some prairie stream for the evening drink; or better still, marking some stray wolf into a valley where he thought himself unseen, and dashing down upon him with wild hulloo ready for the charge, while the silent echoes wake to the clash of hoof and ring of cheer. All these things, and many more, had filled the hours of our life in the past month to such a degree, that our spirits seemed to have widened out to grasp the sense of a freedom as boundless as the wilderness itself.

It was on the third day following the conversation above recorded, that we came in sight of a low dark ridge, showing itself faintly above the northern horizon.

Flowing in many serpentine bends, a small creek wound through the prairie at our left hand, cotton-wood clusters fringed the "points" of this stream, and long grass grew luxuriantly between the deep bends, which sometimes formed almost a figure eight in the roundness of their curves. Our party moved in a straight line, which almost touched the outer points of these deep curves, and from the higher ground along which we marched, the eye could at times catch the glint of water amid the ends of grasses, and mark the wild ducks sailing thickly on the rushy pools. I had used my gun frequently during the morning, and when the mid-day hour had come we had a plentiful supply of wild ducks hanging to our saddles.

In this life in the wilderness I had early learned the lesson of killing only what was needed to supply the wants of the party. When wild ducks were so plentiful, it would of course have been easy to shoot any quantity of them; but that habit of civilized sport which seeks only the " bag " had long since ceased to influence me, and I had come to regard the wild creatures of the prairie, birds and beasts, as far more worthy of study in life than in death. That terrible misnomer "good sport" had for me a truer significance. It meant watching the game by little and little, and killing only what was actually required for the use of our fellow-travellers and myself. During the mid-day halt on this day Red Cloud held a long conversation with the other Indians upon the place they were now tending to. The Assineboine had never visited the spot, the Cree had been there on a war-party two summers ago; but it was now, he thought, so late in the season that there would be little danger of meeting any roving bands of Blackfeet, and the Crees he knew to be far away towards the eastern prairies.

It would have been difficult to have imagined a more perfect scene of a mid-day camp than that in which our little party found itself on this bright autumnal day.

The camp fire was made at the base of a round knoll, which ran from the higher plateau of the prairie into one of the deep bends of the creek; upon three sides a thick fringe of cotton-wood lined the edges of the stream; the golden leaves of poplars and the bronzed foliage of the bastard maple hung still and bright in the quiet September day. Immediately around the camp grew small bushes of wild plum, covered thickly with crimson and yellow fruits of delicious flavour.

Ah, what a desert that was! When the wild ducks and the flour gelettes had been eaten, a single shake of the bush brought down showers of wild sweet fruit, and when we had eaten all we could, bags were filled for future use.

But even such prairie repasts must come to an end, and it was soon time to saddle and be off. So the horses were driven in, and resuming our course, the evening found us on the banks of the Red Deer river, not far from its point of junction with the Medicine. We camped that night upon the banks of the stream, and early next day reached the point of junction. A ford was soon found, and to the Sioux' great joy no trace of fire was to be seen in the meadows between the rivers, or on the range of hills that lay to the north and east; all was still and peaceful as he had last seen it. The pine bluff yet stood dark and solemn at the point where the rivers met, and the meadows, as our party rode through them, were knee-deep in grasses and long trailing plants.

And now began in earnest a period of hard work. First the small lodge of dressed skins was pitched upon a knoll amid the pine-trees; then the saddles and stores were all made safe, upon a rough stage supported upon poles driven fast into the ground. Next began the clearing of trees and brushwood on the site selected for the hut. It was a spot close to the point formed by the meeting of the two rivers, but raised about twenty feet above the water, and partly hidden by trees and bushes. Tall pines grew on the site, but the axe of the Sioux and the scout soon brought down these giants, and made clear the space around where the hut was to stand.

It was wonderful to watch the ready manner in which the Indians worked their hatchets; never a blow missed its mark, each falling with unerring aim upon the spot where the preceding one had struck; then a lower-struck cut would cause the huge splinters to fly from the trunk, until, in a few moments the tree crashed to the earth in the exact line the Indians wished it to fall.

Although a novice at woodman's craft, I was no idle spectator of the work. If a man has a quick eye, a ready hand, and a willing heart, the difficulties that lie in things that are unknown to us are soon overcome. Every hour's toil made a sensible improvement in my work. I soon learnt how to roughly square the logs, and to notch the ends of them so that one log fitted closely to the other.

Donogh and the wounded Cree meantime looked after the horses, gathered fuel for the fire, and cooked the daily meals of our party, and often gave a hand at the lifting of log or labour of construction. Thus the work went on without intermission, and day by day the little hut grew in size. All day long the sound of wood-chopping echoed through the pine wood at the point, over the silent rivers, causing some passing wolf to pause in his gallop and listen to the unwonted noise; but no human ear was there to catch it, or human eye to mark the thin column of blue smoke that rose at eventime above the dark pine-tops when the day's work was over. There was no lack of food either. With a few hooks and lines Donogh managed to do good work among the fishes in the rivers. The creeks and ponds still held large flocks of wild ducks, and many a fat black duck fell to a steady stalk of the Cree, whose crawling powers were simply unmatched. The black-tailed buck were numerous in the thickets around, and with so many things the larder never wanted for game, venison, wild fowl, or fish.

Thus the days went by, and at last the hut was finished and ready for occupation. It was an oblong structure, measuring twenty-five feet by twenty. A low door gave admission upon the south side; east and west held windows of parchment-skin drawn over a wooden frame that opened and shut on leather hinges. At the north side stood the fireplace, a large hearth, and a chimney capable of holding a quantity of pine logs. Half the wooden door frame was also bound with parchment skins; thus plenty of light could be obtained in rough weather, and when the days would be still and fine both door and windows could be open.

"When the snow has fallen," said Red Cloud to us, "the light from the ground will be very great. The snow hanging on the pine boughs will also light up the place, and the winter's day will be brighter than you can imagine. At night our logs will blaze brightly upon the hearth."

The fireplace and chimney were built of stones and mud. The Indians had carefully mixed the latter so as to ensure its standing the great heat of the winter fires. The logs composing the walls were all of pines, or, more properly speaking, of white spruce; they had been roughly squared and notched at the end, to allow of their catching each other and fitting tightly together; mud and moss had then been pressed into the interstices so as to make them perfectly air-tight. The roof was composed of long reed-grass, cut from a neighbouring swamp and dried in the sun. The floor was plastered with a coating of mud, which, when fully dry, made a smooth and firm surface. Altogether the interior presented an aspect of great comfort—rude, it is true, but still clean, bright, and cheerful.

It was a marvel to me how all this labour had been done, and this result achieved, with only a few rude implements— a couple of axes, a saw, a few gimlets and awls, and those wonderful knives which the Indians themselves make from old files—those knives with which a ready man can fashion a canoe, a dog-sled, or a snow-shoe, with a beauty of design which no civilized art can excel.

But although shelter for the winter had been thus provided, an equally important want had still to be attended to; a supply of meat sufficient to last three months had to be obtained.

The Red Cloud had often spoken to me of the expedition which we had still before us in the first month of the winter, and now that the hut was finished the time had come for setting out in quest of buffalo.

"Of all the winter food which the prairie can give," said he to me, "there is no food like the meat of the buffalo. The time has now come when the frost is sufficiently keen all day to keep the meat frozen, therefore all we kill can be brought in; none of it will be lost. The last buffalo we saw," he continued, "were on the plains south of the Elk river; they were scattered herds of bulls. The cows were then absent three days' march south of that ground; the herds were moving very slowly to the west. About a week's journey from here there is a small lake in the plains, called the Lake of the Wind. from the ceaseless movement of its waters. Day and night, even when the winds are still, the waters of that lake move and dash with noise against the pebbles on the shore. It is a favourite haunt for buffalo. To that lake we shall steer our course; for four days we shall have to cross a bare plain, on which no tree or bush grows; but at the lake there will be wood in the caverns around the shores, and we can get shelter for our tent, and fuel for fire, there. The horses are now all strong and fat, and they will be able to stand the cold, no matter how severe it may come."

The Sioux spoke truly; a prairie horse is all right if he be fat. It matters little in winter what he may be in speed, or strength, or activity; as long as he is thick fat there is always a month's work in him.

Early on the day following the completion of the hut, all the horses were driven in from the meadows in which they had spent the last three weeks. They all looked fat and strong.

During some days past the Cree had been busy preparing sleds, for light snow had now fallen; and although it had not lain long upon the ground, it was, nevertheless, likely that ere the time for the return of our party had arrived the ground would be white with its winter covering. These sleds would be carried crossways upon a horse until the snow would allow of their being drawn along the ground; they would each carry about 500 pounds of meat, and that would form an ample supply for the winter, with the venison and wild game that could be obtained in a ten-mile circle around the hut.

All preparations having been finished, Red Cloud, Donogh, the scout, and myself started on the following morning, bound for the south-west. We took with us a small tent, six horses, and plenty of powder and ball. The Cree and the dog remained to take charge of the hut. We expected to be absent about one month. It was the 20th of October, a bright, fair autumn day; hill and plain lay basking in a quiet sunlight, the sky was clear and cloudless, the air had in it that crisp of frost which made exercise a pleasure.

Winding along the meadows of the Red Deer, the pine bluff at the Forks was soon lost to sight behind its circling hills.

The evening of the third day after quitting the hut at the Forks found our little party camped on the edge of that treeless waste which spreads in unbroken desolation from the banks of the Eagle Creek near the North Saskatchewan to the Missouri. The spot where the lodge was pitched bore among the half-breed hunters of the plains the title of Les Trois Arbres.

It would have been difficult to have found a wilder scene than that which spread itself to the south and west from this lonely group of trees.

"Beyond the farthest verge of sight," said the Sioux, as

he pointed out the general direction he proposed to follow on the morrow, "lies the lake which the Indians have named the Lake of the Wind. From yonder group of trees to the shore of that lake, four long days' journey, there does not grow one tree or bush upon the prairie. We must halt here to-morrow, to bake bread and cut wood, to carry on the sleds, sufficient to last us across this bare expanse. Once at the lake we shall find wood in plenty, and I think the buffalo will not be far distant."

The sight upon which we now gazed was in truth almost sublime in its vast desolation. The sun, just descended beneath the rim of the western prairie, cast up into the sky one great shaft of light.

The intense rarity of the atmosphere made the landscape visible to its most remote depths. A few aspen clumps, and the three trees already mentioned, grew near the standpoint from which we looked; but in front no speck of tree met the eye, and the unbroken west lay waiting for the night in all the length and breadth of its lonely distance.

Never before had I beheld so vast an extent of treeless ground. The other prairies over which we had journeyed were dwarfed in my mind by the one now before me. I seemed to be standing upon the shore of a rigid sea—an ocean, whose motionless waves of short brown grass' appeared to lie in a vast torpor up to, and beyond, the sunset itself; and this sense of enormous space was heightened by the low but profound murmur of the wind, as it swept by our standpoint, from vast distance, into distance still as vast.

The whole of the following day was spent in preparations for crossing this great waste. A quantity of dry poplar sticks were cut into lengths suitable for packing upon the sleds.

The fire in the leather tent was kept briskly going, and a good supply of gelettes was baked before it.

"We will need all the wood we can carry with us," said the Sioux, "for the work of boiling the morning and evening kettle."

When the sunset hour had again come, I was out again upon the hill top to watch the sun set over the immeasurable waste. My wanderings had taught me that it was at this hour of sunset that the wilderness put on its grandest aspect; and often was it my wont to watch its varying shades, as, slowly sinking into twilight, the vagueness of night stole over the prairie.

It was at these times of sunset, too, that I seemed to see again all the well-remembered scenes of my early days in the old glen. Out of the vast silent wilderness came the brown hill of Seefin, and the gorse-covered sides of Knockmore. I could fancy that my ear caught the murmur of the west wind through the heather. How far off it all seemed —dreamlike in its vividness and its vast distance!

Very early next morning the tent was struck, the horses

were driven in, loads packed, and all made ready for the launch of the little expedition upon the great prairie sea.

The Sioux led the advance. Long ere mid-day the last glimpse of the Trois Arbres had vanished beneath the plain. In the afternoon a snow-storm swept across the waste, wrapping earth and heaven in its blinding drift. Still the Indian held his way at the same steady pace.

"It is well," he said to me as I rode close behind him. "If there are any roving bands on the borders of this great prairie, they will not see us in this storm."

Before sunset the storm ceased, the clouds rolled away to the south, and the boundless plain lay around us on all sides, one dazzling expanse of snow.

Camp was pitched at sunset in the bottom of a deep *coulee*. A night of intense cold followed the storm; but within the leather lodge the fire soon gave light and warmth; and as soon as supper was over we lay down on each side of the embers, wrapped in our robes.

Thus we journeyed on for some days, until, on the afternoon of the fourth from quitting Les Trois Arbres, we drew near the Lake of the Wind.

The weather had again become fine, and, for the season, mild. The snow had partly vanished, and the sun shone with a gentle lustre, that made bright and golden the yellow grasses of the great waste.

For several hours before the lake was reached, the trees

that grew near its shores had become visible. I had noticed that these clumps had risen out of the blank horizon straight in front of us, showing how accurate had been the steering of the Sioux across a waste that had presented to the eye of the ordinary beholder apparently not one landmark for guidance.

I asked the Indian by what marks he had directed his course.

"I could not tell you," replied the Sioux. "It is an instinct born in us; it comes as easy to us as it does to the birds, or to the buffalo. Look up," he went on; "see that long line of 'wavies' sailing to the south. Night and day they keep that line; a week ago they were at the North Sea; in a few days they will be where winter never comes. Before man gave up this free life of the open air, while yet the forest and the plain were his homes, he knew all these things better even than did the birds or the beasts; he knew when the storm was coming; the day and the night were alike to him when he travelled his path through the forest; his course across the lake was clear to him: but when he grew to be what you call civlized, then he lost the knowledge of the sky, and of the earth; he became helpless. It is so with the red men; year by year, we lose something of the craft and knowledge of wood, plain, and river. One hundred years ago, our young men hunted the buffalo and the wapiti with the weapons they had themselves made; now it is the gun or the rifle of the white man that is used by them. Without these things, which they buy from the traders, they would die, because they have mostly forgotten the old methods of the chase. Before the horse came to us from the Spaniard, we hunted the buffalo on foot, and our young men could chase the herds from sunrise until dusk of evening; before the gun came to us from the French we killed even the grizzly bears with our arrows, and straight and true they flew from the bow drawn on horseback or on foot."

As thus the Sioux showed how deeply he had studied the past history of his race, the scattered woods that fringed the lake took better defined form, and soon the sheen of water became visible through openings in the belts of forest.

As we drew still nearer, the whole outline of the lake was to be seen. It lay between deeply indented shores at its northern, or nearer end, but farther off to the south it stretched out into a broader expanse of water. The evening was perfectly calm, the branches of the trees did not move, but the water, still unfrozen in the centre of the lake, was agitated with many waves, and a restless surge broke upon the edges of ice with a noise which was plainly audible on the shore. It was a singular scene, this restless lake lying amid this vast rigid waste. The Sioux bent his way into one of the long promontories, and soon a spot was selected amid a thick screen of aspens and maple, where the tent was pitched in shelter, and all made comfortable against the now approaching night.

Next day broke fresh and fair; the air was keen and cold, but the dry fuel, now obtainable in plenty, had kept the lodge warm; and soon after sunrise the sun came out, glistening upon the white branches of the leafless trees, and the hoar-frosted grass, and shallow snow of the plain, and making all things look bright and cheerful. We were soon in the saddle. The Sioux led the advance, and swinging round by the southern end of the lake we gained some high and broken ground. The Sioux had ridden on some distance in advance, and I was about to quicken my pace in order to overtake him, when suddenly I caught sight of a dark object appearing above a depression in a ridge some way to my right; the ridge itself concealed lower ground beyond it, and the object, which for a second had caught my eye was the back of some animal that was standing partially hidden within this lower space.

I was glad to have thus caught first sight of game, before even the quick eye of the Sioux had lighted upon it. Keeping low upon my horse, I galloped forward, and told my companion what I had seen. He immediately reconnoitred the hollow, and came back to say that it held three animals, two buffalo cows and one calf. As I had first discovered the game, I was to have first shot. We both dismounted, and crept cautiously up to the edge of the ridge and looked over. From this edge to where the animals stood was about one hundred and fifty yards. I laid my rifle over the ridge top, took a steady aim, and fired at the cow that stood nearest to me. Then we both sprang to our feet, and ran with all speed down the hill towards the animals. The cow I had fired at moved off with difficulty, the others bounded away up the opposite ridge. It was now the Sioux' turn. Stopping short in his long stride he fired quickly, and ran on again. The buffalo at which he fired had gained the summit of the distant ridge, and was for a moment clearly shown on the white hill-top and against the blue sky beyond it. I was so intent upon watching my own animal that I had no time to take note of whether his shot had struck; but, reloading as I ran, I soon reached the bottom of the little valley. My buffalo was still moving quietly up the incline, evidently sorely wounded. Another shot from my rifle ere the beast had reached the top of the ridge brought her to the ground, no more to rise. We breasted quickly up the incline until the top was gained, and there, just beyond the summit, lay the Sioux' buffalo, quite dead in the snow. What a scene it was as we stood on this prairie ridge! Away on all sides spread the white and yellow prairie, the longer grasses still showing golden in the sunlight above the sparkling layer of snow; there was not a cloud in the vast blue vault that hung over this glistening immensity; the Lake of the Wind lay below us, its line of

We both sprang to our feet, and ran with all speed towards the animals.
[*Page* 168.

shore-wood showing partially dark against its snow, and its centre of open water lying blue as the sky above it, set in a frame of snow-crusted ice. Close at hand, on either side of the ridge where we stood, lay the dark bodies of our buffalo, stretched upon the shallow snow.

Both animals proved to be in very good condition. "You will taste to-night," said the Sioux to me, "the best bit of meat to be got in the prairie—the flesh of a fat cow buffalo; the finest beef is but poor food compared to it."

We were still so near our camp that we determined to get the sleds out and drag it in, before night would give the wolves a chance of plundering our winter store of meat. The Sioux began to skin and cut up the buffalo, and I went back to where we had left the horses, and then rode to the camp to bring Donogh, the scout, and the sled to the scene. It was astonishing to see the rapid manner with which the two Indians cut up these large animals. Early in the afternoon we were all back in the camp, with three sled-loads of primest meat; we brought skins, marrow-bones, tongues, and tit-bits; and the remainder of the daylight was spent in arranging the supplies safe from the ravage of prowling wolves and in preparing for a good feast after the labours of the day.

Pleasant it was that night, when the darkness had fallen over the silent wilderness, to look at the cosy scene presented by our camp. We had swept clear of brushwood and snow a large space on one side of our leather lodge. Maple-trees grew thickly around it; in the centre burned clear and bright a fire of dry logs. Steaks were roasting before glowing embers, the kettle was steaming from a cross-stick, marrow-bones were toasting, gelettes were baking in a pan set facing the fire and backed up with hot embers, while, seated on buffalo robes, around the fire we sat, canopied by the starlight, circled by the vast and lonely wilderness.

The next morning found us again in the saddle, but this time Donogh came to share our sport. Our course now lay in a westerly direction from the lake. It was in that line that the yearling calf had retreated on the previous day, and there it was likely we should fall in with buffalo. It was mid-day however before the sight of buffalo gladdened our eyes. Far away to the south dim dark specks were visible. Ascending a ridge in the direction of the animals, we had a better view of the plains. A large herd was distinctly visible, moving slowly towards the north-west. We watched them for some minutes. "We must cross them on their line of march," said the Sioux to me; then we rode briskly off towards the south-west keeping our horses along the hollows of the prairie. It was his intention to take up a position in advance of the herd, and then await its coming. He preferred this mode of attack in the present instance to running the buffalo upon horseback: the light covering of snow was sufficient to render the prairie dangerous, since it had partially hidden the badger holes, and the surface was hard with frost. "Our horses have to carry us home to the Red Deer river," he said as we cantered along; we must be careful how we use them. We soon reached the edge of what seemed to be a channel of a stream through the prairie; but there was no water in the wide grassy hollow that ran in sweeping curves over the plains, nor could a stream of water ever have flowed in it, because it followed the general undulations of the land around, although the floor or bottom of it was always lower than the land that bordered it on either side. We now saw that the line of the buffalo's advance was up this grassy hollow, and as the wind was favourable we would only have to conceal ourselves in the floor of this depression and to await the approach of the herd. Leaving the horses in a deep hollow, we gained a spot in the grassy channel where we could lie concealed behind tufts of grass and snow; here we lay down to await the buffalo. It was not very long before the leading ones came in sight of our hiding-place, round a curve in the depression about four hundred yards distant.

Then in scattered files more came into view, walking slowly and deliberately forward in that complete unconstraint with which the wild animals of the earth take their leisure when they fancy their great enemy, man, is far away from them.

A very old bull led the advance, moving some distance in front of any other beast.

The snow of many a winter's storm, the gleam of many a summer's sun, had matted and tangled his shaggy mane and sweeping frontlet.

As he approached nearer to us we could see his eyes gleaming brightly from beneath the thick masses of hair that hung from his forehead; but there was no trace of that anger or fright such as the hunter sees when in pursuit of a flying herd. The look now was calm and tranquil; the great beast was at home in this solitary waste, as his race through countless generations had been at home here; for in these wilds, so green in summer, so white in winter, he and his had roamed since time began.

"Do not fire at him," said the Sioux in a low tone to me. "He would be useless to us."

The old veteran had now come to a halt, about thirty paces in front of where we lay. He was so close to us that we could mark with ease every movement of his shaggy head, every expression of his eye. Some vague idea that there was danger in front seemed to have come upon him, for once or twice he turned his head round, as if to see whether his comrades were close at hand.

As they came closing up to him from behind, the same vague feeling of fear or suspicion seemed to have communicated itself to them, for they also paused irresolute on their way. That the suspicion was not directed towards any particular point, was evident from the looks which the huge animals continued to turn to either side. As thus they stood, gradually closing up from behind upon the leader, a storm that for some time had been threatening, broke over the prairie, whirling snow in dense drifts before it, and wrapping the scene in chaotic desolation.

Truly, a weird wild picture was that before us—the great waste narrowed for the moment by the curtain clouds of wintry tempest, the dark animals vaguely seen through the wrack of drift, and the huge form of the monarch of the prairie standing out against the background of gloom. It is many a long day now since I looked upon that scene, but I see it still before me, through time and distance.

The old buffalo, as though reassured by the proximity of his friends, now began to move forward again.

The Sioux whispered to me to aim at a young bull that had come up towards the front. He was some little way behind the old leader, but his side was partly visible to me. I aimed low behind his shoulder, and fired. In a second, the scene had changed; all was wild confusion among the herd. Where all had been torpor, all became movement; to sense of security followed intense fright; and away in wild stampede, through drift and storm, fled the suddenly startled animals. The young bull had, however, received his death-wound; he soon dropped from the ranks of the flying herd, and lay down to die.

It was now so late in the day that we could not hope to

get the beast home to our camp before the morrow. But to leave the dead animal as he was, on the prairies, exposed for the night to the ravage of wolves and foxes, would have been to find little remaining save his bones next day. The Sioux stuck his ramrod into the ribs of the buffalo, and fastened his powder-flask to the rod, letting it swing in the wind. This precaution made the carcase safe from attack, at least for one night; for keener than the scent of food with the wolf is his scent for powder, and he will long continue to circle around meat thus protected, ere his greed will bring him close to it for plunder.

As we rode home to the camp, the snowstorm that had swept the plains abated; but a bitterly cold wind was blowing across the prairie, and a lurid sunset foreshadowed a continuance of wild weather.

The stock of dry wood for fuel was, however, large; and sheltered amid the thickets, our camp-fire blazed brightly, while again we brought back from our long day's work those keen appetites to relish the good things of steak and bone and tit-bit that only the prairie hunter can ever know. Pleasant used it to be on such nights to sit before the camp fire and watch the wind, as, blowing in gusts, it whirled the yellow flames through the dry logs, while the peeled willows baked by the embers.

On this evening the scout brought out a plentiful supply

of willow rods, which he had cut during our absence along a part of the lake shore to which he had wandered. The outer bark of these willows was a bright red colour. This outer bark the scout had peeled off, leaving beneath it a soft inner skin. Having carefully peeled down this inner skin, so as to make it form ringlets or curls of bark at the knots on the willow rods, the ends of the rods were now stuck in the ground close by the fire. The heat soon caused the strips of bark to become crisp, and fit for smoking. It is in this manner that the Indians make their "Kinni-kinnick" tobacco.

Wherever the red willow grows, by margin of lake or shore of river, along the edge of swamp or thicket, there the tobacco pouch of the red man is easily replenished; and mixed with real tobacco, this inner bark of the willow forms the universal smoking-mixture of the tribes that roam the northern wastes.

In the "thick wood" country, lying between lakes Superior and Winnipeg, the red willow is scarce, but a weed not unlike dwarf box is found. Dried before a fire, its leaves form kinni-kinnick, like the willow bark. True to his habit, of taking a last look at the horses before lying down for the night, the Sioux arose from his robe at the fire and went out into the open. The horses had sought the shelter of the thicket; the wind was beginning to rise;

no stars were visible, the branches of the dwarf trees sent forth a mournful sigh as the night-winds passed through them.

"To-morrow," he said, when he came back to the tent, "winter will be on all the land."

It did not matter. We wrapped ourselves in our robes and lay down to sleep, heedless alike of rising storm and falling snowflake.

CHAPTER X.

Winter—wolves—A night's trapping—A retreat—In the teeth of the north wind—The carcajou—A miss and a hit—News of Indians—Danger ahead—A friendly storm—The hut again.

THE next morning, plain and thicket, hill and lake, lay wrapt in a white mantle. The storm had sunk to calm, the snow had ceased, but winter was on all the land, no more to leave it until the winds and showers of spring should come from the south to chase him back into his northern home. It was piercingly cold when we issued from the tent to begin the day's work. The cold was different from anything I had yet experienced. The slightest touch of metal sufficed instantly to freeze the fingers. A gun-barrel, the buckle of a girth, the iron of a bit, struck so deadly cold upon the hands, that I found it was only by running to the embers of the fire, and holding my fingers for a moment in the blaze that I could restore them to working power.

Red Cloud and the Assineboine appeared, however, to take slight notice of this great cold. The work was done as usual, quickly and neatly; packs and saddles were arranged, the two spare horses were got ready to bring back the buffalo killed on the previous evening, and in a very short time our little party trooped out from the sheltering thicket into the great prairie.

All was now a dazzling sheet of most intense white. The clouds had cleared away, and the sun shone out, making the vast surface glisten as though millions of diamonds had been scattered over it. The snow was not yet deep upon the prairie; the wind of the preceding night had driven it into the hollows, or flattened it down amid the grass, so that the horses were able to make their way along.

About two hours' ride brought us in sight of the dead buffalo. It was visible a long way off, showing very dark upon the white surface of the plain. The scene around it was a curious one. Fully a score of wolves were circling and dodging around the carcase, some looking anxiously at the longed-for meat, others sitting farther away, as though they had determined to await the discoveries of their more venturesome comrades ere they would approach the dead animal.

Red Cloud looked at them for some time.

"There are a good many warm skins," he said, "in that lot, and they are easily carried compared with the skin of those buffalo cows we shot yesterday. If we had a few of those wolf robes, we could make our winter beds warm enough in the hut at the Forks."

He thought a moment, and then continued,—

"There are so many wolves here that it would be worth while to camp near this to-night and trap some of them. We will take two loads of meat back to the camp at the lake, then return here, bringing with us the tent, and wood sufficient for the night. We will fetch hither all the traps we have with us, and then see if we cannot catch some of these white and grey wolves."

We had now reached the buffalo, and the work of skinning and cutting up went on apace. Soon light loads for the horses were ready, and I and the scout set out for the lake, leaving the Sioux to keep watch over the carcase.

When we had departed, the Sioux set to work to outwit the cunning wolves, who still lurked around, hiding behind the hillock, and looking every now and again over the skyline of a hill to watch their much-coveted food.

Noticing that a small ravine ran curving through the prairie within easy rifle-shot of the dead buffalo, he followed our tracks for some distance, until reaching a depression in the ground, he turned aside into it; then bending down so as to be completely hidden from the wolves, he gained the ravine at a considerable distance from where the buffalo lay. Following the many windings of this *coulee*, he reached at last the neighbourhood of the animal. He did not need to look up above the ledge of the ravine, because ere he set out upon his stalk he had marked a tuft of tall dry grass which grew at the curve which was nearest the buffalo, and now keeping the bottom of the ravine, he saw this tuft appear in view as he rounded a bend in the hollow. Looking cautiously up from the base of the dry tuft, he saw, about a hundred yards distant, several wolves busily engaged at tearing at the hide and legs yet remaining of the buffalo. Singling out the largest wolf, he took a quick but steady aim, and as the report rang out, he saw the wolf spring into the air and fall dead beside the buffalo carcase. A second shot, fired as the other wolves galloped rapidly away, was not so successful. The bullet cut the snow beneath their feet, and in another few seconds they were out of range.

When we again appeared upon the scene, bringing the tent and traps, we found a magnificent wolf's skin added to our stock of winter goods.

Pitching the leather lodge in the shelter of the ravine, all was made comfortable against the night. The spare horses had been left at the old camping-place, and only those ridden by the hunters had been brought to this exposed place.

Just before nightfall the Sioux set his traps in a circle round the spot where the buffalo lay. I watched with interest the precautions by which he hoped to baffle the cunning of the wolves. To the chain of each trap a heavy stick was attached. This weight would prevent the wolf dragging the trap any considerable distance; but both the trap and the stick had to be concealed in the snow, and care taken to prevent the fine powdery snow drifting in underneath the plate, so as to allow the pressure of an animal's foot to spring the trap.

The circle of traps was soon complete, and just at dusk we were all ensconced within our lodge, busily preparing the evening meal.

"About an hour after dark the wolves will grow bold," said the Sioux. "They are circling round now, but they are too cautious to go near just at first. We will go round the traps when supper is done, and again before we turn in for the night."

When supper was finished, we crept out of the lodge and went to visit the traps. The night was intensely cold; the stars were shining with wonderful brilliancy over the vast white prairie. The first trap we approached held nothing, —and so on until we reached the fourth. Here we saw a dark object struggling hard in the snow. As we drew nearer to it I was able to distinguish an animal closely resembling a huge grey dog. The Sioux had brought with him a stout pole four feet in length, Coming close to the wolf he struck him a violent blow with this pole, killing him instantly. Then he re-set the trap, and dragging the dead wolf along, we proceeded to finish our round. All the other traps were empty. But two hours later, when another visit was made, a coyote and a kit fox were found, so that the stock of winter skins began to increase rapidly.

Another wolf was captured during the night; but when morning came we found that he had succeeded in dragging the trap, and the stick to which it was attached, a long way over the prairie. It was the trap which had been set by me.

"Curious," said I. "The wolf caught last night was just able to move the trap, and now this one carries trap and stick far over the prairie. He must be a stronger wolf than the first one."

"No," replied the Sioux. "But do you see the track that the stick has made in the snow? Does it not run straight, end on, after the wolf?"

I noticed that it did so.

"Well," said Red Cloud, "that is because you did not select the exact centre of the stick in which to place the chain. The consequence is that one end of the stick is heavier than the other. This heavy end trails after the chain, so that the wolf has less difficulty in dragging it along. It glides over the snow easily, whereas when both ends of the stick are evenly balanced, it lies across the animal's line of flight. That is the reason why this wolf has got away so far. But we will reach him yet."

Following rapidly along, we overtook the trapped animal in the bottom of a *coulee*, in the soft snow of which he could not make much way. He was quickly despatched, and dragged back to the tent, his skin to be added to those already taken.

The weather was now so intensely cold that Red Cloud began to fear the horses would be unable to drag the load of meat back to the Forks. There was meat fully sufficient to load the three sleds we had brought to their utmost capacity. Fortunately the spare horses had had an easy time of it up to the present. They were still in fair condition; but the riding horses already showed signs of feeling the terrible severity of these exposed treeless plains, and to delay the return to the Forks longer than was absolutely necessary, would only be to imperil the lives of the most valuable animals possessed by us.

Accordingly the lodge was struck, and the retreat to the hut at the Forks began.

During four days our line of sleds and men toiled slowly over the treeless waste, dark specs upon a waste of white. The north wind blew with merciless rigour. Sometimes the air was still, and the sun shone; but at other times terrible storms swept the wild landscape, whirling powdery snow over hills and ravines. With downbent heads men and horses plodded on; at night the lodge was pitched in some *coulee* for better shelter, and in the early morning so black and cold and desolate looked all visible nature, that I used to long to be again in the tent. Still I struggled hard to keep a bold front before my Indian comrades; they did not complain, why should I? One good thing was, we had plenty of buffalo meat, and we could be fairly warm at night by lying close together in the "lodge."

At last, on the fifth day, the wood at Les Trois Arbres was reached, and piling on the firewood, that night the tent was made warm and comfortable.

The poor horses were now very weak. On the treeless plains the grass had been short and covered in many places with snow; but in the thickets wild vetch and pea grew, twining, through the brushwood, and these succulent grasses, sweetened by the frost, were eagerly sought for by the hungry steeds. It was decided to give a day's rest here, for the worst portion of the journey was now over. Accordingly the lodge was pitched in a sheltered spot amid thickets, and the horses turned adrift in what at this season of the year was good pasturage.

The next day we spent in a long hunt on foot amid the thickets and open prairies. The "poire" tree grew in many places amid the aspen groves, and the Indians declared that where the poire flourished there the bear was to be found— so our hunt this day was to the sleeping-place of the bear. When the last berry has disappeared, and the first snow has come, Bruin begins to bethink himself of seeking a place wherein he can sleep away the long winter months.

Beneath the trunk of a fallen tree, under a rock, often-times on the level ground of aspen or poplar thicket, he digs his hole. When it is deep enough to hold his fat body he backs into it, and placing his nose between his fore paws goes fast asleep. Sometimes the sleep is for four or five months duration; but at other times, when the sun comes out warm and bright in mid-winter, he will crawl forth from his burrow, roam a little way around, and then retire again into his den. It is no easy matter to find his nest. Like all wild things he selects his place of rest with an eye to security; but hide it as he may, the Indian's sharp eye pierces through all disguises, and in the time before the snow has fallen deep enough to cover tree stumps and hollow in one undistinguishably level of white, the couch which Bruin has made with so much care for his winter's sleep becomes his death-bed ere his first doze has well begun.

Red Cloud and I took one direction, the scout set off in another. The day was calm and fine; scarcely a breath of wind stirred over the prairie, and the rays of the sun fell brightly upon the snowy surface, through which the yellow grass still showed in many places. Dressed in a light leather shirt, and Indian leggings and moccasins to match, I stepped briskly along, following in the footsteps of the Sioux. In and out of aspen thickets, over open patches of prairie land, along the tops of small ridges quite bare of snow, the Indian held his way with rapid stride. At length we emerged upon the edge of a deep *coulee*. In the bottom of this ravine a few pools of frozen water were visible. The sides of the ravine were steep, but in the bottom the ground was level; some stunted bushes grew at intervals along it. As we stood on the sharp edge of the prairie looking down this depression, the eye of the Indian suddenly caught sight of a moving object some distance away to his right. It was an animal that had plunged over the edge and quickly disappeared in the valley. Before many seconds had elapsed a second object crossed over the ridge and dived into the *coulee*. The Indian exclaimed, "Lie down, it is a carcajou; he is hunting a deer. The deer will follow the *coulee*, and will pass right beneath where we stand; we should get them both." We lay flat upon the prairie edge with rifles ready. Presently along the bottom of the gorge appeared a large jumping moose. He was evidently sorely pressed by his pursuer, who, only about fifty yards behind, came along at that slouching gallop peculiar to his species. Red Cloud whispered to me, "Fire as the deer passes. Aim in front, and low, for it is down hill. I'll take the carcajou." My heart beat fast; the distance was under seventy yards, but the pace was good. A shot rang out. "Missed," cried the Sioux as the deer went bounding by. Quick as thought I pulled again, this time aiming well in front and very low. The deer staggered—fell—rose again to his feet, and then plunged over upon his side, dead. Meantime the wolverine was coming along at a tremendous pace. All at once a shot rang out in front; then another. His pace was too rapid to be checked in an instant; but the reports from the ridge to his left caused him to swerve from the bottom of the *coulee*, and to ascend the bank nearly opposite the spot where we lay. As he went up the steep bank he presented a beautiful mark to the Indian's rifle. For an instant the weapon followed the upward course of the animal, then it poured forth its unerring fire. The carcajou staggered in his gallop, and slipped back a short way down the steep hill side; then he recovered himself, and began again to ascend. But now a second report rang out, and, shot quite dead, the beast rolled down the shingly side, and lay still, within a few yards of the deer he had followed to the death.

My first shot had not allowed sufficiently for the depth of the *coulee;* the bullet had just gone over the deer's back, but the second had passed clean through the animal's ribs.

And now to carry the game home to camp. It was no easy matter; the Sioux, however, proved himself, as usual, fully equal to the difficulty.

In a very short time he had skinned both the animals. The flesh of the wolverine was useless, but the skin was a very fine one.

When the skin of the deer was removed, it was placed upon the snow, with the side that had been next the body of the animal turned downwards upon the ground. Then the venison was packed upon the hairy side, and the ends of the skin wrapped over it to prevent the pieces falling off;

then to the two fore-legs of the skin the Sioux fastened the string of leather called "shagganappi," which he always carried with him, and passing the band of the line round his shoulders, he drew the load of meat easily over the snow. We followed the *coulee* for some distance, until coming to a spot where the bank was less abrupt, we were able to draw the load to the level of the prairie; then trudging along over snow and grass, we arrived at the lodge ere yet the winter's sun had touched the horizon.

It was still later when the scout returned. He had much to say about his day's work. Soon after setting out in the morning he had struck the trail of a moose, and had followed it for a long distance. The moose had travelled far, and ere the day was half done the scout found himself a long way from camp. Still he persisted in keeping the trail. At last he beheld a sight that made him think of other things besides his game. From a ridge over which the trail led, he espied some Indian lodges pitched on the edge of the woods. The hunter instantly became the brave; he approached the neighbourhood of the tents with the utmost caution. He waited long enough until he discovered the tribe to which the Indians belonged; then he returned with all speed to tell his tidings to his comrades. The band, he said, belonged to the Cree tribe; they were trapping and hunting in the vicinity of the elbow of the South Saskatchewan, and had now been here for some days. This was bad news for us. We had hoped that our winter hut at the Forks would remain unknown to any Indians ; and now this band of Crees were close upon us. Unless a fall of snow would quickly come, our homeward trail to the hut must be struck by some Cree brave in the next few days, and once struck it was sure to be followed. The Crees were not hostile, but that was a fact upon which we could not long count. Besides, the news of the existence of a hut at that point would soon spread among the tribe, and other Indians would hear of it before the winter was over. Mischief might easily come from it. We must endeavour to hide our trail by some stratagem.

For hours that evening the Sioux sat silently before the tent fire, buried in deep thought. A snow-storm would have put an end to all his difficulties ; but the night looked fine and clear, the stars were shining over the prairie, the yellow lustre of the sunset still hung in the western sky.

It was possible to branch away at right angles from our present line, and to continue that course until the weather changed, and then to resume the old direction and make straight for the hut ; but that would entail much extra marching upon the horses already thin and weak, and would probably lead to the loss of some of them. Under all circumstances the best course to adopt seemed to be to remain camped in the neighbourhood until a change of weather would obliterate the trail. Accordingly next morning a move was made a few miles further away from the Crees, and camp was again pitched in a spot not likely to catch the eye of any roving Indian.

The next night brought a change in the weather; the wind began to rise, clouds came drifting up from the northeast, and ere midnight came the snow was falling over the plain. We were ready for it; the horses had all been driven in at nightfall; the sleds got ready for the march. By the light of the fire the tent was struck and packed, and long ere morning began to break upon the driving scene of snow and storm our little cavalcade was far [away on its march to the hut. All day the storm blew, the snow fell; and all day too, Red Cloud led the march through blinding drift, and small chance was there of keenest eyes ever finding our trail. The wind blew the surface of the snow before it, quickly filling every cavity, and piling up the fine drift in dazzling heaps. We carried on all day, and camp was only made long after nightfall, when many a mile of snow-clad wilderness lay between us and the Crees.

Another day's march brought us within sight of the pine-bluff at the Forks, and that night the tired horses were turned adrift in the sheltered meadow by the river, and we lay down to rest in the hut at the Pascopee.

CHAPTER XI.

Winter comfort—Snowshoe-making—Snow and storm—The moose woods—A night camp—Memories—A midnight visitor—Maskeypeton the Iroquois—Danger—A moose hunt—Indian stalking—The red man's happy hunting-grounds—Plans—Raft-building.

ALL was well in the hut; the Cree had kept watch and ward. No Indians had found the place. Everything promised a quiet, peaceful winter, with ample time to mature plans for the spring. The stage which had been built soon after our first arrival at the spot was now filled with prime buffalo meat; the flour, blankets, and other stores taken from the trader, were stored carefully away on shelves in the hut. The Cree and the scout dried and rough-tanned the wolf, carcajou, and buffalo skins; rude bedsteads were put up along the walls, and upon them dried grass, skins, and blankets made most comfortable beds. A large store of fuel was chopped, and piled outside the door; and harness, guns, skins, axes, &c., gave a furnished appearance to the interior, which, when lighted up by the pine-logs in the evening presented a look of comfort, in striking contrast with the savage desolation of the wilderness without when the mid-winter rigour came full upon it.

As the end of the year drew nigh the storms increased in intensity. The snow deepened over all the land, but the meadow chosen for the horses held such an abundance of food that the animals stood the cold well. When the vetch and wild peas were exhausted, a swamp, which in summer grew a thick sedge-like grass, gave excellent sustenance to them. The snow was easily pawed away by the horses' fore-feet, and the coarse grass, sweetened by the frost, was laid bare beneath. Day after day the Sioux, with myself, or the scout, or Donogh, set out on a hunt for venison, and many a buck fell to our rifles in the valleys and thickets of the surrounding hills.

As the snow deepened over the land, the use of the snow-shoe became a necessity in walking. Before the want had arisen the Indians had taken measures to supply it. Birch-wood had been cut and seasoned, the gut of the jumping moose dried and prepared, and the rough framework put together, afterwards to be strung, and turned into the required shape.

As I watched the clever manner with which the wood was pared down and shaped, and with what beautiful accuracy the cross-pieces, the toes and heels, were fitted, turned, and made ready for the sinew strings—all done too with only a small knife and an awl, and done with such apparent ease,

I felt tempted to say, "I too will make a pair of snow-shoes;" but it was only to find how futile was the effort to imitate the handicraft of the wild man in the work of the wilderness.

By the time the snowshoes were finished the snow was deep enough on the river and the plains to fully test their capabilities. I determined to accustom myself early to the use of the shoes, so that I might be able to keep pace with my friends, whose power of snowshoe-walking had grown from infancy. With this object I was out every morning as soon as breakfast was over, tramping along the frozen and snow-covered expanse of the rivers, or forcing my way through the thicket-lined shores, and up the hills and slopes of the surrounding country. At first I found it no easy matter to tread my way over soft and deep snow, or through places where the brambles and weeds lay half-buried in the drifts and dazzling banks; but in a few days my step grew more firm, my stride became longer and more rapid, and after a week I was not ashamed to join Red Cloud for a hunt after game.

Thus we four denizens of this wild and lonely spot ranged over the land surrounding our solitary dwelling; and ere the new year had come there was not a pine-bluff or a thicket of aspens—there was not a bend on the rivers, or a glade among the hills, which was not known and explored.

O

It was a strange, wild life, this winter roving over the great untamed wilderness of snow.

At times the days were bright and calm—the sun shone with dazzling lustre upon the unspotted surface of the earth. The branches of the trees glistened in the white rime of the morning, the dry powdery snow sounded hard as sand under the shoe.

Again the scene would change, and wild storms swept sky and earth; the bitter blast howled through the thickets, the pine-trees rocked and waved, and the short daylight closed into a night of wrack and tempest. Such days and nights would run their courses, and again the scene would change; the wild wind would sink away, the snow would cease to fall or to drift, a death-like stillness would ensue, and with a brilliancy of untold beauty the moon would be seen above the still and tapering pine-tops, and the white light of frosted silver, set with myriad sparkling gems, would overlay all the land.

The new year came; January drew to a close. Colder and colder the iron hand of winter seemed to grasp the forest and the ridge, the silent frozen rivers, and the lonely hills.

One day the Sioux set out with me to visit a large wood of pines and poplars, the tops of which could be discerned from a ridge lying a few miles away from the hut. It was a long tramp, and the dogs were taken to carry kettle, blankets, and food, in preparation for camping during the night in the wood in order to continue the hunt on the following day.

As the morning was fine, the sun shone brightly on the snow, and the dogs followed closely in the footsteps of the Sioux, as with rapid strides he passed over the white ridges and intervening gullies drifted deep in snow. I walked behind the sled that carried the supplies for the camp.

The day passed away, varied by nothing save exercise, broken only by the mid-day halt for food. It was the middle of the afternoon when we drew near the broad belt of wood which was to be our home for the night.

For some miles we had followed a tract of low meadow-land along the river; but now the Sioux led across the frozen stream, and slipping his feet from the snowshoe-strings as he gained the farther shore, he began to ascend a very steep ridge that rose directly from the opposite bank.

The dogs worked might and main to follow their leader. I urged them with voice and whip from behind; and up the slippery ridge we scrambled until the top was gained. Here a halt was made, to recover breath and take a survey of the scene.

Beneath, spreading away for many a mile, lay a broken and wooded region, over which patches of dark green pine-trees stood in marked contrast to the snowy surface of level and ridge. Here and there the eye caught glimpses of unbroken sheets of snow, telling the presence of frozen lakelets beneath. Indeed, the pine-trees were themselves sufficient to indicate the fact of water in abundance being there, for it was water alone that had protected them in the dry autumn days from the wild ravage of the prairie fire.

The Sioux scanned with careful sweep of vision all the wide scene from east to west. Then seemingly satisfied with his scrutiny, he resumed his snowshoes, and struck down a long gradual incline towards the belt of woodland.

It wanted but an hour of sunset when the first pine-trees were reached; and shortly after, the small grey owl's hoot sounding through the vast solitude bade us select a thick clump of firs, in the midst of which a cosey camp was quickly made.

Few who have not experienced it can realize the full measure of comfort which the wilderness, even in the depth of winter, can hold forth to its denizens. It seems difficult to believe that a camp, made in the open snow, amid a clump of fir-trees, with nought save the branches between the traveller and the sky, with only the frozen earth swept clear of snow for his floor, and with blankets and a skin for bed and covering, could be anything save the most miserable of lodging-places. But it is marvellous how quickly the wild hunter will change these unpromising materials into a spot where genial warmth can be felt, where rest can come to weary limbs, where food can fill hungry stomachs, and the pipe of peace can be smoked in pleasant repose.

At first the night was still and fine; but as the midnight hour drew on the wind arose, and the tree-tops began to bend their heads, and the melancholy cadence of the swaying branches fell upon our ears as we slept.

Long habit had given the Sioux the faculty of consciousness in sleep; the senses, all save that of sight, still carried to his brain their various messages.

The swaying of the branches soon roused him to wakefulness, and throwing aside his robe he looked out at the night. The fire had burned down to ashes, which the night-wind, when its gusts came strongly now and again, blew into dull red embers. The snow-light made visible the tree-trunks around. Overhead he could mark the clouds moving rapidly from the east; the storm was rising.

He got up, raked the ashes together, threw some wood upon the embers, and sat down to watch the flickering flames and to wait for the dawn. The noise awoke me, and I watched him from where I lay. Oftentimes it was his wont thus to sit watching in those hours of the late night. More than once I had, on other occasions, looked out from my robe, to see thus seated before a few embers the figure of my friend. Who can tell the thoughts that at such moments passed through the mind of this strange man? Memories of that great wilderness he loved so well—of these vast solitudes, which to him had nothing awful. Glimpses of far-stretching prairies—of rivers flowing in wide curves through endless distances—of trees sinking beneath waves of meadow-land. Such were the scenes he saw in the pine-fire embers. Then too he would listen to the voice of the tempest in far-off forests; and as the sound swept through the lone hours of the night, there came to him many a thought of boyhood in the land lost to his tribe. But always, as he has often told me, his mind running along those grooves found the same resting-place—the spot where, in the island of the mountains, lay the bones of his murdered father. And then, with all the bitter wrath of his heart fanned into flame, he would rise to his feet, and stalk away into the dark forest or the silent prairie, and looking up at the cold stars he would cry, "Father, thy son does not sleep. He wanders over the earth only to revenge thy fate."

As now he sat, with head sunken on his hands, and eyes fixed on the embers, there sounded close by a noise as of human steps upon the snow. The Sioux turned towards the side from whence the sound proceeded, and saw in the dim light of the snow the figure of a man. Calm as he habitually was—accustomed to regard the sudden indications of danger with the outward semblance of repose, he nevertheless on this occasion felt creep upon him the sensation of fear. Weird and ghostly, the figure seemed to have risen out of the white ground. Instinctively the Sioux grasped the rifle that lay near him. The strange figure seemed to catch the movement: he spoke.

"As a friend I have sought your camp," he said. "Had I come as an enemy, you would not have seen me."

Red Cloud relinquished his half-grasped rifle, and rose to meet the stranger.

"Who are you?"

"I am Maskeypeton the Iroquois."

The wind still rising, now blew a strong gust, which swept the camp, causing the flames to flare for a moment through the dry wood of the fire. The light fell full upon the face of the stranger, revealing features well known to the Sioux.

"Maskeypeton the Iroquois," he said, "no matter what has brought your steps at this hour to my camp, you are welcome. Sit down and share my fire."

The stranger answered, "There was a day, years ago, when you turned your horse's head to take a wounded Iroquois from under the guns of the Long-knives by the banks of the Yellowstone. Maskeypeton is here to-night because of that day. Last evening," he said, "I struck your trail on the ice of the Pascopee. I was then bound for where I had heard your hut lay. I followed your trail while daylight lasted, rested until the moon rose, and then kept the track that led me hither."

The Sioux listened in silence.

"I have not come," went on the Iroquois, "without a reason; that reason is a warning. Enemies watch for you. They have found the spot where you have built your winter hut; and when the snow leaves the prairies, and the ice breaks in the rivers, the Sircies will seek your life."

"But I have no quarrel with the Sircies," answered the Sioux. "No man of the tribe has ever known injury at my hand. Why should they now try to harm me?"

"Because there is another enemy hidden behind them," said the Iroquois.. "The white trader finds many weapons with which he strikes his blows."

The eyes of the Sioux reflected with a strange wild glare, the fitful light of the fire, but he said nothing. After a while he asked,—

"Is the trader with the Sircies?"

"No, he is living at the white man's fort by the river of the Gros Ventres."

The Sioux thought in silence over the tidings the Iroquois had unfolded to him, and already his mind had formed its plan, but he did not even thank his informant for the timely warning.

Looking towards the northern sky, he saw by the position of the Great Bear that morning was drawing near, and that it was time to prepare for the work of the coming day. The conversation with the new comer had been carried on in a low tone. To me it was unintelligible at the time, but later on I became aware of its meaning.

Of the purport of the stranger's visit, Red Cloud now said nothing, he simply explained the presence of the Iroquois, by remarking that he had struck and followed our trail of the previous day, that he was an old friend, and would join them in hunting the moose during the next few days. The morning already gave every indication of being followed by a day well suited to the pursuit of the moose; the trees rocked and swung under the gusts of storm, and the moan of the wind through the stretch of pine forest promised the hunters the best guarantee of a noiseless approach to the resting-place of that most suspicious and far-hearing denizen of the waste. Breakfast over, we set out from the camp, leaving the sled and harness suspended in the fork of a tree to save the leather fastenings from the attacks of the dogs. Red Cloud led the way, plunging directly into a labyrinth of wood, which soon opened upon a frozen and snow-covered lakelet. At the farther side of this open, a profusion of willow bushes were seen; along these we bent our steps, and soon, in the deep snow that had drifted around the willow stems, a series of large hoof-prints became visible, now leading around the edge of the thickets, now into the midst of them, while the tops in many places hung down, bruised and broken, as though some tall animal had been browsing upon them as he travelled along. The Indians looked at the tracks intently, and then pushed their way through the thicket to the edge of the forest at the farther side; here a perfect network of footmarks seemed to lead in every direction, crossing each other in apparently hopeless confusion. But the Sioux did not appear to have any doubt as to the line he should follow. Passing again into the forest, he held his way without pause through tangled brake and thicket. I, however, noticed that we were now following a double track, that is to say, a track made by an animal which had gone to and returned from the willows by the same line, but the double marks were not always distinctly defined. On the contrary, it required the most careful scrutiny to discover the existence of a double footprint in the holes, so exactly had the animal appeared to place one footstep in the impression already made by him in the snow. I noted that the Sioux, when he did bend down to examine the holes, paid particular attention to the edge of the snow at the point where the hoof of the moose had last quitted the track. At this edge a few fine grains of snow lay on the surface of the older fallen mass, and these light particles seemed to give to the tracker his test of proximity to his game. Sometimes he would blow gently upon them, sometimes he would content himself with pushing the muzzle of his leather-covered gun into the footmarks.

All at once a change passed over his mode of pursuit. His pace slackened; his step was more carefully planted, and his eye scanned more closely the surroundings of copse, brake, and thicket. He now motioned the Iroquois to stay in one spot, and whispering me to keep close behind him, and to tread as much as possible in his footsteps, he turned aside at a right angle and bore away deep into the forest, apparently following no track of any kind.

Following closely behind, I noticed that the course was not straight—it bent inwards in a wide circle, so that if continued it must again strike the trail of the moose. It was so; with long drawn steps the Sioux came back again upon his old line at a point some quarter of a mile from where he had quitted it. Arrived near the line of tracks he made a most careful study of the ground, and noted each footprint with great care; then he bent his steps back again in the way he had come, and again bent round so as to make another half circle, this time a considerably shorter one. His course I can but illustrate by the following diagram—

The straight lines representing the original track of the moose, and the curved ones the course which we followed, in lessening half-circles, that ended and began again some few yards short of the trail.

The object of these curious tactics was not at once apparent to me; but I noted two points that threw some light upon them. One was the fact that the circles were always made to the side away from the wind; and the other was, that the Sioux on arriving near the line of trail invariably directed his scrutiny of bush and thicket to the space lying between us and the line, little care being taken to examine the forest directly along the trail to the front.

Three circles had thus been made without any result, and we had once more drawn nigh the line of trail. A few steps, more carefully taken than any that had gone before, brought us to their limit, some few yards short of the line.

To the left front as we looked towards the trail there stood a small clump of broken and tangled wood, lying within twenty paces of the trail. The Sioux looked long and steadfastly, then he advanced half-a-dozen paces to his front, noiseless as the footfall of a hare in a thicket; all at once he stopped. As yet the gun-cloth had not been taken from his gun, but now I noticed that the barrel was uncovered; still the hammer remained upon half-cock. I had not gone forward the last ten paces, for I instinctively realized from the manner of my companion that the final moment of the stalk was at hand.

Without changing his position Red Cloud now beckoned

me to his side, with a gesture impressing the utmost caution. Both of us had long since taken off our snowshoes, and our moccasined feet scarcely sounded in the snow. When we were close together Red Cloud said, in a low whisper,—

" Look in the centre of yonder thicket."

I looked, and saw nothing beyond the maze of tangled branch half-sunken in soft snow. Red Cloud now raised his gun, but it still remained at the half-cock. I looked, and looked again, but could make out nothing. All at once the sharp click of the hammer, drawn to full cock with somewhat unusual strength, and therefore noise, struck the ear; a second later and there rose up in the thicket centre, fifty yards from where he stood, a huge, dusky animal. The Sioux seemed in no hurry, he took matters as coolly as though the moose was working in obedience to his own movements; the moose stared blankly at us, the Sioux looked quietly at the moose. The pause was only for four seconds, but to me it seemed an age. All at once the spell was broken. Quick as lightning the gun was raised to the shoulder, the shot rang out, and the moose bounded like a ball from a cannon, crashing out of the thicket. " Missed," thought I —no; not a bit of it. Thirty paces were not covered ere the great beast plunged forward in the snow, a struggling mass amid the spotless white.

We drew near the quarry. He was a noble animal. The Sioux regarded him with looks of pride. It was a stalk well done; it had been a triumph fairly gained over an animal remarkable over all the wild animals of the North American forest for cunning and sagacity.

And now as we waited for the Iroquois, I had fully explained to me the tactics I had just witnessed. When the time for lying down comes, in the early dawn, the moose selects a safe spot to the leeward side of the trail he has followed; in fact, he retraces his trail for some distance before deviating from it. He takes up his resting-place for the day, guided by instinct to select a spot from which he can catch the wind of any person following his footsteps. To defeat this excessive caution was the object of those curious lines of approach taken by the Sioux; each time he came out within sight of the line on which he knew that the moose was to be looked for in some adjoining thicket. Thus each brake had been scanned. To have followed the trail would have been to have given the animal warning of our approach. It was only by cautiously examining all possible lurking-places from behind them, *i.e.* to leeward of them, that the result we have seen could be attained.

The work of skinning and cutting up the moose was now proceeded with. The distance from the camp was not far, and while the Sioux made ready the carcase, I went back along our track to bring the dogs for the meat. When I got back from the camp with the sleds all was ready. Skin, marrow-bones, and meat were all packed away, and before the low-set sun had touched the pine-tops in the west we were back again in our camp.

It was a grand feast that evening for both dogs and men. We sat long in the red light of the fire, frying the delicious marrow-bones, and toasting rich bits of meat. The Iroquois looked the picture of content. He had had a hard time of it for some weeks he told us; his gun had not shot straight; the moose had been wild, the days calm; but now plenty had come, and he seemed determined to make up for past misfortunes. He spoke English fairly well.

"White Brother," he said to me, amid one of the pauses in our repast, "these are the happy moments in our lives; these are the moments which, when we think of them in civilization, draw us out again into the wilds. Months of hunger and cold are forgotten in a day such as we have spent to-day."

"But," said I, "you are a stranger here; your people dwelt far away beyond the great lakes, where the white man's cities now cover the land, and where the rivers are furrowed by the wheels of his fire-boats."

"Yes," he answered, "that was my home, and a remnant of my race still dwell by the shores of the St. Lawrence; but for me it would not do. I came here twenty years ago, a youth, in the canoe of a trader. I have lived in these woods and prairies ever since. In my own land I was a stranger, in this strange land I found myself at home."

Next morning the return march to the hut was begun. The Iroquois formed one of our party. We moved over the snow-clad wilderness in silence. Red Cloud was busily engaged in forming plans by which we might hope to elude the designs of his enemies The Iroquois, always reserved and taciturn, moved along wrapped in his blanket, silent and impassive; and I felt in no humour to break in upon the plans or meditations of my companions.

Darkness had quite fallen when the dogs, tired by the weight of the moose meat which they were hauling, came in sight of the hollow in which the hut lay. Then the weary load grew light in anticipation of home, and, pulling vigorously at the traces, the fire-lit doorway of the little hut was soon reached.

But long before the journey was over, Red Cloud had fully matured in his brain a plan which promised him escape from the toils that encompassed him. That plan he briefly explained to me as follows,—

On the ice-covered little indentation, or mimic bay, close beneath the east wall of the hut, we would construct a large and solid raft of dry pine-trees. The raft when finished would be lashed to the trees on the shore to await the disruption of the frozen river. The ice once gone and the structure afloat, the work of loading goods and chattels, guns and ammunition, would begin; then, at the first signal of assault from hostile Sircies, the hut and its fixtures would be fired, and down the swift-rolling flood of the loosened rivers would glide the ark, bearing to realms of safety our little party from the ruined site of our winter home. Such were the means by which he hoped to defeat once more the machinations of his foes.

The next morning saw the beginning of the refuge raft. The pine bluff echoed with the ringing strokes of well-wielded axes, and soon a dozen dead and dry pine-trees had fallen, and their trunks were rapidly being cleared of branches and cut into even lengths of fourteen feet, and others of ten and twelve. The dry trees were the only ones fit for the work; the green ones, heavy with sap, would have floated too low in the water to allow of weights being placed on them.

When a sufficient number of dry trees had been felled and cut into lengths, the work of drawing them to the little bay began. Every one worked with a will; but many of the trees had been cut at a considerable distance from the hut, and it was laborious work to get the larger pieces into position upon the ice. Then was done the work of notching and shaping the various parts of the raft, and forming the outer framework upon which the higher platform was to be built. The two longest and thickest trunks were placed as outside pieces, these two were connected together by cross sticks at either end, and all formed a massive frame twenty feet in length by eight feet across; over these in turn were placed eight pieces of lesser bulk and size, crossed and held together by transverse sticks.

While these preparations were going on, the Cree was busily engaged in cutting up and stretching into pliable lengths long strips of "Shahanappi," or buffalo and moose skin; these, when fully stretched, were passed around the trunks, lacing the entire structure into a most compact and powerful raft.

In three days' time the raft was finished, and as it had been in the first instance laid upon the exact spot on the ice which it was meant to occupy when afloat, no further labour was necessary to drag the ponderous mass into position, and nothing remained but to complete the arranging and sorting of the stores, and many minor details, and to make everything ready for rapid embarkation when the hour of movement would have arrived.

The first object aimed at by Red Cloud was to avoid leaving in the hands of his enemies any token of his defeat. He was determined that, if he could help it, not a gun or trophy should be shown as things that had been taken from the wandering Sioux. Nothing in fact save the possession of a barren site should be left to his enemies. The chief difficulty lay in the horses. How were they to be removed? There could be no reason to expect that the Sircies would allow a day of practicable weather to elapse after the melting of the snow before their scouts would be on the alert, around a wide circle of the banks, to prevent the escape of the party by land. It looked as if all the horses must be sacrificed. The idea of killing his favourite horse, his long-tried, faithful friend, was a thought that Red Cloud could not endure. He spent many hours in thinking out some method of escape. At last he hit upon what seemed to promise success. He would build another raft, and putting himself upon it, and his steed swimming behind it, he would run the river alone; the others would go on the first raft. He told me his plan. I proposed that the raft should be made large enough to carry two people, and that I should also take my horse, and still continue to share the fortunes of my friend.

The Sioux consented to this arrangement, and the work of building soon began. Some changes were made in the shape and construction of the second raft, to enable it to bear the unequal strain likely to be put on it. In the course of a few days it was declared finished, and, moored side by side with the one first built, was in readiness to receive its cargo whenever the moment would arrive. Thus we found ourselves ere the close of winter preparing to meet as best we could a formidable attack from powerful enemies. The forewarning given by the Iroquois had enabled us to forearm, and it now only remained to await the attack when the breaking up of the ice would let loose the passions of our enemies, and the flood-gates of our friends —the Pascopee and the Red Deer rivers.

CHAPTER XII.

The winter draws to an end—A keen look-out—Signs—The break-up of the rivers—An ice block—The enemy approaches—A noiseless arrow—The ice still fast—The ice flows—The war-cry of assault—A parley—We embark on the rafts—The hut in flames—On shore again—Freedom—Winter gone.

THE end of the long winter was drawing nigh: the snow yet lay on plain and forest, the ice held dominion as firm as ever over lake and river, the frost at night was still severe; nevertheless, there were many signs of approaching spring. The knolls and edges facing the mid-day sun had become bare of snow; the air, during the hour of noon, felt warm and balmy; the surface of the snow became soft under the sun; and there was in the atmosphere an indescribable sense of freshness, that presaged the near retreat into more northern realms of the grim winter king who had so long ruled with iron grasp the subject land.

As the first symptom of the enemy's approach might now be looked for in the neighbourhood, it became necessary to adopt all precautions against surprise, and to get the horses under the protection of the hut.

There remained from last summer a total of five horses, two having been lost after the prairie expedition in the end of November. The five were now driven in from their wintering ground; they were found to be in excellent condition after their three-and-a-half months in the snow; two of them were, however, of little value, and it was decided that it would be better to sacrifice these at once —not only because their ultimate fate was sealed, but also because the means of keeping the remainder in food were extremely limited, no supply of hay having been stored in the previous autumn.

The roof of the hut held, however, a large stock of the long reedy grass that horses love so well to feed upon, and the thick covering of snow which, during the entire winter had overlaid this thatch had kept the grass clean and succulent. One side of the roof was now divested gradually of its covering, and enough of provender was obtained to keep the three horses alive during the few remaining days they had to wait. We had already erected a small stockade, which covered the approach to the rafts, in case an attempt should be made to rush the place.

It was the habit of Red Cloud to spend many hours of the day in reconnoitring the line by which alone it was possible for any hostile party to approach the hut. The time had now arrived when signs of scouts must be evident if the expected attack was to take place. The ice had begun to loosen in the rivers, and the snows were vanishing quickly from the face of the prairies.

About the fourth day after the Sioux had begun to reconnoitre, the Iroquois started out to examine the country along the North river. Keeping the low ground between ridge and river, he watched intently the drifts and open spaces by which a scout would have been likely to pass. At a spot lying about a mile from the Forks, he came upon a footprint that had not, he thought, been made by any denizen of the hut. He brought the Sioux to the place, and a comparison of the snow-shoes of the party with that of the impression in the snow, showed the surmise to be correct. There had been strange Indians lurking about.

But the Sioux was now quite prepared for any movement of his enemies. The ice still held in the rivers, but each hour gave increasing symptoms of its disruption; great seams and rents had opened in it; in the central portion channels of open water were to be seen, where the current ran with immense velocity, escaping for a moment from the superincumbent weight of ice, and again vanishing beneath it. The ravines that seamed the plain were daily pouring down streams of water to swell the volume of the river, causing the ice to rise, and producing the rents and chasms already spoken of.

Strange footprints.

[*Page* 214.

At last the change occurred. It was night-time. A great tremor seemed to vibrate along the entire surface; water sprang in innumerable places through the fissures; great blocks of ice reared up and fell crashing upon their fellows, and the mighty mass began slowly to move.

When daylight came a whirling volume of crashing ice-floe was seen, and the rapidly rising river told the story of a complete break-up along the entire channels.

The rafts held well to their moorings. A few hours more must settle the question of escape. The river had now risen to a height of seven or eight feet above its frozen surface, and soon it must begin to subside; then the larger ice would rapidly disappear. Red Cloud watched the water-mark; so long as the floes kept drifting, the water was rising, or stationary; when the floes would show stranded along the shores, then the time of subsidence had come.

At last the tide turned and the river began to fall. The ice in the little bay had been rent and broken, and the water rising, from beneath, had submerged it; the rafts were half floating.

And now began the work of loading stores: saddles, food, guns, blankets, kettles, and sundries, were ranged in carefully prepared lots upon the raft destined for them, and in an hour's time everything was ready for departure—everything save the river; another block had taken place in the ice below the junction, and the pent waters were again beginning to rise.

Mid-day came, and yet the block continued; fortunately the rising water had ample room to spread itself over the low-lying grounds along the rivers, and the rise was not sudden. Still the danger of some huge block of ice being forced upon the rafts was considerable, and it was necessary to watch narrowly the rising tide, and to stand by the rafts, with poles ready, to keep them afloat in case of a rapid subsidence setting in.

The evening was drawing near. All day the Iroquois had watched the plain at the top of the point, from the screen of forest that fringed its edge. The Sioux and I had spent the time between this advanced post and the scene at the rafts, and the scout had stood ready with rifle and pole. Donogh and the Cree had charge of the horses. Dry grass and wood shavings had been piled inside the now empty hut, ready for the match; but still the scene remained unchanged—no enemy appeared; the river was yet blocked.

All at once there came a low signal-call from the Iroquois upon the ridge. Red Cloud and I rapidly ascended to the look-out point. The Iroquois had seen a strange figure emerge from a thicket half-a-mile distant, and disappear over the edge of the ridge. Then half-a-dozen others followed, one by one, and glided over the edge. The sight had been for an instant only; but it was enough—the enemy was at hand.

Leaving the Iroquois at his post, Red Cloud and I turned off along the slope of the ridge, on the side towards which the figures had been seen to disappear. About one hundred yards from the hut, a landslip on the steep bank had carried away all trees and brushwood, leaving the sandy sloping bank quite bare of cover. This open space of fifty yards across had already been marked by us as a *glacis* over which an advancing enemy must expose himself to view. On the edge of this open, we now awaited the further approach of our enemies. It was in fact the only vulnerable side; the rivers protecting the point upon two sides, while the rest of the angle was completely commanded by the look-out ridge.

Keeping now well within cover, we silently watched the open landslip. The Sioux carried his double-barrelled rifle, his short bow, and a quiverful of arrows.

"They make no noise," he whispered to me, "and at this distance are better than bullets."

It was now sunset: there was still about half an hour of good light. Would the hostile party await darkness, or make its advance without further delay?

"Had they meant to attack after dark," said the Sioux, "they would not have shown in the open. They will come on at once."

He had scarcely whispered this to me, when from the brushwood on the opposite side of the slip appeared the dark figure of an Indian. He was quickly followed by others. They came full into the open, heading directly across for the spot where we stood; they thus presented only a single file to us. Ere the leading figure had gained a quarter of the way, a noiseless arrow sped from the bow of the Sioux. The aim was a true one! The shaft struck the leader in the shoulder, and brought the whole party to a halt.

At forty yards the arrows from a practised hand will follow each other in rapid succession. Scarcely had the first arrow struck, ere another was winging its way, narrowly grazing the now startled band. Instinctively the entire party fell back upon the cover which they had just quitted, and ere they had gained its shelter another shaft found its billet amongst their rearmost ranks.

"Go quickly to the rafts," whispered Red Cloud to me; "see if the river runs. I shall remain here; the enemy will not attempt to cross the open again for some time. When it is quite dark I will fall back upon the hut, and before morning the channel must be clear."

The war party of Sircies made no further attempt to cross the open. They formed, in fact, only an advanced party of the main war-trail, and they decided to wait the arrival of the entire force before making any onward move.

They had hoped to surprise us; but we were fully upon the alert, and neither the hour nor the strange silent method of our defence induced them to advance.

The river still remained fast. Darkness came on. We were now within the hut. The hostile Indians had as yet made no further sign of their proximity; but any moment might find them full upon the place, and all depended upon their method of attack. If they decided to make an assault in force upon the defences, their numbers must prevail; but as they were in ignorance of the existence of the rafts, and looked upon the ultimate capture of the little party at the hut as a certainty, there was every reason to suppose that they would not press an assault upon what in time, they deemed, must be their own.

Slowly the night wore on. Towards midnight the river showed symptoms of subsiding; the water slowly ebbed along the edge of the little bay, and the ice began to strand upon the shore; but the subsidence was so gradual that it was impossible to say whether it really meant a final break in the barrier below. About three hours before daylight, however, the decrease in the water-level grew more rapid; not only did the shore give its symptoms, but the central portions of the streams were heard in movement. At first slowly the downward motion began, then faster and faster it became, until soon, in many a wild whirling eddy, the vast mass of broken-ice poured along.

The river had fully broken up, and the time of escape was at hand.

Just at this moment there sounded from the high ridge above a wild and well-known cry. It was the war-whoop of the Sircies.

The hills at the opposite side caught up the sound, and sent it ringing back in answering echoes. It was the signal for assault upon the hut.

The main body of the war party had in fact arrived upon the scene, and there no longer existed any reason for delaying the attack. The cry was rapidly followed by a ringing volley from the brushwood at the farther side of the stockade. The bullets struck right and left among the trees, but did no damage to any of our little party. As yet we made no sign by voice or weapon of our existence. Screened behind the stockade, the Sioux and the Iroquois watched with eagle eyes the open space around the hut. The Cree stood by the horses, Donogh and I watched the raft.

Another volley came crashing around the hut, but still no response was made; no shot sounded from the stockade.

The first silent flight of arrows had made the Sircies careful in their advance, and now not a brave ventured to show himself outside the sheltering screen of wood. While thus the enemy contented himself with firing at random into the surrounding trees, the river continued to pour down its flood of ice-floes, and to decrease in level; but the difficulties of withdrawing from the position in front of a watchful foe during daylight were so great that the Sioux determined to abandon the stockade before day had set in, and to attempt the work of embarkation under cover of darkness.

In order to prevent the enemy from making an assault during the last moments of night he now engaged in a pretended negotiation for surrender with them. He began by inquiring the reason for this attack. He reminded them that he had no quarrel with them, but that he was fully prepared to resist to the utmost every attack, and to sell his life as dearly as possible.

After a time a response came from the leader of the Sircies. It is easy to find cause of quarrel when quarrels be once determined on. In this respect the wild man is not a whit behind his more civilized brother; so on the present occasion there was little difficulty in showing, to the satisfaction at least of the Sircie braves, that there existed ample reasons for the attack upon our hut at the Forks.

"Why was the hut there at all?" demanded the Sircie leader. "Was the ground on which it stood Sioux ground! Was it Cree ground? And had not the Sireies hunted over it for many generations?"

To these questions Red Cloud replied,—

"That he had come to winter there, believing the place to be neutral territory; but that if the Sircies could prove to him their right to it, he was willing to pay compensation for his occupancy; but," he continued, "this compensation must be the result of peaceful negotiation and not evoked from him by war. He would meet peace with peace, and he was equally ready to oppose war with war."

These sentiments, expressed at much greater length than I have here recorded, carried the waning hours of the night further towards the day, darkness still blotted out the features of the landscape, but the stars told us there was not much time to lose. Ere the harangues were finished, the work of embarkation had begun and was being swiftly proceeded with; the raft with the baggage was ready, save to take on board its human freight, and the horses were to be led into the water astern of the second raft at the moment it was to be shoved from the shore, and allowed to swim after it in its descent of the stream.

A low whistle from the little bay now announced to the Sioux that all was ready for the final move. He again expressed aloud to the enemy his resolve to defend himself to the last, then falling back silently and swiftly to the rafts he saw that all was ready; so far as we could see, the river was now free of ice. Then the Sioux went back to the hut again, struck a match, and threw it into the dry hay and shavings which had been piled against the wooden walls. The blaze kindled rapidly, but we had previously taken the precaution to close up the windows with clay and pieces of skin, so that no appearance of light could be seen from without; leaving the hut, the Sioux closed the door carefully behind him. In another moment he was with us at the raft. The word was given to shove out from the little cove. As the first raft glided into the current we unfastened the horses from the tree and stepped upon our own raft; a word of encouragement, a tightening of the reins, and the two horses followed us into the flood.

Then we pushed cautiously out; the current caught the raft and bent its course down river. At first the horses as they began to lose their footing showed many signs of fright, snorting and breathing fast; but after a few seconds they seemed assured, by the low-spoken words of encouragement as well as by the facility with which they swam.

And now, as the distance lengthened out between the point and our raft, a change occurred in the scene. From out the dark grove of pines there came a bright flame; at first it broke in fitful flashes from amid the trees; but anon it cast a clear and steady light on trunk and branch. Quickly it grew in strength; up through the motionless pines at last it rose, a pyramid of flame, so bright and clear that no longer could even the Sircies doubt its cause.

It was the hut in flames!

Struck with astonishment, and deeming the conflagration to be a ruse of the Sioux for some further onslaught upon them, they still hesitated what to do.

At last one or two, bolder than their comrades, pushed

over the open space and passed the stockade. All was silence save the sharp crackling of the still rising flame. Then others followed; and at last the whole band approached the point. The enemy was gone! No horse, no gun remained; and as the fire poured forth through roof and door and walls, the discomfited Sircies ran hither and thither, vainly seeking for that prey whose capture, but a few moments before, they had counted upon as assured.

Far down the river by this time we stood on the raft, spectators of this strange scene. The leading raft, a few yards ahead, also held its course undisturbed; and as now the towering flame shot up high above the pine clump, and cast its reflection on the steep bordering ridges, every point of which was so well known to us, I knelt upon the moving raft, and thanked God for an escape from a terrible situation which but a short time before had seemed hopeless enough.

Gamely the horses held their way down the river in the wake of the last raft. Every now and again the Sioux spoke some well-known Indian word to them. Both horses had been so fully accustomed to obey a single word of command from their masters that the instinct had reached that stage when it becomes the highest form of discipline—perfect obedience.

The rafts reached the end of the long river-reach that lay below the Forks. Another minute, and the bend of the river would hide from our eyes the last glimpse of flaming hut and surrounding hill. There was a strong temptation on the part of some of the men on board the first raft to fire back a parting salute of defiance and triumph; but it was wiser to give the Sircies no token or trace of their flight. Doubtless the daylight would reveal the track which we had taken, by showing the footprints in the soft mud of the shore where the rafts had touched; but by that time many miles would intervene between us and our foes, and all chance of pursuit would be impossible for the present. So round the curve the rafts ran swiftly, and then nothing was visible but the river, showing grey under the sky, and the dark outline of the wooded shores on either side.

After half an hour's work, Red Cloud hailed the leading raft to carry on until mid-day, and then to put in to the south side of the river; to make camp by the shore, and to send the scout up to the high ground where the more open country began, to watch for our approach by land.

The horses had had quite enough of the water. We would put to shore, select a good landing-place, and leaving the raft, follow the upper bank of the river for the remainder of the journey.

The two rafts now separated, and were finally lost to each other.

Cautiously drawing near the south side, the horses soon

found their feet upon a bank, which in the summer would have been dry ground. The shore was but ten yards beyond; it shelved up in an easy ascent from the water. We pushed in until the end of the raft grounded, then we stepped into the water and led our dripping and tired horses on to dry earth.

We had taken with us from the hut only saddles, arms, and ammunition, and some pemmican, and tea, and axes; these were soon brought on shore, then moving further into the wood, we made a fire. The horses stood close to the flame, which soon dried their dripping flanks. Here we passed half an hour; the morning air was very cold, and it was pleasant to sit before the genial warmth of the fire. Often we spoke of the past escape, and often our conversation wandered on to the future, with its plans and outlooks.

As the daylight began to show objects distinctly we set out, leading our horses by the bridles through the tangled maze of thicket, up the steep ridge that rose directly from the river bank.

The summit gained, the course lay to the east, along the edge of woods that here filled the space between the prairies and the water. But now the horses carried their owners, and right glad were we to feel ourselves once more in the saddle, free to steer where we pleased over the open plains. Right glad too seemed the horses to find themselves on firm ground.

The snow yet lingered in hollow places, but the prairie was clear and dry. The grass of last year lay in yellow tufts around; the leafless trees and bushes looked bright in the early sun; and the earth smelt fresh and pure as it once more gave forth its odours to the air. The long winter at last was gone.

CHAPTER XIII.

Horses wanted—New plans—We start south—The prairie in Spring—No buffalo in sight—Starvation—A last resort—Buffalo at last—We fall in with Blood Indians—The camp—Tashota—A trade—Rumours of war—We depart from the Blood camp.

RIDING quietly along the edge of the open ground for many hours, we drew in sight of the spot where the first raft had stopped at mid-day.

The camp had been made in the low ground near the river, and the Iroquois was at his post on the upper level, alert and watchful.

By evening our little band was again united together, and a substantial meal was laid out, at which we all joined, with appetites not the less keen because of the exertions and anxieties of the past twenty-four hours. A long council followed the meal.

It was necessary to decide upon a course which should embrace in its plans the next six months of the summer season.

The latest acquisition to the strength of the party—the

Iroquois—had declared his wish to share the fortunes of our band for some months. To this no one objected. Indeed, it might have been said that all owed to him their safety. Had it not been for his timely warning, it was impossible to say what fate might not have befallen us, unsuspicious as we had been of attack or molestation.

We therefore numbered four on the raft, and two horsemen. Now in the season which was beginning horses would be a necessity of life on the plains; therefore the first and most pressing want was a horse for each of the dismounted men.

Another necessity was the safe stowing away of the surplus goods which we possessed. These could not be carried without seriously retarding the freedom of movement across the prairie. It was therefore decided that the stock should be placed in *cache* some four days' journey further down the stream, and that at the point where they would be stored the four men would wait in camp the arrival of the other two, whose duty it would be to go in search of horses for the complete equipment of the whole band.

After every man had in his possession a horse, then it would be time to form plans for future action.

But it was one thing to say that each man should possess a horse, and quite another thing to provide the required number. True, horses could be obtained from many bands of Indians by barter; but to hit off the whereabouts of a band on the open plains was no easy matter.

Out of many courses open to him the Sioux determined upon one. He would start with me on the following morning, and directing his course due south would seek for buffalo in the great prairie. Once with the herds, he need have no further difficulty on the score of food. They might then wander on as the buffalo moved, keeping the great herd in sight; by this means they would be certain to fall in with Indians out upon their spring hunting expeditions. From some of these bands horses could readily be exchanged for some articles of arms, which we could easily carry on the horses in addition to our own weapons.

So far went the plan.

It was computed that in three days we should fall in with buffalo, that a week more might elapse ere Indians were met with, and that perhaps a month might altogether intervene ere we would be back again at the point agreed upon for the *cache*.

All these matters having been talked over and arranged, preparations for the journey were next undertaken.

A couple of revolvers and an American repeating rifle, together with a few other items—all of which had originally formed a portion of the trader's cargo—were taken from the raft and packed between the two horses. Blankets, a kettle, two tin cups, two axes, extra flints and steels, provisions to last four days—all the requisites, in fact, for prairie travel —were packed in bundles easily attached to the saddles, and everything made ready for a start at daybreak the following morning.

These preparations, together with the arrangements to be made by the party at the *cache*, occupied the remainder of the afternoon, and soon after dark we all lay down to sleep —the sleep to which our long-borne exertions had so well entitled us.

The dawn of a very fair spring morning saw Red Cloud and myself on the move; nor had its light long to shine ere the raft was bearing the other four down the swift current of the Red Deer river.

From the edge of the ridge where wood and plain met, we looked back to the river bank to catch a last glimpse of our friends. The raft was well in the centre of the stream going merrily along. The keen eyes of its occupants caught quick sight of the horsemen on the sky-line above them; there was a wave of hands, a faint shout of farewell, and then the frail link of sight was broken.

All day we held our southern way at an easy pace.

The horses were all too unused to work, to allow of more than a walk or trot being used; but the calculations of time had been based upon easy going, and there was no necessity for rapid movement.

I have already spoken of the general character of the

prairie through which we travelled. Here and there small copsewood studded the face of the great expanse of rolling grass-land; at times, the sheen of a blue lakelet caught the eye; and as the morning sun flashed over the scene, strange glimpses of hill-top, rock, and large trees were visible on the far-away horizon—those tricks of mirage which so frequently deceive the sight of the traveller while the morning and evening beams are slanting along the wilderness.

Pleasant is this every-day life of travel over these great northern prairies, when the spring has come up from his southern home, bringing all his wealth of bird and bud to deck his roadway to the Polar Sea.

How fresh are the cotton-wood thickets where the paired partridges nestle, and roll in the dry scented leaves of last year's autumn! How sweet are the early flowers that seem to burst all at once from the yellow grass, specking the knolls with pale blue buds, that open to look at the midday sun as he passes overhead, and then close again as the evening chills creep over the scene!

Over the ridge-line to the south, long V-shaped lines of wild geese come sailing on their northern way, some trailing behind as though they fain would cry halt along the margins of many of these soft and quiet lakes, whose blue waters spread invitingly below them; but inexorable instinct bids them follow on behind the wide arms of the moving wedge-shape column, into regions where yet the spring is a laggard, but in which man is a total stranger.

Yes, it is pleasant work that daily routine of prairie travel —work that brings to the heart of man as much of the simple satisfaction that exists in breathing, seeing, living, as can perhaps be found the whole earth over.

Over such a scene we now held our way, and evening found us camped by a tiny lake many miles from the starting-point.

The next day and the next day beheld us still holding south. But a change had gradually crept over the landscape. The thickets had become few, the lakelets scarce. Long stretches of unbroken plain lay before us, and, rolling away to east and west, the same treeless and yellow grassy hills spread out to the farthest verge of vision.

But there were no buffalo to be seen. Far and near the eye of the Sioux scanned in vain for a trace of those dark specks so welcome to the hunter's sight—those moving specks, so infinitely small on the horizon, so impressive in the nearer distance, that tell him the great herds are at hand.

The fourth day had arrived, the last day for which food had been brought. More than 100 miles had been travelled, and yet not one trace of buffalo was visible on any side. From the evening camp that day we made a long survey of the plains. A ridge higher than its neighbours gave us a far extending view over the prairies, and as we stood upon its summit while the sun was nearing the western horizon, vast indeed was the scene that lay within the compass of a single glance. If ever the mere fact of space can be thoroughly realized by man on earth, instantly embodied as it were in a single sweep of vision, brought home to the mind by the simple process of sight, it is when the eye sweeps over such a scene as this upon which we now looked. Not a cloud obscured it; no mist arose from stream or river; no blur of smoke crossed its immense depth. To the west, all was brilliant colour; to the east, the pale tints of the coming night were faintly visible above the horizon.

A grand sight surely! but one, nevertheless, upon which we now looked with a keen sense of disappointment; for all this scene of lonely distance held in its vast area no hope of food.

Still the Sioux was determined to hold his course further out into the waste.

"For two days more," he said, as we finished the last bit of pemmican in a hollow beneath the hill from which our survey had been made—"for two days we will journey on to the south."

"And then," I inquired, "if we should not fall in with buffalo what will you do?"

"And then," said the Sioux, "I will show you how we still can live and still can travel."

Next morning we were off at daybreak, and all the long day through a steady pace was maintained to the south. Evening fell—morning dawned—and yet no food or sign of food appeared. The bird-life of the park-like prairie that lay to the north had wholly vanished. The lakelets lay at long intervals apart. Trace of buffalo there was none.

Still the Sioux kept his course unchanged, and so confidently had he spoken of the certainty of finding food that evening, that I never doubted for an instant that all would yet be well.

Each ridge that lay before us seemed to me to be the one that would bring to view the much desired game; but as ridge after ridge was passed and yet no sign of life became visible, I often bent my gaze to the west in order to measure the moments of daylight yet remaining.

At last, from one of those innumerable eminences that dot the surface of the prairie the Sioux drew rein and dismounted. All was unchanged. The vast circle of sky-line held no living creature in its embrace. Close by there lay a small sheet of water, and by its margin we two hungry men, unsaddled for the night.

But this time the Sioux did not perform the usual process of hobbling and turning adrift his horse.

"I promised you that you should have food to-night," he said to me, "and now you shall see how it is to be done."

So saying, he drew from his leather coat a small pocket-knife, and took from the pack of his saddle a tin cup holding about a pint. Then he passed the larêt with a running noose round his horse's neck, drawing it tight as he did so. He then spoke a few words of encouragement to the horse, and the faithful animal answered by turning his head and rubbing his nostrils against his master's arm.

Watching these proceedings with great interest, I saw to my astonishment the Sioux open a vein in the horse's neck, and begin to draw from it a thin stream of blood. The horse never winced at the puncture, nor indeed did he appear to be aware of what was going on. In a few minutes the little vessel was quite full; the cord was slackened, and the drain ceased.

Approaching the small fire of old buffalo chips and small sage stalks, which had just been lighted, the Sioux placed the vessel of blood upon the flame. Into it he crushed a few leaves of the wild sage which grew so profusely around. When the mixture had simmered for some minutes, he handed the cup to me. It did not look an inviting repast; but hunger borne for two days will make palatable most of the dishes that it is possible to put before a man.

The feeling that gnawed my stomach was something more than mere hunger, and urged by its raging pangs I took with eagerness what would otherwise have been to me a nauseous compound. Strange as it may appear, it really was palatable, and what was still more important, it was nourishing and sustaining. While half of the contents of the tin yet remained, I handed it to the Indian, and our supper was soon over.

Strange shifts are those the red man learns in order to sustain his life amid the perils of the wilderness. Many of these shifts I had been taught in the past year, but none so strange as this one.

"See," said the Sioux, when the scanty meal was finished, "the white man would have killed his horse when hunger had come upon him; he would have lived for three days, or four, and then he would have died. On these two horses we can live, if necessary, for many days, and they will still carry us along our way."

At dawn next morning we were astir.

The Sioux ascended the hill at once. I remained in the camp. It was yet indistinct light, and the eye failed for a time to reach even midway across the vast field of vision that lay around. But at length the reddening eastern sky cast its reflection deeper into the west, and pierced the prairie in every direction. Suddenly the Sioux waved his hand, and shouted a wild whoop of triumph! The buffalo were in sight!

Far off and faint, dwarfed down by distance to mere dark specks, they dotted the horizon to the south-west, and spread nearer into the scene in atoms that were ever growing more distinct.

I was quickly at his side. Well indeed might the Indian have called his war-note. The sight would have been one to call forth no scant measure of enthusiasm, even had it been looked upon by men whose minds had not been strung by hunger to most anxious intensity, for in itself it was a glorious prospect.

Upon this vast silent plain had come, during the dark hours, a mighty invasion. The frontier of the horizon had been passed; the columns had spread out like some great fan-shaped cloud, and where the evening sun had gone down over a landscape lonely and untenanted, the glory of the morning beams had come flushing up upon the myriad surges of that wild animal life which, in size, majesty, and numbers, stands all unequalled over the earth.

"How far are they away?" I asked, after I had for some moments gazed upon this grand scene.

"Three hours' riding will take us to the foremost bulls," answered the Indian. "The cows are a day or two farther off; but we cannot afford to pick our animals. We must take the first that comes."

Descending the ridge we were soon in movement towards the sky-line of the south-west.

Towards mid-day the leading files of the herd were close at hand.

The ground was broken into many ridges, having between them valleys that afforded perfect facilities for approach.

It was not long, therefore, ere a shot from the rifle of the Sioux had brought down a young bull, near whose prostrate body our camp was at once made, and hunger fully satisfied—the tongue and some of the marrow bones being quickly put to roast over a fire made of sage sticks and dry grass.

The plan now formed by Red Cloud was to keep along the outskirts of the main body of the advancing column, which he judged to be many miles in length.

It was not, he thought, necessary to proceed much farther on our present course, as the Indians with whom he hoped to fall in, would be sure to follow the movements of the buffalo, and to have their camp one day or so behind the main body.

In this his surmises were perfectly correct. The next day saw the herd moving steadily towards the north-east; but it also brought a body of Indians into sight, whose quick eyes were not slow to detect the presence of strangers in the vicinity.

Having scouted for a time along ridges that commanded a view of our camp, a body of six braves, satisfied with their observations, came riding up at a gallop. They proved to belong to a branch of the Blood Indians, the main body of which tribe was now "pitching" two days farther south, near the range of wooded hills known as the Cypress Mountains.

The buffalo, they said, had only recently passed the American boundary-line; and there had been some conflicts between Indian bands which had followed them over British territory, and the people of their own (the Blood) tribe.

Their cousins and allies, the Peaginoos, Blackfeet, and Sircies, were away to the west and north; but doubtless they would all soon draw near the buffalo, when they heard the news that they had reached " the great prairie."

These were not altogether cheering tidings for us. The presence of the Sircies would undoubtedly lead to hostilities; and although there existed no actual cause of quarrel between the Sioux and the Blackfeet or their kindred tribes, still their known hostility to almost all other races of red men around the wide circle of their boundaries, made it more than likely they would not hesitate to attack a solitary wanderer in their midst.

To the inquiry of the Sioux as to their having horses to barter, they replied that there were many horses with their tribe; and that if the Sioux and the white man would visit the camp, they had little doubt but that a trade could be readily entered upon.

It was arranged that the visit would be paid, and then the braves rode away in the direction from which they had come.

The object which the Sioux had hoped to attain was to procure the horses he stood in need of before any of the kindred tribes already mentioned had joined the Bloods.

Once in possession of half-a-dozen horses, and with one day's start, he would defy the united efforts of all the Sircies, Blackfeet, and Peaginoos to overtake him; but our position he well knew would be most hazardous if one or all of these bands should arrive ere his trade was concluded.

Early next morning, accordingly, we moved in the trail of the six Blood Indians, and by evening drew near the camp of the main body at the base of the Cypress hills.

The lodges were pitched along a level piece of ground a short distance away from a stream, which had its source in the neighbouring hills. The banks of this stream held growth of poplar, and bastard maple, and willow, which kept the camp in fuel, and yielded materials for the work of hide stretching and pemmican making—all which operations were in full swing in front of the lodges.

The arrival of the strangers was the signal for the coming forth of many braves; but etiquette did not permit the chief to come out from his lodge until the visit of ceremony had been duly paid to him by the strangers.

As we entered the camp we shook hands with the warriors and men of lesser note, who stood around on every side.

Finally dismounting near the chief's lodge, and beckoning me to follow him, Red Cloud passed in beneath the low opening, and shaking hands with the chief, sat down on a buffalo robe at the farther side of the fire which smouldered in the centre.

The chief Tashota, or the Left-handed, was a tall and powerful-looking man, just past the prime of life. He sat reclining on his robe, looking straight into the fire before him, and blowing slow puffs from a calumet of green pipe-stone, curiously carved into the body and head of a bird. I also shook hands, and then seated myself in silence.

A minute or two passed, and Tashota, taking his pipe from his lips, spoke.

"Have my friends come far?"

"Yes. Seven days have passed since we left the Red Deer river."

Then followed questions at slow intervals on most of the subjects of interest in prairie land—the game, the news of war, the movements of tribes, the doings of the white traders; but all semblance of curiosity on the part of the chief to know the objects of the present visit was carefully avoided, and that eagerness which, in civilization, is so prone to go at once "to the point" was nowhere observable.

Nor was the Sioux, anxious though he felt on the score of time, over hasty to develop his object. Of course he said nothing about the party left at the cache. He merely accounted for his presence in that part of the country by his desire to fall in with buffalo after the winter; and while expressing his willingness to become the purchaser of a few horses, he also adroitly touched upon the chances of the other tribes shortly expected to arrive, being possessed of many superfluous animals which they would be eager to dispose of.

This was a clever bit of trade tactics. Tashota was not anxious to see a customer go even to his cousins; so after a time he asked what kind of animals the Sioux might require, and what he had to offer in exchange for them?

He wanted five or six animals of average size and speed. He had only a few weapons to offer in exchange; but they were good ones. He would show them to the chief.

Whereupon he took out a short but very handy American repeating rifle, carrying in its magazine fourteen cartridges, which, by a simple action of the trigger-bar, were passed one by one into the barrel, and fired in succession with great rapidity; and he also laid on the ground a bag of cartridges and three revolver pistols.

The eyes of Tashota glistened as they looked at these weapons, and in his mind he resolved that they should be his.

Calling in one of his braves he ordered his band of horses to be driven in. Meantime his wife had been busily engaged in preparing dinner for us strangers. A plentiful supply of the best bits of the buffalo were put to boil over the replenished fire, and a meal was soon ready, to which the memory of the long fast so recently endured caused ample justice to be done.

A lodge had been pitched for us, and when dinner was over we withdrew to it for the night, to await the arrival of the horses on the following morning.

But Red Cloud well knew that our position was anything but secure; there were other dangers threatening him besides those that lay in the expected arrival of the Blackfeet or of the Sircies. He reckoned that at least a week must elapse ere that portion of the Sircies which had attacked the hut at the Forks could reach the Cypress hills; so far as they were concerned he was safe. But the stray rumours he had caught of war between the Ogahalla branch of his own race and the Bloods were ominous of trouble to him.

If the Bloods had suffered at the hands of his race, they would not hesitate to revenge their injuries or their losses upon him. One thing was certain, and that was that the sooner he got away from his present position the better.

These thoughts gave him ample material for reflection during the night. Early next morning the horses had been driven in, and word came to the hut where we were lodged that Tashota was ready to do a trade.

It was not long before the Sioux had selected five horses from the band. The terms of barter were quickly settled, and the chosen horses having been caught, were duly handed over to their new owner, whose rifles, revolvers, and ammunition passed over to the Blood chief.

By this time it was mid-day. The camp was quiet, but the mind of the Sioux was not easy. Things seemed to him to have run too smoothly in their exchange. His quick eye had detected what he considered to be faint indications of an intention to take back, if possible, the horses now bartered. In the camp he knew he was safe; the laws of hospitality forbade a guest, once received, being ill-treated; but once outside the last lodge he would have all his tact and watchfulness put to the test—so at least he surmised, and we shall soon see how true were his fears.

It was necessary for him, however, to hide completely from our hosts all tokens of suspicion. If our escape was to be effected it must be done soon, and before the Bloods could have taken steps to secure our capture. He determined, however, to make no secret of his intention to depart, judging truly that it would have been impossible to have got away unnoticed, and that it was better to maintain a show of confidence in the good faith and loyalty of the Bloods until the moment of any hostile act of theirs had actually arrived.

His plan was to leave the camp two hours before nightfall, so that our movements might be fully visible to the Bloods, and that they might see the direction we had chosen to take; for the rest, his real intention would be developed only when night had fallen.

It was about three o'clock in the afternoon when we directed our steps to the lodge of Tashota. The chief was alone; not a movement of eye or feature betrayed that he meant mischief to the person or property of his visitors. Yet all the while a deep-laid plot had been arranged, to rob, and if necessary to kill, the Sioux after he had quitted the camp.

"I am starting this evening," said the Sioux as he seated himself at the fire. "I am going north to the posts of the white traders, and the journey is long. I have come to bid my brother farewell."

The chief nodded, and Red Cloud continued: "I have heard rumours of war between the Ogahalla Sioux and your people. For myself, I raise my hand against no red man; the quarrel of the Ogahallas is their own."

The chief still kept silence.

Red Cloud arose, and held out his hand across the fire; the Blood shook it. Then the Sioux lifted the door-curtain of the lodge, and we passed out into the open.

Ten minutes later we two men, with seven horses, rode slowly from the camp.

CHAPTER XIV.

On the trail—A pursuit—The mark is overshot—A night march—Morning—The curtain rises—We are prisoners—Blackfeet—Penoquam—The Far-Off Dawn—His history—His medicine-robe—Interrogations—New arrivals—The trader again.

WELL watched by sharp and restless eyes were we that evening as our figures grew fainter in the grey of the prairie.

Tashota had already laid his plans; and although no overt act had yet been taken, everything was ready to ensure a rapid pursuit when the proper moment had arrived.

Two hours passed, and darkness began to close over the plains. Then over both sides—the travellers and the camp—a marvellous change suddenly passed.

It is true that, long before darkness had begun, preparations must have been rife within the camp; and horses ready for a foray, and braves busy getting arms and ammunition together, must have been visible on all sides. The red man is ever more or less equipped for war, and it takes little time for twenty men to be in all respects ready for a week's raid.

As the sun went down, each man of the war-party stood

ready by the lodges for the signal to pursue, and many anxious eyes doubtless followed us and our band of led horses, grudging every step that daylight permitted us to take farther on our way.

But darkness was not thus descending upon us to find us wrapt in a false sense of security. Scarcely had the camp been left behind, ere the Sioux imparted to me all his forebodings of evil and his plans for averting it.

"When night has come," he said, "these men will pursue us. If they fail to overtake us to-night, they will continue on our trail day after day. It is impossible we can escape them by fair riding, encumbered as we are with these horses. They will, in the long-run be certain to outpace us.

"At the same time it is impossible for us to leave the direction we are now following and to strike on a new line home. We have not food sufficient to last us six days, and we could not draw upon our horses for more, except in case of actual starvation. What I intend to try is this. When it is quite dark, we will turn abruptly from the present line and seek shelter in the ravine of that stream on our left. The pursuing party will push on in the darkness thinking we will have travelled all through the night.

"At daybreak they will separate to seek our trail. They will search all day, but will not find it; their horses will then be dead tired; they will rest, but they will not give up the attempt to overtake us. As we have not been found in front or to the right or left, they will determine to seek us on the back trail; but they will not have come to that decision until to-morrow evening, when their horses will be useless for pursuit.

"On to-morrow evening at nightfall we will start from here with horses all fresh, and we will direct our course to the right of the line we followed when leaving the camp. So as to hit off the buffalo two days from here. We will travel all night, change saddles at daybreak, and travel all day to-morrow; by that time we should be far away from our pursuers."

Soon the evening hour drew on. The short twilight rapidly deepened into night, and as the last glimmer of light vanished, the plan was put into operation. Turning sharp to the left, we plunged down amid some broken ground that led to the ravine by the stream, and were soon securely ensconced amid the bluffs and rocks that fringed its lowest levels.

It was a dark moonless night, and once amid the broken ground all objects became a shapeless blank.

The Sioux pulled up as soon as he found himself at the bottom of the ravine. He dismounted, and gave me his horse and the larêt which ran through the bits of the three he led.

"I will go back on foot and lie near the trail," he said. "Sit you down here until I return." So saying he vanished on foot into the darkness, and reaching the neighbourhood of his former trail, lay down in the grass to watch.

He had not long to wait.

Through the gloom there suddenly passed, riding at a hard pace, a body of men. They had swept by almost as soon as the keen ear of the Sioux had detected their approach, and quick as they had come they were gone.

The Sioux came back to the ravine and the night passed slowly away.

When dawn revealed the features of the surrounding neighbourhood, we moved into a more sheltered position, where, amid rock and bushes, we remained perfectly screened even from any observer who might have stood at the edge of the ravine. Here during the day we relieved each other in the work of allowing the horses to graze with a larêt passing from one to another.

At length evening came again. The meal of dried meat was eaten, with water from the rill that trickled through the bottom of the glen; then saddles were adjusted; girths were drawn, and as night wrapped its black mantle around the waste, we emerged upon the level prairie to begin our long march to the north.

It was quite dark; not a sound stirred over the wilderness. The Sioux led the advance; he had three horses to his larêt. I followed, leading two. The pace was a sharp trot, and the course lay with undeviating precision to the east of north.

At last the long monotony of the night was over.

Light, faint enough it is true, but still light, began to show itself along the line where the prairie and the sky touched each other in the east; then it grew into a broader band of pale yellow, and soon stray tints of rose began to streak it, and to push the first faint reflection still higher into the heavens.

How weird and distant it used to look, that first dawn over the virgin wilderness! Shadow-land, grim darkness going, glorious light approaching—approaching so stilly, with such solemn steps that seemed ever to hesitate as they trod the gloomy sands of the shore of the night! Then gradually growing bolder, they rolled back the waves of darkness, and drew from the abyss hill-top after hill-top, until all the wondrous beauty of the sun was flashed upon the silent land.

Little time had I to think of these things as now, in hot haste, the saddles were taken from the two old horses and placed upon the backs of two of the recent purchases.

Then away we went again, and the morning wore on to mid-day, and the evening came and found us still moving to the north-east.

When night again fell we stopped, unsaddled, and turned the weary horses out to rest.

We were one hundred miles from the camp of the Indians.

Morning again; a thin rain fell. The south-west wind carried with it fleecy folds of mist, that at times completely obscured the prairie and wrapt ridges and hollows in veils of vapour.

As we pursued our course and the mid-day sun began to exercise more influence upon the vapoury clouds, the mists drew up from the valleys and drifted slowly along from the ridges and elevations. All at once the wind changed; a light, dry breeze swept over the land, driving before it all traces of fog and mist, until the whole plain stood revealed to its depths before our eyes.

The first sight that greeted us was ominous. A little to the west a long cavalcade of Indians was passing towards the south. Scarcely a mile intervened between us and them; the ground on all sides was bare and open; recognition by the cavalcade was immediate; from its front, centre, and rear braves were seen to start simultaneously towards us, and ere five minutes had elapsed twenty or thirty Indians had surrounded us. The meeting was not a hostile one; the Indians were not on a war-trail. It was the whole camp which was on the move, and though trouble might afterwards arise from the meeting no violence was now offered or threatened. Still there was a display of force on the part of the new comers that made compliance with their wishes necessary, and when they turned their horses' heads back towards the cavalcade it was evident that the Sioux and I were virtually prisoners.

"There is trouble before us," said Red Cloud to me, as we rode towards the spot where already, in anticipation of our arrival, camp was being pitched. "These are Blackfeet; but they will not detain you."

Upon reaching the camp, we were conducted at once into a circle of Indians who were seated upon the ground, apparently waiting to receive us. Prominent amid the circle sat a powerful Indian, whose dress and bearing proclaimed him chief. He wore a deer-skin shirt beautifully embroidered on the breast with stars, and circles of coloured porcupine-quill work. The sleeves were fringed with human hair. On his head he carried a sort of helmet or cap, of ermine tails and eagle feathers, and his leggings and moccasins bore similar tokens of elaborate handiwork.

In common with many of the surrounding braves he smoked in solemn silence.

Penoquam, or the Far-Off Dawn, was indeed a savage well worthy of the name he bore, and of the power which he wielded. His fame had for years spread far over prairie land. Twenty years before the time we speak of, his reputation for dauntless bravery had been for ever established by an extraordinary raid which he had made alone, far down the Missouri River, into the countries of the Mandan and Minatarree Sioux. A few years later he had engaged in single combat with a celebrated Crow chieftain named Octoo, or the Lightning. The combat had been in full view of the rival tribes, and both Blackfeet and Crows had fairly kept the conditions of the conflict and abided faithfully by its issue.

A favourite tale by Blackfeet camp-fire for many years after, was that long and varying struggle. The old men loved to dilate upon the joy that filled the hearts of the onlookers when they saw the horse of the Crow chief fall pierced by an arrow, leaving his rider on foot, almost at the mercy of his still mounted antagonist; and how that feeling of wild exultation changed to anxious suspense when they beheld their champion spring from his horse, disdaining to accept the fortunes thus given to him, and advance on foot to meet his foe on equal terms of ground and weapon.

Not less terrible were the feelings with which they watched the closing moments of the fight. When the combatants met in the last deadly embrace, from which one should never rise; and how at last that deadly struggle ended in the victory of the Far-Off Dawn, who, bleeding at many wounds, rose alone from the sandy soil, gained with a great effort his saddle, and rode slowly back to his people, to fall into their ready arms, while their shouts of triumph fell unheard upon his ears.

On the medicine robe of the Far-Off Dawn's history, the central figure, representing a man standing over the prostrate form of another man, and holding aloft the scalp of his enemy, still commemorated that great victory.

At the time of which I write, his power over the Blackfeet and their confederates was very great. His possessions too, in the light of Indian wealth, were very large. Fully four hundred horses ran in his bands. His weapons for war and for the chase included almost every specimen of modern fire-arms. His generosity was said to be in keeping with his courage; he gave freely away his share of the booty that fell to his lot. Altogether Penoquam was a chief whose reputation for valour, capacity, and wealth, might favourably compare with that of any Indian leader from Texas to the great Sub-Arctic Forest.

Such was the man in whose presence we now found ourselves. A buffalo robe was spread for us in a break of the circle directly facing the spot where Penoquam sat, and the discourse began at once.

Interrogated as to place from whence we had come, destination, and object of our journey, the Sioux replied in answers as short as they could well be made, consistently with replying to the main questions put to him. He was coming from a camp of the Blood Indians near the Cypress hills. He was returning to the banks of the Red Deer river, and the object of his journey had been to get horses. He had purchased some of his present band from the chief.

When Red Cloud had finished replying to the questions

which had been put to him in the Sioux language, some conversation was carried on in Blackfeet among the men who sat around. Presently one of them spoke:—

"Our young men who have lately been to their cousins the Sircies, have spoken about a wandering Sioux having built himself a hut at the forks of the Red Deer and Pascopee rivers, and of war that was carried on between him and their tribe. Are you not that Sioux against whom our cousins have had war?"

To which Red Cloud replied,—

"I built a hut at the spot you speak of, and dwelt in it during the past winter; but I made no war on the Sircies or with any other tribe."

The others consulted together for a few minutes, and then the chief spoke,—

"Our cousins the Sircies are only two camps' distance behind us on this trail," he said; "they can be here by to-morrow's sunset. If they have no quarrel with you, I shall be your friend; but my cousins' quarrel must be mine also. You can stay in my lodge until our cousins have arrived, and then you shall be free to go if your hands are clean of their blood. As for the white man who is your companion, we have no quarrel with him; he is at liberty to depart or to stay with you, as he pleases."

In fact the Sioux was a prisoner. His horses and arms were taken away, and he found himself treated, it is true, with no indignity of durance, but bereft of any means of flight or of fight, and constrained to await the arrival of those very foes whose unprovoked attack on him a few days before was now to be brought as evidence against him of enmity to the Blackfeet confederated tribes.

In the lodge which was now given to us (for it is needless to say I gave not a second thought to the permission to depart) there was ample time to con over the position, and to realize fully its dangers. The arrival of the Sircies would undoubtedly be the signal for an outbreak of angry feeling against the Sioux on the part of the united camps of Blackfeet and Sircies. The defeat and disappointment which the latter had suffered at his hands, to say nothing of the wounds he had inflicted upon at least two of their braves, would now be counted heavily against him—all added to whatever incentive to his destruction the trader had originally held before them. These thoughts were by no means reassuring as we sat moodily through the night in the lodge; but long before morning he had determined upon a plan which would at least defeat in some measure the machinations of his enemies, and might eventually be the means of freeing him altogether from danger.

From two quarters next day there arrived at the Blackfeet camp enemies to the Sioux. A party of Bloods from the Cypress hills, and the Sircies from the Medicine, appeared upon the scene ere the sun had set.

As may be supposed, their joy at hearing of the capture of the Sioux was very great; but there was this difference between them—that whereas the Bloods only sought the property of their enemy, the Sircies longed for his life.

The trader had laid his schemes this time with no uncertain purpose, and the price to be paid to the Sircie chief was for the life of his enemy, not for his horses or weapons. Little wonder was it then that when they found actually in their possession the same man who had recently completely baffled all their machinations, escaping from their snares in a most mysterious and unaccountable manner at the very moment they had deemed his capture most assured, that they should give vent to their feelings in loud yells and shouts of savage triumph, the sounds of which told but too surely to Red Cloud the confirmation of his worst anticipations.

In a large council held this evening, and at which all the chiefs and leading men were present, it was almost unanimously resolved that the Sioux was a lawful prize. Firstly, by reason of the aggression made by the Ogahalla tribe upon the Bloods; and secondly, by the wounds inflicted upon the bodies of two Sircies at the hut at the forks of the Red Deer river.

It was decided, however, that before any final decision was come to with reference to the punishment which the captive was to suffer he should be heard in full council, and an opportunity given him of putting forward anything he had to say in his defence. This was done more on account of my presence in the camp than from any idea of justice to the Sioux. It was thought that the white man might carry to the forts on the Saskatchewan information that might afterwards lead to trouble between the white man and the Indians, and it was therefore advisable to carry out as many of the forms of justice as it was possible to arrange.

This council was to meet on the following day, and to it were summoned the chiefs and leading men of the Bloods, Sircies, and Blackfeet here assembled.

CHAPTER XV.

The council of the nation—The wager of battle—Signs of friendship—A private interview—A fair field and no favour—The trader on the scene—I leave the camp—I camp alone—The rock on the hill—The skulking figure—Preparations for the start—The race for life—The snake in the grass—A desperate strait—The odds are made even—Hand to hand—A last chance—Out of range.

IT was an imposing spectacle this council of the Blackfeet on the next morning. On the rounded top of a prairie knoll sat the chief and old men of the tribes; the space surrounding the knoll held the fighting-men seated in circles. I sat with the Sioux on the slope. Penoquam occupied the centre of all. For a time the silence was only broken by low murmurs of voices; everybody smoked. At length the tall and majestic figure of the Far-Off Dawn rose in the centre; every eye became fixed upon him. Wrapping his robe around his body, he spoke,—

"Chiefs and braves of the Blackfeet nation. When the father of our tribes crossed the mountains of the setting sun, and pitched his lodge in this great prairie, he traced for his sons the paths they were to follow in life. To one he gave fleetness of foot, to another he gave strength of arm, to another he gave sight to track the buffalo, the elk, and the moose; but to all alike he said, Be thy courage big in battle, and thy tongue just in council. Brothers, we are here in council to speak the straight word. Our brothers the Sircies are here; our cousin the Sioux is here; they have had quarrel with each other. We will ask our brothers the Sircies to tell us why there has been war between them and our cousin; and we will ask our cousin to say why he has quarrelled with our brothers. Then, when we have heard each the word which he has to speak, our judgment will be given with a straight tongue."

Then Penoquam called upon the Sircie chief to state the cause of his quarrel with the Sioux.

The Sircie now told his version of the attack upon the hut at the Forks, dwelling at length upon the wounds suffered by his braves, but keeping carefully concealed the part played by the trader in the affair. He represented the attack as made because the ground on which the hut had been built was a portion of the hunting-grounds of the Sircie tribe; and he also spoke of the presence at the hut of Indians belonging to tribes that were at war with his people. In conclusion he demanded that the Sioux should be given up to him for punishment.

Then the Sioux, rising from the ground to his feet, spoke in answer.

"Chiefs and men of the great Blackfeet nation. It is true that I fought against the Sircies, but I fought only in self-defence. Who is there among you who will not push aside a falling tree, or hold his shield against a hostile arrow? I am known to you all. My hand has never been raised against a red man's life, save to defend my own; but if this Sircie thinks I owe him blood for blood, I am free to offer him the trial of my life against his own. Here, on horseback or on foot, I am ready to meet him in the combat."

A murmur of approval ran round the dusky circle. The Sircie was for the moment abashed; this was the last turn he could have wished the affair to take. The Sioux, he was well aware, was more than a match for him at any weapon; nevertheless he could not openly decline the proferred combat. He would pretend to accept the battle wager. When he announced his readiness to fight, his followers at once demurred:

It was not combat they wanted, they said, but the death of their enemy. The Sioux had already shed the blood of their brethren; why should he be given an opportunity of shedding more? His own life should now be the penalty.

It was clear that a considerable portion of the Blackfeet shared this view. Nor was it to be wondered at; their brotherhood with the Sircie was stronger than their cousinship with the Sioux. But as I watched the faces around, and took note of each varying expression, I thought I could see in the face of the chief Penoquam indications of other feelings towards my friend. It seemed to me that he wished if possible to stand between the Sircies and their prey.

The face of the red man is slow to betray his thoughts, but the eye of true friendship is quick to read sign of favour or affection towards a friend, when the balance of fate hangs suspended between his life and his death.

I was right in my surmise. Penoquam wished well to the Sioux. He had heard through his spies the true story of the under-current which the trader had set to work for the destruction of Red Cloud, and he was determined if possible to save him; but neither his power over his own people, nor his influence with other tribes, great though they undoubtedly were, could enable him openly to avow his intention. He must dissemble his real motives, and pretend acquiescence in the demands of the Sircies. His voice was now heard above the murmurs of the chiefs and braves.

"It is right," he said " that our brothers the Sircies should ask the blood penalty, but it is also right that our cousin should be given the chances of the custom of our people. The Blackfeet are strong in battle, they do not fear any tribe on the prairie, or in the thick wood; but as they are brave, so are they just. This Sioux has offered fight; our brother is ready to meet him in the combat; but if the

Sioux should gain the battle, the reckoning for the blood already shed would still be due. No; we will not grant the combat to the Sioux, nor shall we give to the Sircies the life of our cousin. Seven days from to-day we will say what shall be done with the Sioux; until that time he is our prisoner."

The council now broke up, and I was soon alone with Red Cloud in our lodge. It was after nightfall that a messenger came to say Penoquam desired our presence in his tent.

It was only a few yards distant.

We found the chief alone, seated before a small fire, smoking. He motioned us to sit by him, and when we had all smoked for a while in silence, he spoke. He had only a few words to say, but they meant a great deal to us.

"In seven days," he said, "the Sioux would be given a chance of his life. He would have his own horse again, and his freedom would then rest with himself. He would be given a clear start of three bow-shots' distance. His enemies, the Sircies might catch him if they were able. For four days Penoquam would say nothing to the tribe of this resolve, but on the fifth day he would announce to them his decision."

We went back to our tent and silently thought over this proposal. It had many things to recommend it, so far as the chances of ultimate safety were concerned. It is true the horse of the Sioux was yet unused to trial of speed after the winter's snow, but those of the Sircies were no better prepared, perhaps not so well. But on the other hand, the proud heart of my friend revolted at the idea of having to fly before his enemies. So galling did this thought seem to him that he actually determined to refuse the chance offered to him, and to tell Penoquam that he was ready to die facing his foes, but not to fly with his back towards them.

I tried to dissuade him from this resolve, but all my efforts were useless, and I lay down to sleep that night with the gloomiest forebodings of approaching evil.

It was yet early on the following morning when there arrived in the Sircie camp one whose presence soon caused a change in the resolution formed by the Sioux; it was the trader McDermott. What connexion this arrival could have with the determination of Red Cloud to accept the offer of Penoquam I could not discover, but that the presence of the trader was the cause of this acceptance I could not doubt; indeed it was easy to see that the resolution to decline the chance of flight was at once abandoned when the news of McDermott's arrival was received.

So far things began to look brighter. I had such complete faith in my friend that I felt he could not fail unless the odds were altogether against him, and I knew that there could not be many horses on the plains whose speed would outmatch his. So the few days passed away, and at last came the morning that was to announce, to Blackfeet, Sircies, and trader alike, the judgment of Penoquam.

The announcement was received by the braves with much excitement. It promised them a spectacle that was dear to the red man's heart; for the Sircies or the Sioux the majority cared little, but their interest in the race for life was keen. Three days had still to elapse before the race.

It was necessary that I should decide upon some line of movement for myself. If the Sioux escaped, I would still be a denizen of the camp. If he fell, I felt that I could not meet his enemies save as my own. And yet I could not bear the idea of leaving him to face alone this ordeal. True, I could be of no service to him; but that did not seem to lessen the horror of deserting him at such a time. It was on the evening of this day that he spoke his wishes to me,—

"I want you, my friend, to do me a great service. Penoquam has told me that I am to be set free on the east side of this camp. I will make for the east at first. If I find that I am not likely to be overtaken I will bend away to the north in the direction of our *cache*. You must go before me on that course. You have three spare horses besides the one you ride. Take these horses at nightfall to-morrow out of camp. Depart on your way to the north. Halt some little way to the east of north. When morning breaks choose some ground where you can remain safe during the day and night, and then on the forenoon of the second day from to-morrow look out to the south for me. If the Sircies follow me with fresh horses I may want your help then. If I should not come by the evening of that day, wait for me no longer, but endeavour to get to the *cache* as best you can, and tell them what has happened."

The next day I made my preparations quietly for departure, and when evening came I quitted the camp. A son of Penoquam came to see me clear of the lodges. I had not dared to do more than silently press the hand of my friend. He sat in his tent composed and quiet, as though to-morrow was to bring to him the usual routine of prairie life. Once clear of the camp, I held on straight towards the north, steering by the pole star. I travelled without halting all night, and the first streak of dawn found me many miles from the Blackfeet camp. I turned off towards the light, and held on for some time longer. The sun was now drawing near the horizon. It was time to halt, I looked about for hollow ground in which to camp, and soon found it; then I hobbled the horses, spread out a robe, and lay down. But I could not sleep; the thought of what was so near at hand kept my mind on the stretch, and the confidence which I had before felt as to the result of the race for life, seemed now to vanish in swift-recurring fears of disaster to my friend. The dew lay wet upon the prairie. I pulled the short green grass, and bathed my feverish forehead in it; then I arose and began to ascend a ridge that lay to the southward of my camping-place. From the top I could see far over the prairie; dew-freshened and silent it spread around; not a sign of life was to be seen upon any side. Far away to the south, and somewhat to the east of where I was, a ridge stood out high over other elevations; there appeared to be on its summit something like a large boulder. I remembered, one day when strolling around the Blackfeet camp, having noticed a similar object far away to the north-east; it was the same hill. A thought now struck me; I might go in the night towards this hill, and at daylight gain its northern side. The camp would then be in view, and I would see something of what took place. I determined to do this as soon as darkness had come.

I descended the hill and lay down again on my robe. Still I could not rest. The trader McDermott seemed to haunt my mind; his presence in the camp filled me with vague apprehensions. I felt that he would strain every effort to destroy the man he held in so much dread, and who was now almost in his power. At last the day wore to an end. When it was quite dark I set out for the rock hill. I only took my own riding-horse; I carried a double rifle. I steered a course slightly east of south. When the night was about two-thirds over I stopped to wait for daylight. I was afraid lest in the darkness I should overshoot the rocky hill. When day broke I saw the rock still before me, but further off than I had expected. Keeping the hollow ground as well as I could, I went on. It was sunrise when I reached it. I then haltered my horse in a hollow on the north side of the ridge, and went up the hill on foot. The rock at the top proved to be a granite boulder, here stranded cycles ago from some iceberg fleet sailing south, when this ocean of grass had been a still vaster ocean of water. I did not then trouble myself much to think what it had been in the past; to me now it was everything I wanted—vantage-point, shelter, position.

I looked out from the edge of the rock over the prairie to the south and west. Far off, I saw the lodges of the Blackfeet camp, with thin pillars of light blue smoke ascending in the morning air.

The atmosphere was very clear, and objects were visible to a great distance; everything was quiet in the intervening distance. I stood some time leaning against the boulder, surveying the scene outspread beneath. Suddenly I saw a figure on horseback appear in the middle distance. It was only for a moment, and he was lost again in some prairie hollow. Keeping my eyes on the place I soon saw the figure show again—this time the head and upper part of a man's body. This also soon vanished, but only to reappear again and again at intervals. The man, whoever he was, seemed to be making across the line that led to the camp.

He was nearly midway between the camp and my standpoint. At first I thought it might be the Sioux, but a little reflection told me it could not be my friend. At last I saw the figure stop, and dismount from his horse. Following with my eyes the line he had taken, I noticed that there seemed to be a marked depression in the prairie in that quarter. Standing on high ground, I could see into portions of this depression, but to a person on the level the figure would have been almost wholly invisible. It was evident the figure was that of some person who desired, like myself, to keep concealed from view. What object could he have in thus keeping so far out in the plain from the camp on the line the Sioux would take. Then it occurred to me that this man might be the trader McDermott. Could it be? Every circumstance I had noted—the line followed—the care taken to conceal himself—all tended to convince me that it must be the trader. My heart sank within me at the thought; a cold perspiration broke upon my forehead, and I leant against the granite rock for support. Then came the thought—could I not do something to defeat this stealthy scoundrel, who was thus hiding to intercept the escape of my friend and strike him a traitor's blow? Alas, what could I do? Fully five miles of open prairie lay between me and the hollow where this wolf had taken up his ground. Long before I could reach the spot I must be observed from the camp. While I was yet thinking what to do, I observed in the far distance, on the confines of the camp, signs as of the movement of men and horses. I could see specks moving to and from on the level plain of grass that lay on the side of the camp nearest to me. It was not long before I saw these specks assume shape. A line of horsemen was distinguishable, with one mounted figure in advance; this was only for a moment. Then I saw the whole move forward almost in an easterly direction, and to the left front of where I stood. My heart beat so that I could hear its throbbing like the tick of a clock. I was wildly excited, but with the fever of heart and brain came strength and power of thought such as I had never before experienced. Concealment was no longer necessary. I ran back to the hollow where I had left my horse, drew tight the saddle-girths, jumped into the saddle, and rode up to the rock again. The short interval had changed the scene. The horsemen had come on, but the line was no longer uniform; there were stragglers already dropping behind, and there were others who, at the distance from which I saw them, seemed to be almost nearer the leading horseman than they had been before.

I saw that the direction of the leading horseman was changing a little towards the north, but for what reason it was impossible to say. This change of direction if continued would leave the place where I had last observed the skulking figure considerably to the right.

I now observed that this man appeared to be aware of

the alteration of direction, for he began to move further to to the west on the line he had already been pursuing.

In the time I have taken to tell these changes and movements the main scene itself was sweeping rapidly along. Scarcely two miles now separated the Sioux from the figure in ambush, but I saw with joy that in his efforts to keep concealed from view the horseman in the hollow was quickly losing the great advantage of position which he had first held, and that there was every chance that instead of being able to cut off the Sioux on a line at right angles to that of the original pursuit, he would be compelled to strike at him on the longer course of an acute angle. On the other hand, I knew that while the horse ridden by my friend must now be showing signs of the pace at which he had come for four miles, that belonging to the man in ambush was almost fresh.

All at once the horseman in the hollow came out into full view. He rode at topmost speed to cross the line on which the Sioux was moving. To avoid the fresh attack I saw the Sioux bend further away to his left, and I noticed that his course was now directed almost straight upon my standpoint.

Nearer and nearer he came; the original pursuers were now far behind, in fact only four or five of them were still in the race; the rest had ridden their horses to a standstill. But I thought little about these Sircie braves; my eyes followed the course of the new enemy; my heart sank as I marked the rapidity of his advance, and the evident freshness of his strong black horse.

As I have already remarked, the line upon which he advanced was calculated to meet that upon which the Sioux was moving; and the point at which they would meet if continued as they were now directed, would be not very far away from where I was standing.

Of the two horsemen, the trader was the nearest to me; he was still a couple of miles away, but I judged that when he passed the western base of my hill he would not be half a mile distant.

Red Cloud was evidently in no hurry to edge away to his left and thus make the chase a stern one. Perhaps he feared that any change of direction westward would throw him back up to the Sircies, or it may have been that he felt his gallant horse still strong beneath him. Anyhow, on he held his course, apparently little heeding his dangerous enemy on the right.

It is difficult for me to tell the exact process of thought which my brain went through while my eyes were fastened on this scene. What I must have thought the subsequent action proves; but I cannot recall any distinct effort of thinking, or any line of reasoning guiding me to action. I saw and acted. After all, in the real crises of existence it is on such action that our lives turn.

T

I hastily turned my horse down the northern slope of the hill, and sweeping round by the north-west base, galloped out into the open prairie.

And now I beheld a strange sight. Less than a mile distant, straight in front of me, the trader was riding furiously, following hard upon the Sioux. The latter had turned his horse full towards the west. There did not seem to be two hundred yards interval between pursuer and pursued; and judging by the terrific pace at which the trader's horse was going, that short distance was rapidly being lessened. No other figures were anywhere to be seen.

I took in all this as, with spurs hard set into my horse's flanks, I flew in pursuit of the trader.

Once or twice I saw him raise his gun to his shoulder to fire at the Sioux; but he dropped it again to await a nearer and more certain shot.

Fast as the two men were flying before me, my horse was going even faster still. I was gaining at every stride upon them; but of what use was my effort when any moment a shot might end the life of my friend? I was too far off to render assistance. I might, however, avenge his death if he fell.

And now, as straining every nerve, I rode along, expecting every instant to see the puff of white smoke, and hear the report of the fatal shot, I beheld the strangest sight of all that I had looked upon during this eventful morning.

Suddenly I saw the Sioux swerve to the right from his

onward course, and, wheeling with the rapidity which only the Indian can turn, bear down full upon the trader.

So unexpected was the movement, so quick was its execution, that the trader was completely thrown out. Had the Sioux made his wheel to his left hand the advantage of shot across the bridle arm would have been with the trader; but now this wheel to the right brought the Indian upon the off side of his enemy, and put McDermott in a disadvantage, which was instantly increased by the still forward movement of his own horse.

Just as the Sioux's horse had completed his wheel, the trader fired a snap-shot, his gun held straight at the full stretch of his right arm. The range was under one hundred yards, but the rapid motion of his own horse made the shot a difficult one, and I shouted with joy when I saw that neither man nor horse was harmed.

Still the odds were terribly against the Sioux. He had neither gun, nor bow, nor knife, while his opponent was fully armed. More in the hope of distracting McDermott's attention and confusing his aim, than with any expectation of hitting him at the distance I was still away, I now fired two shots at him as he stood out clear from the Sioux, whose wheel had placed him well to one side. Both shots missed their object, but I saw that he turned a quick glance in my direction just as the Sioux came thundering across the short space that still lay between them.

The career which McDermott had long followed made him an expert in all the exercises of wild life on the prairies. He could pull a cool trigger amid the fierce stampede of buffalo, and take a sure aim in battle or in the chase. He would have wagered the best horse in his possession that an unarmed enemy charging him on the open prairie, if such a man were found mad enough to attempt the venture, would have been a dead man within twenty paces of his standpoint; and even now, although coward conscience trembled in his heart as he faced his enemy, his levelled gun was pressed firmly to his shoulder, and held steady in the bridle-hand, while his horse stood true to the teaching of Indian tactics, the obedient servant and trained auxiliary of its rider.

I saw the Sioux low bent upon his horse; I saw the smoke flash forth from the trader's gun; and then for an instant all was confusion. With a wild convulsive leap forward, the Indian's horse fell, crashing almost at the feet of the trader's steed; and then—so quick was the upward spring that I could mark no interval of time—the red man's grasp was round his enemy, and the game of life or death was at last being played on even terms.

I reached the spot at the final moment. The Sioux, with one knee firmly planted against the trader's saddle, had clasped both arms around his enemy, wrenching him by a mighty effort from his horse. In the struggle McDermott

I struck the iron butt heavily down upon the trader's head.
[*Page* 277.

had flung aside his empty gun in order to better grapple with his assailant; so the fight was now without weapons. Both men rose from the ground still locked in a fierce embrace. For a moment it seemed that the heavier frame and greater bulk of the white man must prevail over the lither figure of the Indian. Once or twice the trader lifted his assailant almost off his feet; but the marvellous agility of the Sioux again gave him the advantage, and after a long and desperate rally the white man was borne backward and forced upon his knees.

So far not a word had escaped the two men; they had fought in grim silence. But now when victory seemed about to declare itself for the Sioux, a savage laugh broke from the trader, and with a mighty effort he locked his arms around the Indian, intent only upon holding him in his grasp. Well might he think the game was still his own. A low ridge three hundred yards to the south, suddenly darkened with galloping horsemen, and with loud war-cries of triumph, a dozen Sircies came sweeping down upon us. One chance yet remained to us. I pushed my horse close to the struggling men, and with my gun held by the barrel, I struck the iron butt heavily down upon the trader's head. The strong tension of his grasp relaxed, and he sank, apparently lifeless, to the ground.

But so intent was the Sioux upon his enemy that he resented my interference, and glared at me for a moment;

then I saw him seeking for a weapon, heedless of the approaching danger, now so close upon us.

"Quick," I cried to him, "or we are lost! Jump upon the trader's horse."

My word recalled him from the frenzy of passion which had absorbed every faculty of heart and brain.

The horse had stood quietly during the struggle, as his old training had taught him; the trader's gun lay at his feet. To seize the gun from the ground and spring into the vacant saddle was the work of an instant, and ere the headmost braves were quite upon us, we were off at headlong speed towards the north; one arrow quivering through the flesh of my right leg, and two or three others hurtling harmlessly around us. Twenty seconds more, and our fleet horses had carried us out of range.

CHAPTER XVI.

Revulsion—Home again—New plans—We depart for the mountains—The Hand hills—The great range—Home memories—A murderous volley—Donogh sees "the land beyond the grave"—Vain regrets—We enter the mountains—The island—A lonely grave—The Indian's home.

We rode hard for a couple of hours. I led the way towards the place where, on the previous evening, I had left my three horses. Long ere we reached it, the Sircies had abandoned their pursuit, and turned back towards their camp. Now we had time to talk over the past. For many hours that morning, and all the previous night, I had been moving as though in a dream. During the past two hours I seemed to have lived an age; there had been moments of agony so acute, that my brain reeled when I thought over them. But now all was past; the long night of doubt and captivity was over, and the fair morning of hope and freedom shone full upon us.

My heart soon answered the helm of such thoughts, and my spirits rose in unison with them. Not so with the Sioux. The abstraction of the flight seemed to be still upon him;

for a long time he rode on, looking vacantly before him. Once or twice I spoke to him, but he did not seem to hear what I said. At length he roused himself and spoke.

"If you had ever said to me that one day I should have had that man within my grasp, and that I would have failed to take his life, I would have told you that it was impossible. And yet," he went on, "it is better that he should still live. Had he fallen at the hands of another, my father's spirit would have remained unavenged."

"Live?" I answered. "He fell, when I struck him with my gun, as though life had left him."

"For all that he is not dead. Men like him do not die so easily. He was stunned by the blow; he will be laid up for a week, and then he will be as well as ever."

I confess to feeling glad at this. Although I had struck the trader to save my friend's life, I cared not to have on my hands his blood. It is true that had my gun been loaded at the moment when he held the Sioux tightly locked in his embrace, I would not have hesitated shooting him dead to set free my friend, but I would always have regretted being compelled to do so.

It was better as it was; the Sioux was safe. McDermott still lived.

We then spoke of the earlier events of the morning. I heard how Red Cloud had always counted upon his enemy forming part of the pursuing force. It was that belief which had induced him first of all to accept the chance of flight offered by the Blackfoot chief. I asked him how he had hoped to resist the trader successfully, seeing that he was without arms of any kind.

"The spirit of his dead father would watch over him," he said. And when I told him of my fears and anxieties on the previous day, and how I had determined to turn back to the rock hill, with a vague purpose of helping him in his need, he again remarked,—

"It was the spirit of my father that led you."

Of the loss of his favourite horse he thought much.

"Had I done my work as well as he did his," he said, "my enemy would not have escaped me."

"But you have gained even a better animal," I said, "than the one lost."

"No, not better to me," he replied. "For three years, through every change of land and season, through danger and difficulty, through fight and chase, that poor beast bore me—and all only to fall at last by the bullet of my enemy. Well, it adds another name to the list. It will perhaps be longer before it is closed."

We now reached the place where I had left the horses. They were feeding together almost on the same ground; and without any delay longer than was necessary to get them together, we started for the *cache*. Although the events of the morning made the time appear an age, the day was yet young. I had dry meat sufficient for both our needs, a lake gave us water; with only a halt of a minute or two we held on until long after nightfall, and when daylight broke next morning the woods were in sight. Bearing away to the east we kept in sight of these woods all day, and at evening drew in towards their shelter, camping once more amid the pleasant leaves of trees, and enjoying a couple of partridges for our supper.

We were at a point considerably below where we had left our party less than three weeks before, but still above the place where the *cache* was to have been made.

Continuing our course next day, we reached, early in the afternoon, a spot which commanded a long view of the river valley. Far winding between partly wooded banks, it lay for many a mile amid the silent wilderness—the shallows at curves catching the sunlight, the quiet reaches reflecting the clear blue sky.

How calm and tranquil it all looked! The contrast between its peacefulness and the strife I had just witnessed struck me with profound wonder. Here was a bit of the earth as it came from the Creator's hands, bright with the glow of summer, decked in the dress of leaf and blossom, sweet with the perfume of wild flower, fresh with the breezes of untold distance; and there below the southern horizon, but two days' riding away, man's passion, guilt, and greed ruled rampant in the land. According to the directions which the

Sioux had given as to the place for the *cache* to be formed, we must now be near the camp of our comrades.

So indeed it proved. On the edge of the woods we came suddenly upon the Iroquois; he had seen us from a lofty lookout point which he had established on the far side of the river, and had crossed over to meet us and show the way to the camp. It was formed upon an island in the river. There we found Donogh, the scout, and the Cree, all well, and longing for our return. They were amply provided with food; moose were plentiful, they had trapped several young beavers, and smaller game was abundant. We sat late that evening talking over our adventures.

The Indians listened with breathless interest to the story of the capture by the Blackfeet—the pursuit, the fight, and the escape. Donogh was never tired asking questions about my share in the final struggle with the trader. Had he been there to help, he said, McDermott would not have got off so easily.

A week now passed quietly away; the horses wanted rest after their arduous travel; plans had to be made for future movements. It was not likely that we should be left long unmolested in this neighbourhood. If the Sioux was right in the belief that a week or ten days would suffice to cure the injuries which the trader had suffered, then the Blackfeet, the Sircies, or Bloods, would soon beat up our quiet camp. Besides, the life of the wilderness must ever be a life of wandering. The bird seeks the sunlit atmosphere to try his wings; the horseman on the prairie roams because he cannot sit down and call a patch of the earth his home. His home is sky-bound; and when he can no longer wander, his grave is not far off.

Farther to the west there yet lay a vast region, into which we had not entered. At its western extremity rose the pine-clad sides and icy peaks of the Rocky Mountains, whose deep-rent valleys and vast glaciers fed this stream upon which we were now camped, as well as countless other streams and rivers, whose waters eventually seek the far separated seas of Hudson's Bay and the Gulf of Mexico. To this region of prairie bordering upon mountain we would direct our course, and remain until the autumn must again make us think of winter-quarters.

We had four full months of summer before us; we had horses, arms, and goods; our guns would give us food.

So we were once more on the move. We divided our stores and goods evenly among the five horses, and being one horse deficient, Donogh, the Iroquois, and the scout took it in turn to walk. As the weather was now very fine and warm, we *cached* the leather tent, and some other items for which there was no use. We travelled quietly, but by starting early and camping late managed to make good distances each day. Our course lay along the line of mixed wooded and prairie country which bordered the Red

Deer river. We kept a sharp look out for hostile Indians, and took precautions at night to secure the horses from attack.

As thus we journeyed towards the west, we entered upon a very beautiful land; grassy hills spread away beyond each other in a constant succession, long winding lakes came in view as we gained the summits of ridges, and the valleys and lake shores held groves of mixed cottonwood and pine-trees, which gave camping grounds of fairy-like beauty amid the vast stillness of the wilderness. One evening, it was about the end of June, we gained a range of hills which during two days had bounded our horizon on the west.

Long ere we reached them, Red Cloud had promised me a view from their ridges surpassing anything I had yet looked at in the great prairie.

Slowly up the east side of the hill we held our way, while every now and again a long-eared hare sprang from the grass before us, and vanished into brake or coppice. At last the top was gained. The sun yet shone on the bare ridge, but the prairie beneath on either side was in shadow, and already the blue line of shade was creeping up the hill to where we stood. Fifty miles away to the west the vast plain came to an end. A huge rampart mountain rose up into the sunset skies, poising for a moment the great orb of the sun on its loftiest pinnacles of snow. Far away to north and south this rampart range was laid along the horizon, until the edges of mountain tops were only faintly visible above the plain on the verge of vision to south-west and north-west.

"The Rocky Mountains at last," I said, half musing, to myself, as thus I beheld this grand range lying in all the glory of the summer sunset.

"That is the name the first fur-traders gave them," said Red Cloud; "but the Indian has better titles for them; 'The Mountains of the Setting Sun,' 'The Ridge of the World.' He who would scale the icy peaks, they say, would see the land beyond the grave."

As now I looked across the great intervening plain, slowly fading into twilight, and saw the glittering edge of the long line of mountain top, clear cut against the lustrous afterglow, the red man's thought which would make this giant range the line of separation between life and death seemed to be no far-fetched fancy. Here ended the great prairie. There was the shore of that vast wilderness, over which my steps had wandered through so many varied scenes of toil, tumult, and adventure. Beyond, all was unknown. And then came back to me a vision of those well-remembered hill-tops of my early days; the heather-covered slopes of Seefin, the wild crags of Cooma-sa-harn, the flat rock that marked the giant's grave on Coolrue.

The sound of a footstep approaching from behind roused me from my reverie of home. I turned; Donogh stood beside me; there was a strange wistful look in his eyes.

"Ah, master!" he said, "it makes me think of the old home again, to look at those mountains, and the sun going down behind them as he used to do in Glencar."

The tone of his voice was sad. I asked him if he felt home-sick?

"No, not home-sick," he replied; "but I have been dreaming for nights past of all the old places—the eagle's nest over Cooma-sa-harn, the rocks that hung over Lough Cluen, the island in the south end of the lake. I saw them just as they were in the old times. It was only last night that I dreamt we were climbing the face of the cliff to the eagle's nest, and I thought the old bird came suddenly swooping down, and that I fell into the lough below."

"Would you like to be back again in the old glen?" I asked him.

"Not unless you were to come too," he answered. "This is a lonesome country sure enough, but I don't mind it so long as you are near."

We made our camp that night in a hollow, lower down on the west slope of the hill. We had killed some hares during the day, and had boiled them into a thick kind of soup, which, flavoured with wild sage, gave us an excellent supper. The meal over, we were sitting around the fire chatting and smoking, when suddenly a volley of musketry rang forth close at hand, and half a dozen bullets struck around us. In the wild confusion that followed, I only remember springing to my feet, and seeing the others spring up too. Not all, alas! for poor Donogh had fallen forward from the place where he was sitting, and the Cree only rose, to fall again. Seizing my gun, I sprang to where Donogh was lying; but at this moment I felt my hand suddenly grasped with iron strength, and I was dragged forward into the dark.

"Lie down," hissed Red Cloud in my ear, "or we are all lost. Look at the fire, and shoot when you see them in the light."

The whole thing had happened so quickly, that ere I had time to collect my senses I was lying in darkness, just over the brow of a knoll fifteen paces from the fire.

I had not long to wait. Suddenly there came a wild war-whoop of savage triumph, and a dusky group of men swept down into the circle of light from the outer darkness.

They thought that the first volley had given them undisputed possession of our camp, and that scalps and spoils had only to be gathered. Now it was our turn. Quick from our dark shelter the shots rang out; but few were thrown away. One brawny savage, with knife in hand, had reached the spot where Donogh was lying, but a bullet from my gun stopped his deadly purpose, and laid him low beside my poor friend.

Another fell dead near the fire, and we saw two more stagger 'neath our bullets. This unexpected reception checked the ardour of the attack, and drove back our assailants.

We took advantage of their repulse to drag our stricken comrades from the light.

Alas! one had already passed from the light of life to the darkness of death. The Cree had ceased to breathe, but Donogh was still alive.

When we had breathing time to think of other matters than our lives, Red Cloud sent the Iroquois and the scout to drive the horses to a place of safety.

"We have given these Sircies something to occupy them," he said; "but after a while they may try to get our horses, since they have failed to take all our lives."

Soon the fire burned itself out, and the darkness of the short summer's night lay around.

Yet how long it seemed to me, as sitting by poor Donogh's side, and with his hand fast in mine, I waited for the dawn! He was quite conscious, but every now and again a stifled moan broke from his lips, and as the night wore on I felt the hand growing cold and clammy. When daylight came I saw that the poor boy's end was near.

The shot had struck him in the chest, and his life-blood was ebbing fast.

I could not trust myself to speak. I could only hold his hand in mine, and try to stanch the red stream from his death-wound,

U

"Master," he said to me, in a very faint voice, "I never knew father nor mother, brother nor sister, and so there's no one that will miss me, except it's yourself. You'll sometimes think of me, sir, won't you—when you see the deer on the hill-top, and the wild ducks on the pond, and the grouse on the mountain side, all the things that we used to hunt together? And master," he went on, "if ever you go back to the old glen again, you'll say to the priest that the poor boy he used to teach of a Sunday didn't forget the lesson at the end. You'll bury me up on the hilltop, where we first saw the mountain from?" he said again, after a pause. "It's something like the top of Seefin, where we used to sit looking out on the world—the big lonesome world."

Then his voice hushed, and after a time the lips only moved as the poor boy repeated some prayer of his childhood.

It was the long summer dawn that had looked upon the scene. As the boy's life ebbed away the glory of the morning had been growing brighter; and the sun, whose setting lustre had recalled the home scenes to his memory on the previous evening, was now close beneath the horizon on the east. But never more was my faithful Donogh to see the sun. When its level rays struck upon our camp on the Red Deer hill, he had gone before us to the icy peaks of the "Mountains of the Setting Sun"—

he had crossed the "Ridge of the World," and was already in "the land beyond the grave."

On the hill-top near at hand we laid the two bodies in a single grave. With knife and axe we dug a trench in a small clump of cottonwood, and there the red man and his white brother slept side by side.

Then we made haste to leave the fatal spot; not from fear of pursuit, as our assailants had suffered too severely to make it likely they would soon follow us up. An examination of the ground convinced Red Cloud that the Sircies had not numbered more than seven men. They had evidently followed us for some time past, and had probably made their attack as much because we were now within the country of their enemies, the Rocky Mountain Assineboines, into which they did not wish to penetrate, as because of the ground being favourable for a surprise. At least five out of the seven had suffered from our fire—two had fallen, and the traces of their retreat showed unmistakable evidence that three others had been wounded. That they were the hired assassins of the trader, there was little doubt. The gun and knife belonging to one of the fallen were similar in pattern to those we had captured from McDermott in the preceding year. He had evidently outfitted this party, as probably he had done the same by many others. That the survivors would fall back upon their main camp, many days' travel distant, was now nearly certain.

Nevertheless, although the chances of immediate molestation were remote, we were in haste to quit a spot that had been so fatal to our fortunes. As for myself, I literally felt heart-broken at the thought that I was no more to have in life the companionship and faithful service of my earliest friend. Never before had I seen death brought home to me with such vividness. Only yesterday I had spoken to Donogh in the full pride of his youth and strength. The fire at which he met his death still smouldered in its ashes; yet he who had gathered its fuel and set it alight was gone, his flame of life extinguished; his gun, bullet-bag, and powder-horn, his saddle and bridle, the horse he used to ride—all were there, yet he had disappeared. My heart was wrung with grief; I felt as though life had been a long dream, and that now I had suddenly awakened to its grim realities. Then there came upon me a thousand bitter thoughts, and unavailing regrets of the long hours we had spent together. Why had I not made more of my poor friend? Why had I not treasured those hours when he was with me? It seemed as though death, in taking him away from me had taken away too all the mist of selfishness, and that I saw clear and distinctly the worth of the friendship I had lost.

I had remained for some time sitting by the lonely grave, sunk in these sad thoughts, when I felt a hand laid upon my shoulder. Red Cloud stood beside me.

"It is time to go," he said. "Your poor brother's name is one more added to the long list that cry for vengeance."

Mechanically I obeyed. The horses were already saddled and loaded.

The Indians moved silently about; the light of our little party seemed to have gone out.

Slowly we filed off from the fatal spot, winding down the long incline towards the mountains, until the lonely thicket was lost in the distance.

About three days after this fatal day we entered one of the gorges that led into the mountains.

The scenery had undergone a complete change. The trail led along the bank of the Red Deer river, which had now shrunken to the dimensions of a small and shallow stream; on each side the hills rose steep and pine-clad, while, as side valleys opened upon the larger gorge along which we were travelling, the eye caught glimpses of snow-clad summits far above the world of pine-trees.

Often, as we rode along, my mind kept going back to that fatal night on the Hand hills. Here we were now amid those mountains whose fastnesses Donogh had so often wished to reach, while he, poor boy, was lying out in the great wilderness. But the work of travel, and the rough road our horses had now to follow, kept my mind engaged, and gave distraction to my thoughts.

Pursuing our course for a couple of days deeper into the

mountains, we gained at last a beautiful level meadow, set round on all sides by lofty hills, backed by still loftier mountains. A small clear lake occupied one end of this level plain.

We had quitted the valley of the Red Deer river, and crossing a height of land had entered the valley of the parent stream of the Saskatchewan, which here, after passing through the lake, foamed down a ledge of rock, precipitating its waters perpendicularly from a great height into a deep pool, with a roar that was audible at the farther end of the valley.

Above this fall a small rocky island stood, in the centre of the river. One end of this island was level with the edge of the cataract, the other was in smooth water, not very far from where the river issued out of the lake. As the water approached the edge of the fall it ran in many eddies and rapids, but at the end nearest to the lake the stream was smooth enough to permit a canoe to reach the island.

This rocky wedge, set between the lake and the cataract, was covered with trees, and, excepting at the upper end in the smooth river, its sides were steep and water-worn. I noticed that as soon as we came in sight of this wooded isle Red Cloud's usually passive face wore a look of unwonted interest.

I inquired if he knew the spot.

"Know it?" he replied. "Yes, it is the only place I can call my home in all this great wilderness. To-morrow we shall reach it, and then you will know why I call it my home."

We camped that evening near the spot where the river came out of the lake. There was a clump of pine-trees close at hand, and before night had closed in the well-wielded axes of the Sioux and the Iroquois had felled some dead trees, and lopped their trunks into lengths of twelve feet.

Early next morning, they had put together a small raft. Dropping down stream on this raft, Red Cloud landed alone on the little island. I had rambled off to the upper end of the lake while the morning was yet young; when I got back to camp I found the Sioux had returned, and that a small canoe was moored to the river bank, where the raft had been built.

Our mid-day meal over, Red Cloud asked me to visit the island with him. He dropped down the stream as before, and steered dexterously into the small spot of quiet water which lay at the head of the island. I then noticed what before I had not seen, that this quiet water was of very limited extent, and that the current on either side of it ran with a speed that became momentarily of greater velocity as it drew nearer the rapid. I saw in fact that it required knowledge of the spot, and skill in the use of the paddle, to hit off this little eddy of waters.

A small indentation between two rocks gave shelter to our canoe, and also held the raft which Red Cloud had built during the morning. The canoe he had found on the island. We landed on the rock, fastened the canoe to a tree, and struck into the forest that covered the entire space. I could tell by the increasing sound of the waterfall, that we were approaching the end of the island which overhung the cataract. We soon reached this spot; a few old pine-trees grew upon it; the density of their branches had destroyed the undergrowth, and the ground between the massive trunks was clear of brushwood. In the centre of this clear space, shadowed by the sombre arms of these old pines, there was a solitary mound. Red Cloud stood before it.

"It is my father's grave," he said. "Eight years ago I carried his bones all that long way from where he was killed to this distant spot. I had intended bearing them with me wherever I wandered as an ever-present reminder of the oath I had sworn, but on first seeing this spot I selected it as a resting-place. Here I made my home; hither have I come when, baffled by my enemy, I have sought for a time rest for myself and my horses; and again from here have I gone forth to seek my enemy, only to find him always too strong or too cunning for me."

CHAPTER XVII.

Signs of trouble—Reconnoitring—Precautions—We retire into the island—Daylight—The enemy shows himself—A search—He prepares to attack the island—A midnight storm—The raft—Aim low and fire fast—In the whirl of waters—On the lip of the fall—The end of crime.

When we got back to the camp near the lake the scout had news that at once excited the suspicions of Red Cloud. He had gone, he said, back upon our trail towards where we had entered the valley, to look for one of our horses which had strayed in that direction. He had found the missing animal, but during the search he had observed a single white wolf standing on the edge of a thicket some distance away. Endeavouring to approach the place in order to get a shot at this beast, he had found the animal gone, and no trace of trail or footmark could he see, but he had noticed the impression of a moccasined foot in the soft clay of the thicket. When he first had noticed this solitary wolf, it appeared to him to be standing three parts within the thicket, only the head and portion of the neck being visible.

Such was the story which roused the suspicions of the Sioux.

The north side of the valley was bounded by a wooded ridge, which commanded a view of the trail by which we had approached our present camp. To this ridge Red Cloud directed his steps, having first taken the precaution to have the horses driven in from the farther end of the meadow to the close vicinity of the camp, and our baggage made ready for any sudden shift of quarters that might be necessary. The Iroquois remained in camp; the scout was to join us on the look-out ridge.

As Red Cloud was fully convinced that our movements were even now under the observation of hostile eyes, he directed that we were to separate as though in pursuit of game, and by circuitous routes gain the points of observation selected. He believed that the object seen by the scout had been a Sircie disguised under the head and skin of a white wolf; these masks were often adopted by the plain Indians, when reconnoitring previous to an attack. They enabled the Indian scout to approach a camp, to lurk along a ravine, or to show himself upon the sky-line of a hill-top, when no other means of concealment could be used.

If the Sioux's surmise was correct, the hostile party to which this wolf-scout belonged was not far away, and it was likely that ere the evening closed in some indication of its presence would be noticeable.

From the top of the look-out hill a view was obtained of the trail leading to our camp, the only path by which men coming from the east could enter the valley of the lake and meadow; but no sign of man, hostile or peaceful, was visible; and the summer winds as they stole gently through the whispering pines, alone made audible sound in the solitude. Nevertheless the suspicions of the Sioux were not to be allayed by the quiet aspect of the trail by which our camp could be approached.

None knew better than he that if the Sircies had really followed us into these hills, they would have come in all the craft and concealment of their race, keeping within the cover of the woods by day, and moving when night hid their presence. He knew too that any party venturing into these solitudes would be strong in numbers, and that nothing but the most powerful incentive could induce men whose natural sphere of life lay in the open prairie country, to venture among those rough rocks and tangled woods.

The day was yet young; there was plenty of time to examine the trail further towards the east; the scout would push his way quietly through the woods, and return by nightfall to our camp. Red Cloud gave him a few directions as to his movements, and we returned back to the meadow, to prepare for action in the event of attack. We at once proceeded to ferry our goods across to the island; the horses were swum one by one in the wake of the canoe, and landed in the little bay between the rocks.

At this season of the year there was ample forage for

them among the rocks and trees, and in several places, where the soil was low and swampy, the goose-grass, so greedily sought for by horses, grew plentifully.

It was evening by the time we had finished this work, and the shadow of the great mountain that rose between us and the west was already darkening our little meadow. The lake surface was broken in a hundred places, by the rising of many trout at the midges and flies brought forth by the approach of night. We still kept our fire lighted at the place of our first camp, but we were ready to fall back at a moment's notice upon the island; in fact, we only awaited the return of the scout before returning to that secure resting-place for the night.

We had not long to wait. The light was still good when his signal-cry sounded from the entrance to the valley, and he was with us a few minutes later. His news was soon told. The Sircies were in force below the ridge which ended the valley of the Red Deer river—they were in fact not six miles distant. He had counted a score of braves, and there were others whom he could not see. There was a white man with them—at least he had seen an English saddle on the back of a strong horse picketted under the trees.

All this was conclusive; our preparations had not been made a moment too soon; the night now closing around us would scarcely pass without an attack.

The small dug-out canoe just held three persons. At the first trip the Iroquois and I landed on the island, then Red Cloud returned to fetch over the scout, who had remained at our camp. The Sioux was absent longer than I had expected; the daylight had now all gone, and it was too dark to discern his movements, but soon we saw the fire burning brightly, and in its red reflection upon the water I made out the canoe, dropping quietly down for the island.

Red Cloud and the scout now landed, and then we all sat quiet in the shade of the trees, waiting for what the night would bring forth. The hours passed by—nothing appeared; the fire still burned at our old camp. Save the rushing of the water by the island shores, and the dull thunder of the cataract below its plunge, all was silent.

Three of us lay down to sleep. The Iroquois remained alone to watch. How long I had slept I could not say, but I was deep in dreams when a touch was laid upon my shoulder, and I awoke instantly to that consciousness to which wild life in the wilderness soon accustoms its followers.

"Look out," whispered Red Cloud. "They are come at last."

I looked out over the water, but I could see nothing. It was yet night, but the first faint ray of light was in the east behind us as we looked from the island, and its indistinct hue made vague and shadowy the whole range of vision. The fire was no longer visible.

As I strove to pierce the gloom, there suddenly flashed forth in the darkness a long volley of musketry, and the echoes from a hundred mountain cliffs rolled in tumultuous thunder around our island; nor had they ceased ere their reverberations were blended in the fierce war-cry of the Sircies, which pealed forth close to our old camp. We lay within our shelter while this wild storm of shot and shout died away. We could then hear a scurrying of feet, and voices raised in tones of rage and disappointment; then all was again quiet.

The daylight was now gaining rapidly upon the darkness; soon we could distinguish figures moving to and fro where our camp had been, and then we could make out with greater precision the dress and faces of individual Indians, some on the borders of the lake, others in the clump of trees, and others along the banks of the river, within one hundred paces of where we lay.

And now as the dawn momentarily filled the valley with increasing light, there appeared upon the scene a figure which centred upon it all our attention. I looked at Red Cloud, to mark how he bore himself within sight of his arch-enemy, for the mounted man who now rode up to our camping-place was none other than the villain trader; but neither in feature nor in gesture did the Sioux show symptoms of those long-cherished feelings which must have filled his heart. There, within easy rifle-shot of where we lay, stood this man, whose slowly accumulated crimes and long-pursued hatred, had brought him even to this remote resting-place of one whose life he had betrayed—to this home of him whose murder he had so often tried to compass; yet the rifle of Red Cloud remained lowered, and his eye betokened neither rage nor astonishment as he thus beheld his enemy.

As yet there seemed to have occurred to the war-party no suspicion that we had retired to the island. Our disappearance from camp was evidently an event which they had not calculated upon; and even now, when the camp was found deserted, while traces of its recent occupation were numerous, they did not imagine that we had done more than conceal ourselves in the surrounding woods.

That our ultimate destruction was assured, naturally appeared certain to them, for excepting the trail by which they had entered the valley, no outlet was apparent to them; and as they now held that sole means of egress, a thorough search seemed certain to promise our capture.

They therefore set to work at once when daylight enabled them to see the ground, to hunt us up amid the rocks and woods that lay between the meadow and the loftier hills, whose rugged and precipitous sides forbade all chance of escape.

At the upper end of the valley, where the river first

entered the level space, the perpendicular walls of a cañon prevented horses going further into the mountains in that direction. It is true that by scrambling over the boulders and many rocks which lay piled on each side at the base of these walls, a man on foot might force his way at low water; but at this time the snows of the upper mountains, the vast glaciers which here formed the parent spring of the Saskatchewan river, were pouring forth their volumes under the influence of the midsummer sun, and the snow-fed river was foaming full through the rocky aperture into the prairie valley.

If they could have found our horses, then the question of the possibility of our escaping on foot up some cleft or landslip in the mountain wall would still have remained an open one; but wherever we had got to, there also must be our horses, and the horses must still be within the confines of the valley. They now set to work diligently to seek us out; while some remained near our old camping-place, the greater number spread themselves along both sides of the lake. Meantime the sun had risen. All through the forenoon the search went on, and when mid-day came there was not a spot in the valley which had not been visited, excepting the island on which we stood. It was now that, returning from their fruitless quest, they turned their attention with more persevering examination to the ground around our old camp. The spot where the little raft had been constructed showed more signs of wood-cutting than the supply of the summer camp would have necessitated; the bank of the river also betrayed our trail at the water's edge. Then we saw them consult together, while their looks and gestures, as they pointed towards the island, clearly told us that the next attempt would be made in our direction.

Coming down upon both sides of the river, they tried to find a place where they could cross the water, and we could see them endeavouring to peer through the close-set branches that fringed the rocks, for indications of our presence. The central portion of our rocky refuge was, however, more depressed in level than the edges, so that our horses would have been quite concealed from view even had the bordering screen of brushwood been less dense.

When they found the current flowing on both sides of the island was everywhere too rapid to permit a man to cross, we saw them gather again about our old camping-place, and again we could discern by their actions that the idea of making a descent upon the point of the island above the rapid—the point where we ourselves had landed—had not escaped their notice.

But to think of the descent was one thing, to carry it out was another. No man could hope to swim to that point, and carry his life to the island, if the men whom they sought were there; on the other hand, a landing in force from a

X

raft would promise far greater chance of security even in daylight, and if made at night there was no reason why they could not gain the island without loss.

That they reasoned thus was evident to us, for they now set to work to cut down several trees, and the remainder of the day was spent by them in drawing out the felled tree trunks, and putting them together in a raft. That this raft was to be a large one we could tell by the number of trees carried out to the place at which it was being built. So the day passed away, the long evening closed in twilight, and darkness at last lay upon the scene.

The night came very dark. The shadow cast by the lofty mountains was rendered still more obscure by a thick canopy of clouds which drifted across the sky as the night closed in. At first this veil of clouds came unaccompanied by wind; but soon we heard a noise of pine-trees swaying in the upper valleys, and later came the crash of storm, as the thunder tempest drew nearer to our glen.

Intense as were the feelings of excitement with which I looked forward to the night that had now begun, I nevertheless could not help almost forgetting the peril of our position, and the proximity of our enemies, in the stupendous spectacle of the warfare of the elements to which we were now spectators.

At first the rapidly succeeding flashes of lightning were at the farther side of the mountains that encircled our valley;

but as the storm rolled on, broad sheets of flame filled the vault above us, and streams of jagged fire poured down on crag and pinnacled pine; while the crash of thunder, multiplied tenfold by echo, seemed to shake the massive mountains to their base. At last the full fury of the storm burst upon us: the rain splashed down in blinding torrents, the trees swayed wildly in the rush of the tempest, and the roar of the cataract grew louder as the swollen waters, hissing under the rainfall, poured down past our island.

It must have been some time after midnight, when the fury of the storm having spent itself, there came a lull in the wind and rain. Everything was still dark—it was the gloom before the dawn: it was also the hour at which we might expect our enemies to attempt a landing upon the island.

We had lain exposed to all the rain and storm during the night. We did not want for food, for we had the meat of an elk, killed by the Iroquois when we first entered the valley; but as a fire lighted on the island would have been seen by the Sircies, we had of course to lie exposed to the violence of the tempest, without chance of drying our dripping clothes or of warming our chilled bodies.

At first I had thought little of these hardships; the expected attack had kept me fully awake and on the alert. But now, as the small hours of the night drew on, a sense of drowsiness began to overcome me, and insensibly I found myself falling into fitful snatches of sleep upon the wet rock against which I was lying. In these brief moments of slumber, the outward surroundings of our position, the rush of the river, the drip of leaves, the occasional flash of still vivid lightnings, and the rumble of the receding thunder, all found semblance in a vague sense of the danger that menaced us, and I would start to sudden wakefulness, to find the reality and the dream so much alike that it was difficult to distinguish one from the other.

I was in this state, the result of overstrung toil and anxiety, when I felt a hand laid upon my shoulder. I started to full wakefulness. Red Cloud whispered in my ear, "Make ready; they are coming down upon us." I seized my gun, and looked out over the edge of the rock behind which I had been lying. There was nothing to be seen; all seemed inky darkness; the rushing river was alone audible.

All at once there came a flash of lightning; it burst from a cloud that had rolled down the valley behind us. It lighted up the rocks, the trees, and the whole valley above us. For an instant the surface of the river shone out in dazzling brilliancy, and upon it, full in the centre of the stream, flowing with the current right in the direction of the spot where we were lying, was the raft, crowded with dark figures.

This flash of light was only instantaneous, but it sufficed to reveal to me the full reality of our position.

Immediately behind where we lay the ground rose, and

the top of the high bank held a few lofty pine-trees, whose dark cones thrown out against the eastern sky, now streaked with the first pale hue of coming day, gave the Sircies a point to steer for amid the darkness.

At the moment of the flash the raft appeared to be distant from the island about 100 or 150 yards. We were all lying behind the same rock, which was immediately over the landing-place, and only a few feet raised above it.

A faint glimmer of light fell now upon the water; we could distinguish the surface some fifty yards away, where it was still glassy and unbroken; beyond that all was still in gloom.

"When you see the raft," said Red Cloud, "I will give the word, and then fire at it as quickly as you can."

During the storm we had kept the locks of our guns carefully covered with leather hoods; these had been now removed, and all was ready. With eyes levelled upon the streak of light water we waited for the Sioux's word.

Out of the darkness into the lighter water came the raft, faint and shadowy.

"Aim low, and fire fast," said the Sioux.

My double gun was stretched along the top of the rock. I dropped the muzzle well below the line of the approaching floating object; then I pulled first one trigger, and then the other. To my right and left shots rang out in quick succession. Again I loaded; and again I fired. We could see nothing now, for the smoke hung in the damp night air. Then Red Cloud called out to stop firing. Eagerly we looked through the murky atmosphere where the raft had been.

It was no longer in the direct line of our landing-place; it had drifted to the left-hand side, and was now in rapid water but still close to the rock, going down stream with momentarily increasing speed. We could see many confused figures, trying with might and main to get the unwieldy craft to the side of our rock. It was only for a short second, and then the raft was borne along into still rougher and faster waters, to be caught in the remorseless grasp of the furious torrent above the falls, now swollen by the thunder deluge of the night.

We could see no more, the trees hid it from sight; but we had no need for further eye-witness or ear-witness of the fate of raft and crew. Once in the grasp of that torrent, there could be no escape. High above the roar of the cataract one loud cry did indeed reach us a very few seconds later, and then there was silence, only broken by the swirl of eddy, the rush of water against the rock, and the dull thunder of the fall.

As the dawn broadened into day I went down to the lower end of the island. From the grave of the Sioux chief the ground sloped steeply up, until it dropped abruptly to the rapid, forming a bold front of rock immediately over the edge of the fall. The top of this rock stood out bare of trees; beneath it was the rapid, the edge of the fall, and the seething whirlpools below the cataract.

Red Cloud had preceded me to this place; when I reached the grave I saw him on the bare summit beyond, looking fixedly down upon the fall. His arms were folded across his breast. I was beside him a moment later. My eyes, following his fixed glance, rested upon a strange spectacle. Almost in the centre of the fall a rock stood, right on the edge of the descending flood. I had seen it on the previous day, when it had been more exposed to view; now the rising water had covered three parts of its surface, and only the top showed above the flood. On this rock there was a figure.

The light was still too indistinct to allow us to discern features, we could only see that some wretched creature was clinging to the rock, on which he had been cast at the moment the fated raft had taken its plunge into the dark abyss.

But although I was unable at this moment to identify this unfortunate castaway, there flashed across my mind, at the first instant of my seeing him, the thought that it was the trader McDermott who was before me in this terrible position, now hopelessly hanging between life and death.

For a glance at the raging mass of water was sufficient to tell me that escape was impossible, and that no hope of extrication remained to the doomed man.

The sight filled me with a strange dread. I feared to think that it was our enemy, our bitter enemy, who had thus been reserved, as it seemed, for a death more awful than any that had already overtaken the poor dupes of his evil counsel and the recipients of his bribes. Then I thought of my poor murdered Donogh, and my heart grew hard; and then again came the whispering of a better nature, and the terrible spectacle before me chased away the promptings of revenge. That the figure was really that of McDermott there could no longer be any doubt. Turning his head wildly towards either shore in the vain hope of obtaining assistance, he had now observed us as we stood on the projecting rock, and his voice, raised in cries for assistance, reached us, even through the din of the cataract and above the whirl of waters.

"Help, help!" he cried, in tones that rang with the terror and the horror that had seized upon him. But the merciless torrent rolled down in a volume ever increasing, still rising higher, and momentarily breaking the frail link that bound him to life. The sight was all too much for me. I forgot everything of the past in the horrible fact before me of a human being in this awful extremity, and turning to the Sioux I exclaimed,—

"Can we save him? Can we reach him by any means?"

But I had little counted on the real depth of the animosity with which Red Cloud regarded his enemy.

"Save him? Reach him?" he cried. "Do you imagine that if I could reach him I would let yon torrent rob me of his death?"

As he spoke, his eyes glared, his frame shook with passion, and in the grasp which he laid upon my arm his fingers closed in iron strength. Wild with rage, he let go my arm only to seize his gun, as he cried in tones of savage exultation,—

"Ho, villain trader, who is it to whom you cry for help? It is the son of him whom you sold to a cruel death. It is he whose life you have sought through years of blood. It is Red Cloud, the Sioux. Behold, you are at the grave of the man you sold and murdered. His spirit is in the air that surrounds you, in the trees that mock at your agony, in those waters that are dragging you to death. But they shall not take you from me. You shall die, villain, by my hand."

He raised his rifle. His hand was now steady, his eye seemed calm; another instant, and the trader's death would have been certain; but I could stand it no longer.

"Forbear," I cried, striking up the levelled barrel. "He is in the hands of Him who has said, Vengeance is Mine. See, through all these long years you strove to compass his punishment, and you failed; but now here, within sight of the grave of his victim, a mightier Power has brought him to his doom."

Red Cloud dropped his rifle—a deep shadow passed over his face.

"You are right," he said slowly. "We are but the children of the Great Spirit. We see the beginning of the trail; He alone can foresee the end."

While he thus spoke the rising waters had completed their task; the trader had been swept into the terrible abyss, and only a splash of spray shooting outwards from the lip of the fall marked the presence of the sunken rock.

CHAPTER XVIII.

The beginning of the end—Deeper into the mountains—The western slope—On the edge of the snow—The golden valley—It is all mine—Night thoughts—Last words—I see him no more.

Two days passed away. They had been days of peace and rest. No further attempt had been made to molest us. Awed by the terrible fate of so many of their bravest men and leaders, who had lost their lives on the raft over the cataract, the Sircies had abandoned the valley and returned to their own country.

When the fact of their departure was fully ascertained by the scout, we moved out again to the meadow by the lake; but before we quitted the island Red Cloud had a long conversation with me regarding our future movements. Seated by his father's grave on the evening next but one after the events recorded in the last chapter had taken place, he began by telling me that the object of his life was now achieved, and that henceforth he was careless as to what might happen to him, or whither he would go. He would probably turn his face towards the south again, and join some scattered remnant of his tribe at the headwaters of the Platte, or in the country of the Yellowstone.

I told him that it was all the same to me which way he urned his steps; I was ready to follow him.

But he replied that it must not be. Already his companionship, he said, had cost me heavy. My faithful friend had lost his life, my own had often been in hazard. He had still many enemies. The Sircies, the Bloods, the Blackfeet, and the Peaginoos, would all bear to him in future an enmity, not the less active because it was based upon wrongs done to him by them in the first instance. For himself, it mattered little now what his enemies might do; his father's spirit could rest in peace. But for me it was different. I had been a true brother to him; he could no longer lead me into danger. There was yet one place to which we would travel on the same road, and when that place was reached we would part.

Such was the substance of what he said to me.

It is needless to say that I felt terribly cast down by this threatened ending of our companionship. It seemed impossible to think of life without Red Cloud. True, only a year had elapsed since he and I had met, but that year had been equal to five. From him I had learnt all I knew about the prairie and its wild things. Would it be possible for me now to face its chances and its trials alone? And where else could I go? I had literally no home.

This wild life, while it taught the lessons of bravery, hardihood, endurance, activity, and energy, did not bring worldly wealth to those who followed it. I had come to the prairie poor. I would leave it even poorer still. As these thoughts crowded upon me, my face no doubt betrayed to the Sioux their presence. He spoke in a cheerier tone,—

"Our parting time," he said, "has not yet come. Wait until it is at hand, and the path you will have to follow will be clearer to you."

Next day, as I have said, we quitted the island, and made our camp again by the lake. On the following day we packed our horses, and moved off to the upper end of the valley. I had thought that there was no outlet in that direction, but in this I had been mistaken, for shortly after mid-day we came to where a steep face of cliff rose before us. The front of this slanting wall held a zigzag narrow path, just wide enough for a single horse or man to move along it. Its beginning in the valley was hidden by a growth of firs and underbush, and was known only to Red Cloud. We ascended by this trail, and having gained the top of the cliff, hit upon a well-defined path, winding in and out between wooded hills. Following this for some hours, we reached before sunset a wild glen high up in the mountains.

On the next day we followed up this glen until evening, and camped amid some dwarf fir-trees at a spot where a small spring trickled from the hill-side and flowed out towards the west. All the other streams had flowed eastwards, but we were now on the "divide," and this westward-flowing spring was one of the parent rills of some mighty Pacific river.

The snow-line was not very far above our camping-place; we could see the mountain sheep upon a bare ridge of hills; and the "bleating" cry of the ptarmigan reached our ears when, next morning, the sunrise was glistening on the snowy summits around us.

We remained at this camp all that day. The scout and the Iroquois set out for a long hunt after mountain sheep, and Red Cloud asked me to go with him in another direction. No one stayed to watch the camp, for we were now high above the usual haunts of men, where the great hill-tops dwelt in utter loneliness. We reached, after a toilsome walk, a deep secluded valley, opening upon the one that held our camp.

A ragged forest of pine-trees fringed its sides, through which we pushed our way for a considerable distance. At length, the Sioux began to look around him, as though he was seeking for some landmark, or spot known to him in other times, and once of twice he looked to the right or left for some remembered mountain peak by which to mark his whereabouts.

The valley had now closed in, until it was only a narrow

cleft between steep overhanging cliffs. It looked as though some long ago convulsion of nature had split open this fissure, over which in time had grown a sparse old forest. Large stone rocks and *débris* half-imbedded in the earth, cumbered the floor of this valley. With a few strokes of his small axe Red Cloud now cut down a dry pine stick, off which he knocked the side branches; then he sat down on one of the rocks, and said, "The valley which holds our camp leads down to the west side of the mountain. If you follow it down for three days you would come to a river flowing for a time towards the north, then bending west, and at last turning south, until it falls into the sea. Far down on that river, on the sandbanks and bars of its course, there are many white men at work. They are washing the sand and the gravel for a yellow dust; that yellow dust is gold. They have killed the Indians, who lived in that part of the country since the world began, but who thought more about the salmon in the river than of the yellow dust that lay amongst its sands. The water that carried that gold to these sand-bars, came from this mountain range where we now are, the gold came from it too."

As he spoke he began to wedge the pine stick between a fragment of rock and the bank to which it partly adhered. The stone, loosened from its place, rolled down to a lower level. Where it had been, there lay exposed to view a hollow space, in which a number of dull yellow lumps were seen, mixed with white stones and withered pine-moss.

Red Cloud laid his stick upon this hollow in the darker rock.

"Look," he said, "there is the yellow dust for which the white man fights, and robs, and kills. There it is in plenty —not in dust, but in stones and lumps; take it. A white man without that yellow stone is like an Indian who has no buffalo. Take it, my friend. You have been a brother to me; you have fought for me, you have lost much for me: here is all I have to give you. Around where we stand this gold lies thick among these rocks. Five years ago an old Shuswap Indian, who had once been in the mining camps of the lower country, showed me this spot, which he had long kept secret, dreading lest the white man should find it out, and come here to kill the Indians as he had done elsewhere. That old Shuswap is dead, and I alone know of this place. See! all around you these white veins run through the rocks! Look up overhead, you will see them glistening in the sun! See below, where the dry stream-bed is choked with the broken masses, and the golden lumps lie thickly about! In a few hours you can knock out from these crumbling pieces gold enough to load a horse with. It is all yours. To me it would be of no use. I would not track the moose better if I had it; my aim with my arrow or rifle would not be truer, my eye would not see clearer, my arm would not be stronger; but you are nothing if you have it not. All your courage, your friendship, your energy, will count for little if you have not plenty of these yellow stones. There, fill this saddle-bag to-day; to-morrow we will come here again, and then on the next day we will move away. Where the valley divides below our camp, our paths in life must separate."

I seemed to be in a dream as I listened to all this. I looked around, and saw plainly enough the truth of what he said. There, running in every direction through the rocks, were the white seams of quartz; and thick amid their snowy surface shone the rich yellow lumps of gold. A few yards away, where the splintered rocks lay piled together, small nuggets lay mixed with gravel and broken stones; and in the hollow beneath the stone which he had at first moved from its position, was the hoard, long since gathered and hidden there by the old Indian who had discovered the place. And now all this was mine—mine to do what I liked with. I who but a day since was a poor wanderer, possessing only a horse, a gun, and a few items of prairie trappings, was now the owner of this golden glen, with enough to purchase all Glencar twice over. And yet I was not elated at the sudden change in my fortunes. I saw that the end of my wild life had come. I saw the future, with its smoke of cities, its crowds chained to the great machine called civilization, pulling slowly along the well-beaten road. No more the great wilderness; no more those vast and gorgeous

Y

sunsets; no more my companionship with this strange lonely man.

The Sioux read my thoughts. "You think the wild life would be better than this gold I have given you. You look upon your life as closed. My friend, you are wrong. Your life is still all before you. You are only setting out upon its prairies. Many long years from now, when you are in sight of the Mountains of the Setting Sun, you will know that I, Red Cloud the Sioux, showed you the right trail, though he could not follow it himself. We cannot change our colours. The red man cannot give up the wilderness; he dies amid the city and the fenced field. You cannot make this wild life your own, even though you may wish to do so. You have other work to do; you must go back and do it."

"And you?" I said, rousing myself from the dream into which I had fallen, "will you not come with me, and share the wealth you have given me? With the hundredth part of the gold lying around us here, we can traverse the earth from side to side. There are vast spaces in other lands as well as in this one. Asia has wilds as lonely as America. There are sky-bounded plains in Southern Africa, where the wild animals roam in savage freedom. Come with me, and we will seek these huge horizons, far away from the bustle of crowds and the smoke of cities."

He shook his head. "My brother," he said, "it would

not do. The great prairies are dying; the buffalo are going. The red man must pass away too. Come, let us to work while there is yet time."

He began to collect together several pieces of gold in the hollow where the old Shuswap had made his store. When many pounds' weight had been gathered, he filled two saddle-bags; but there was still remaining enough to fill two more leather wallets. The Shuswap's store held pieces of pure gold of every shape and size—some flattened pieces, others rugged knobs like walnuts, and rounded nuggets as large as eggs.

It was indeed a wonderful sight, all this treasure lying hidden away in this remote and desolate valley, thousands of feet above the sea level! "Curious!" I thought. "Man struggles and strives for this metal, lives for it, dies for it, forgets every other pursuit, gives up health for it; and here it lies a stone amid other stones. The winds blow heedlessly upon it; the sun looks down in summer; the snow covers it in winter, and the pine-tree rustles in the evening breeze unmindful of its presence."

The sun was getting down behind the western ridges as we started on our way back to camp laden with our golden loads. When we reached the camp the two Indians had returned, both bringing loads of mountain mutton, the result of their hunt. Red Cloud said nothing to them about our day's work. The fewer persons who knew the secret of the

Golden Valley, the better would it be, he thought, for mankind in general, and for Indians in particular. So we ate our supper of wild mutton that night, and lay down under the stars, wrapped in our robes; but all the golden wealth that lay beside me could not reconcile me to accept with contentment the prospect of abandoning this wild roving life for the smoother roads and softer beds of civilized existence.

For a long while I tried in vain to sleep; my mind was dwelling too strongly upon the events of the preceding day to allow my eyes to close in rest. Our camp lay facing towards the east; right opposite, a great tooth-shaped mountain top lifted itself high into the starlit heavens. The stars, wondrously clear in the transparent atmosphere of our lofty position, rose from behind the triple peaks of this giant. I lay watching them as the night wore on; at last there came one lustrous star; right between the forked peaks it rose, throbbing in many-coloured rays of light, until it looked like a gigantic diamond glistening in the icy crown of the mountain king. Then I fell asleep, and dreamt that I had scaled the summits of the Rocky Mountains, and was looking down upon the great prairies of eternity.

The following day was a repetition of the one that preceded it. Again we sought the golden valley, and again we returned to camp with loads of the precious metal. The whole treasure when packed in wallets made a load just sufficient for one horse to carry. Red Cloud did the work of packing the loads himself.

All was completed early on the morning of the second day, and quitting our high camp, we began to descend the valley in a western direction. We soon came in sight of the low country upon that side. It was different in every aspect to the prairie region of the east. There the green meadows had spread out into measureless distance, here ridge after ridge of pine-trees stretched away into the west. Many a rugged range of mountain rose amid the wilderness of pines, and bold summits of naked rock, or snow patch glistened, above the sombre world of endless forest.

Winding along a descending trail we often lost sight of this panorama, as some projecting ridge of our mountain closed the outward view.

By sunset we had reached a spot where the trail forked—one branch descending still westward towards the mining camp on the Fraser river, the other bearing away in a northern direction.

Here we camped. We had come down many hundreds of feet during the day. The forest growth was large and lofty, and the pine grouse and the partridges were again around us. Far down in the plain a light haze of smoke hung above the tree tops.

On the next morning we were to separate. The Iroquois and the scout would accompany me to the first mining camp, from whence they would recross the mountains to their own peoples. Red Cloud would take the northern trail to the Athabasca valley. The preparations were soon ready, but we delayed the moment of parting to the last. At length Red Cloud rose, and began to unfasten his horse from the tree to which it had been tied. It was the signal of separation.

We shook hands in silence.

"See," he said, "the smoke of your people's fires far below; there is your road, and here is mine"—he pointed to the mountain trail. "I could not go with you, I would have to begin life again;—I am too old to change now. There is no one to come after me. The Sioux are nearly all gone, the Buffalo are fast going; but the wilderness will last long enough for me."

"And is there nothing then that I can do for you?" I said. "You have done everything for me: let me do something in return."

"Well, my friend," he replied, "sometimes think of me. When I am camped at night far out on the great prairie, I would like to say to myself, my white brother remembers me. That is all."

Then he turned off to the north, leading his horse by the bridle up the mountain path. I stood watching him as step by step the void of space grew wider between us. How lonely it all seemed, this solitary man turning off into the mountains to go back from the shore of civilization into the great prairie sea! As thus I watched his slowly receding figure, memory was travelling back over the long trail of our companionship—back through all the varied scenes of strife, and chase, and travel, to that distant day when first on the shore of the wilderness our lives came together. " Think of you ! " I said, speaking half aloud my thoughts. " Yes, that I will. Whenever the wind stirs the tree-branch, or rustles the reeds and meadows—wherever the sun goes down over distance of sea or land—in the moonlight of nights, in the snow of long winters, you will be near me still."

At a bend in the trail he turned to look back : it was but a moment, and then the mountain path was vacant, and I saw him no more.

THE END.

ST. DUNSTAN'S HOUSE, FETTER LANE,
LONDON, E.C. 1892.

Select List of Books in all Departments of Literature

PUBLISHED BY

Sampson Low, Marston & Company, Ld.

ABBEY and PARSONS, *Quiet Life*, from drawings; motive by Austin Dobson, 31s. 6d.
ABBOTT, CHARLES C., *Waste Land Wanderings*, 10s. 6d.
ABERDEEN, EARL OF. See Prime Ministers.
ABNEY, CAPT., *Thebes and its Greater Temples*, 40 photos. 63s.
—— and CUNNINGHAM, *Pioneers of the Alps*, new ed. 21s.
About in the World. See Gentle Life Series.
—— *Some Fellows*, from my note-book, by "an Eton boy," 2s. 6d.; new edit. 1s.
ADAMS, CHARLES K., *Historical Literature*, 12s. 6d.
ADDISON, *Sir Roger de Coverley*, from the "Spectator," 6s.
AGASSIZ, ALEX., *Three Cruises of the "Blake,"* illust. 2 vols. 42s.
ALBERT, PRINCE. See Bayard Series.
ALCOTT, L. M. *Jo's Boys*, a sequel to "Little Men," 5s.
—— *Life, Letters and Journals*, by Ednah D. Cheney, 6s.
—— *Lulu's Library*, a story for girls, 3s. 6d.
—— *Old-fashioned Thanksgiving Day*, 3s. 6d.
—— *Proverb Stories*, 3s. 6d.

ALCOTT, L. M., *Recollections of my Childhood's Days*, 3s. 6d.
—— *Silver Pitchers*, 3s. 6d.
—— *Spinning-wheel Stories*, 5s.
—— See also Low's Standard Series and Rose Library.
ALDAM, W. H., *Flies and Fly-making*, with actual specimens on cardboard, 63s.
ALDEN, W. L. See Low's Standard Series.
ALFORD, LADY MARIAN, *Needlework as Art*, 21s.; l. p. 84s.
ALGER, J. G., *Englishmen in the French Revolution*, 7s. 6d.
Amateur Angler in Dove Dale, a three weeks' holiday, by E. M. 1s. 6d., 1s. and 5s.
ANDERSEN, H. C., *Fairy Tales*, illust. in colour by E. V. B. 25s., new edit. 5s.
—— *Fairy Tales*, illust. by Scandinavian artists, 6s.
ANDERSON, W., *Pictorial Arts of Japan*, 4 parts, 168s.; artist's proofs, 252s.
ANDRES, *Varnishes, Lacquers, Siccatives, & Sealing-wax*, 12s. 6d.
Angler's strange Experiences, by Cotswold Isys, new edit., 3s. 6d.
ANNESLEY, C., *Standard Opera Glass*, the plots of eighty operas, 3rd edit., 2s. 6d.

Annual American Catalogue of Books, 1886-89, each 10s. 6d., half morocco, 14s.
—— 1890, cloth, 15s., half morocco, cloth sides, 18s.
Antipodean Notes; a nine months' tour, by Wanderer, 7s. 6d.
APPLETON, *European Guide*, new edit., 2 parts, 10s. each.
ARCHER, W., *English Dramatists of To-day*, 8s. 6d.
ARLOT'S *Coach Painting*, from the French by A. A. Fesquet, 6s.
ARMYTAGE, Hon. Mrs., *Wars of Queen Victoria's Reign*, 5s.
ARNOLD, E., *Birthday Book;* by Kath. L. and Constance Arnold, 4s. 6d.
—— E. L. L., *Summer Holiday in Scandinavia*, 10s. 6d.
—— *On the Indian Hills*, Coffee Planting, &c., 2 vols. 24s.
—— R., *Ammonia and Ammonium Compounds*, illust. 5s.
Artistic Japan, text, woodcuts, and coloured plates, vols. I.-VI., 15s. each.
ASBJÖRNSEN, P. C., *Round the Yule Log*, 7s. 6d.; new edit. 5s.
ASHE, R. P., *Two Kings of Uganda;* six years in Eastern Equatorial Africa, 6s.; new edit. 3s. 6d.
—— *Uganda, England's latest Charge*, stiff cover, 1s.
ASHTON, F. T., *Designing fancy Cotton and Woollen Cloths*, illust. 50s.
ATCHISON, C. C., *Winter Cruise in Summer Seas;* "how I found" health, 16s.
ATKINSON, J. B. *Overbeck*. See Great Artists.
ATTWELL, *Italian Masters*, especially in the National Gallery, 3s. 6d.

AUDSLEY, G. A., *Chromolithography*, 44 coloured plates and text, 63s.
—— *Ornamental Arts of Japan*, 2 vols. morocco, 23l. 2s.; four parts, 15l. 15s.
—— W. and G. A., *Ornament in all Styles*, 31s. 6d.
AUERBACH, B., *Brigitta* (B. Tauchnitz), 2s.; sewed, 1s. 6d.
—— *On the Height* (B. Tauchnitz), 3 vols. 6s.; sewed, 4s. 6d.
—— *Spinoza* (B. Tauchnitz), 2 vols. 4s.
AUSTRALIA. See F. Countries.
AUSTRIA. See F. Countries.
Autumn Cruise in the Ægean, by one of the party. See "Fitzpatrick."
BACH. See Great Musicians.
BACON. See English Philosophers.
—— Delia, *Biography*, 10s. 6d.
BADDELEY, W. St. Clair, *Love's Vintage;* sonnets and lyrics, 5s.
—— *Tchay and Chianti*, a short visit to Russia and Finland, 5s.
—— *Travel-tide*, 7s. 6d.
BAKER, James, *John Westacott*, new edit. 6s. and 3s. 6d.
BALDWIN, J., *Story of Siegfried*, illust. 6s.
—— *Story of Roland*, illust. 6s.
—— *Story of the Golden Age*, illust. 6s.
—— J. D., *Ancient America*, illust. 10s. 6d.
Ballad Stories. See Bayard Series.
Ballads of the Cid, edited by Rev. Gerrard Lewis, 3s. 6d.
BALLANTYNE, T., *Essays*. See Bayard Series.

BALLIN, ADA S., *Science of Dress*, illust. 6s.
BAMFORD, A. J., *Turbans and Tails*, 7s. 6d.
BANCROFT, G., *History of America*, new edit. 6 vols. 73s. 6d.
Barbizon Painters, by J. W. Mollett—I. Millet, T. Rousseau, and Diaz, 3s. 6d. II. Corot, Daubigny and Dupré, 3s. 6d.; the two in one vol. 7s. 6d.
BARING-GOULD. See Foreign Countries.
BARLOW, A., *Weaving*, new edit. 25s.
—— P. W., *Kaipara, New Z.*, 6s.
—— W., *Matter and Force*, 12s.
BARRETT. See Gr. Musicians.
BARROW, J., *Mountain Ascents*, new edit. 5s.
BASSETT, *Legends of the Sea*, 7s. 6d.
BATHGATE, A., *Waitaruna, New Zealand*, 5s.
Bayard Series, edited by the late J. Hain Friswell; flexible cloth extra, 2s. 6d. each.
Chevalier Bayard, by Berville.
De Joinville, St. Louis.
Essays of Cowley.
Abdallah, by Laboullaye.
Table-Talk of Napoleon.
Vathek, by Beckford.
Cavalier and Puritan Songs.
Words of Wellington.
Johnson's Rasselas.
Hazlitt's Round Table.
Browne's Religio Medici.
Ballad Stories of the Affections, by Robert Buchanan.
Coleridge's Christabel, &c.
Chesterfield's Letters.
Essays in Mosaic, by T. Ballantyne.
My Uncle Toby.
Rochefoucauld, Reflections.
Socrates, Memoirs from Xenophon.
Prince Albert's Precepts.

BEACONSFIELD, *Public Life*, 3s. 6d.
—— See also Prime Ministers.
BEAUGRAND, *Young Naturalists*, new edit. 5s.
BECKER, A.L., *First German Book*, 1s.; *Exercises*, 1s.; *Key* to both, 2s. 6d.; *German Idioms*, 1s. 6d.
BECKFORD. See Bayard Series.
BEECHER, H. W., *Biography*, new edit. 10s. 6d.
BEETHOVEN. See Great Musicians.
BEHNKE, E., *Child's Voice*, 3s. 6d.
BELL, *Obeah, Witchcraft in the West Indies*, 2s. 6d.
BELLENGER & WITCOMB'S *French and English Conversations*, new edit. Paris, bds. 2s.
BENJAMIN, *Atlantic Islands as health, &c., resorts*. 16s.
BERLIOZ. See Gr. Musicians.
BERVILLE. See Bayard Series.
BIART, *Young Naturalist*, new edit. 7s. 6d.
—— *Involuntary Voyage*, 7s. 6d. and 5s.
—— *Two Friends*, translated by Mary de Hauteville, 7s. 6d.
See also Low's Standard Books.
BICKERSTETH, ASHLEY, B.A., *Outlines of Roman History*, 2s. 6d.
—— E. H., Exon., *Clergyman in his Home*, 1s.
—— *From Year to Year*, original poetical pieces, morocco or calf, 10s. 6d.; padded roan, 6s.; roan, 5s.; cloth, 3s. 6d.
—— *Hymnal Companion*, full lists post free.
—— *Master's Home Call*, new edit. 1s.
—— *Octave of Hymns*, sewn, 3d., with music, 1s.

BICKERSTETH, E. H., Exon., *Reef, Parables*, &c., illust. 7s. 6d. and 2s. 6d.
—— *Shadowed Home*, n. ed. 5s.
BIGELOW, JOHN, *France and the Confederate Navy*, an international episode, 7s. 6d.
BILBROUGH, *'Twixt France and Spain*, 7s. 6d.
BILLROTH, *Care of the Sick*, 6s.
BIRD, F. J., *Dyer's Companion*, 42s.
—— F. S., *Land of Dykes and Windmills*, 12s. 6d.
—— H. E., *Chess Practice*, 2s. 6d.
BISHOP. See Nursing Record Series.
BLACK, ROBERT, *Horse Racing in France*, 14s.
—— W., *Donald Ross of Heimra*, 3 vols. 31s. 6d.
—— Novels, new and uniform edition in monthly vols. 2s. 6d. ea.
—— See Low's Standard Novels.
BLACKBURN, C. F., *Catalogue Titles, Index Entries*, &c. 14s.
—— H., *Art in the Mountains*, new edit. 5s.
—— *Artists and Arabs*, 7s 6d.
—— *Breton Folk*, new issue, 10s. 6d.
—— *Harz Mountains*, 12s.
—— *Normandy Picturesque*, 16s.
—— *Pyrenees*, illust. by Gustave Doré, new edit. 7s. 6d.
BLACKMORE, R. D., *Georgics*, 4s. 6d.; cheap edit. 1s.
—— *Lorna Doone*, édit. de luxe, 35s., 31s. 6d. & 21s.
—— *Lorna Doone*, illust. by W. Small, 7s. 6d.
—— *Springhaven*, illust. 12s.; new edit. 7s. 6d. & 6s.
—— See also Low's Standard Novels.

BLAIKIE, *How to get Strong*, new edit. 5s.
—— *Sound Bodies for our Boys and Girls*, 2s. 6d.
BLOOMFIELD. See Choice Editions.
Bobby, a Story, by Vesper, 1s.
BOCK, *Head Hunters of Borneo*, 36s.
—— *Temples & Elephants*, 21s.
BONAPARTE, MAD. PATTERSON, *Life*, 10s. 6d.
BONWICK, JAMES, *Colonial Days*, 2s. 6d.
—— *Colonies*, 1s. ea.; 1 vol. 5s.
—— *Daily Life of the Tasmanians*, 12s. 6d.
—— *First Twenty Years of Australia*, 5s.
—— *Last of the Tasmanians*, 16s.
—— *Port Philip*, 21s.
—— *Lost Tasmanian Race*, 4s.
BOSANQUET, C., *Blossoms from the King's Garden*, 6s.
—— *Jehoshaphat*, 1s.
—— *Lenten Meditations*, I. 1s. 6d.; II. 2s.
—— *Tender Grass for Lambs*, 2s. 6d.
BOULTON, N. W. *Rebellions*, Canadian life, 9s.
BOURKE, *On the Border with Crook*, illust., roy. 8vo, 21s.
—— *Snake Dance of Arizona*, 21s.
BOUSSENARD. See Low's Standard Books.
BOWEN, F., *Modern Philosophy*, new ed. 16s.
BOWER. See English Philosophers.
—— *Law of Electric Lighting*, 12s. 6d.
BOYESEN, H. H., *Against Heavy Odds*, 5s.
—— *History of Norway*, 7s. 6d.

BOYESEN, *Modern Vikings*, 6s.
Boy's *Froissart, King Arthur, Mabinogian, Percy*, see "Lanier."
BRADSHAW, *New Zealand as it is*, 12s. 6d.
—— *NewZealandofTo-day*, 14s.
BRANNT, *Fats and Oils*, 35s.
—— *Soap and Candles*, 35s.
—— *Vinegar, Acetates*, 25s.
—— *Distillation of Alcohol*, 12s. 6d.
—— *Metal Worker's Receipts*, 12s. 6d.
—— *Metallic Alloys*, 12s. 6d.
—— and WAHL, *Techno-Chemical Receipt Book*, 10s. 6d.
BRASSEY, LADY, *Tahiti*, 21s.
BRÉMONT. See Low's Standard Novels.
BRETON, JULES, *Life of an Artist*, an autobiography, 7s. 6d.
BRISSE, *Menus and Recipes*, new edit. 5s.
Britons in Brittany, by G. H. F. 2s. 6d.
BROCK-ARNOLD. See Great Artists.
BROOKS, NOAH, *Boy Settlers*, 6s.
BROWN, A. J., *Rejected of Men*, 3s. 6d.
—— A. S. *Madeira and Canary Islands for Invalids*, 2s. 6d.
—— *Northern Atlantic*, for travellers, 4s. 6d.
—— ROBERT. See Low's Standard Novels.
BROWNE, LENNOX, and BEHNKE, *Voice, Song, & Speech*, 15s.; new edit. 5s.
—— *Voice Use*, 3s. 6d.
—— SIR T. See Bayard Series.
BRYCE, G., *Manitoba*, 7s. 6d.
—— *Short History of the Canadian People*, 7s. 6d.

BUCHANAN, R. See Bayard Series.
BULKELEY, OWEN T., *Lesser Antilles*, 2s. 6d.
BUNYAN. See Low's Standard Series.
BURDETT-COUTTS, *Brookfield Stud*, 5s.
BURGOYNE, *Operations in Egypt*, 5s.
BURNABY, F. See Low's Standard Library.
—— MRS., *High Alps in Winter*, 14s.
BURNLEY, JAMES, *History of Wool*, 21s.
BUTLER, COL. SIR W. F., *Campaign of the Cataracts*, 18s.
—— *Red Cloud*, 7s. 6d. & 5s.
—— See also Low's Standard Books.
BUXTON, ETHEL M. WILMOT, *Wee Folk*, 5s.
—— See also Illust. Text Books.
BYNNER. See Low's Standard Novels.
CABLE, G. W., *Bonaventure*, 5s.
CADOGAN, LADY A., *Drawing-room Comedies*, illust. 10s. 6d., acting edit. 6d.
—— *Illustrated Games of Patience*, col. diagrams, 12s. 6d.
—— *New Games of Patience*, with coloured diagrams, 12s. 6d.
CAHUN. See Low's Standard Books.
CALDECOTT, RANDOLPH, *Memoir*, by H. Blackburn, new edit. 7s. 6d. and 5s.
—— *Sketches*, pict. bds. 2s. 6d.
CALL, ANNIE PAYSON, *Power through Repose*, 3s. 6d.
CALLAN, H., M.A., *Wanderings on Wheel and Foot through Europe*, 1s. 6d.
Cambridge Trifles, 2s. 6d.

Cambridge Staircase, 2s. 6d.
CAMPBELL, LADY COLIN, *Book of the Running Brook,* 5s.
—— T. See Choice Editions.
CANTERBURY, ARCHBISHOP. See Preachers.
CARLETON, WILL, *City Ballads,* illust. 12s. 6d.
—— *City Legends,* ill. 12s. 6d.
—— *Farm Festivals,* ill. 12s. 6d.
—— See also Rose Library.
CARLYLE, *Irish Journey in* 1849, 7s. 6d.
CARNEGIE, ANDREW, *American Four-in-hand in Britain,* 10s. 6d.; also 1s.
—— *Round the World,* 10s. 6d.
—— *Triumphant Democracy,* 6s.; new edit. 1s. 6d.; paper, 1s.
CAROVÉ, *Story without an End,* illust. by E. V. B., 7s. 6d.
Celebrated Racehorses, 4 vols. 126s.
CÉLIÈRE. See Low's Standard Books.
Changed Cross, &c., poems, 2s. 6d.
Chant-book Companion to the Common Prayer, 2s.; organ ed. 4s.
CHAPIN, *Mountaineering in Colorado,* 10s. 6d.
CHAPLIN, J. G., *Bookkeeping,* 2s. 6d.
CHATTOCK, *Notes on Etching* new edit. 10s. 6d.
CHERUBINI. See Great Musicians.
CHESTERFIELD. See Bayard Series.
Choice Editions of choice books, illustrated by C. W. Cope, R.A., T. Creswick, R.A., E. Duncan, Birket Foster, J. C. Horsley, A.R.A., G. Hicks, R. Redgrave, R.A., C. Stonehouse, F. Tayler, G. Thomas, H. G. Townsend,

Choice Editions—continued.
E. H. Wehnert, Harrison Weir, &c., cloth extra gilt, gilt edges, 2s. 6d. each; re-issue, 1s. each.
Bloomfield's Farmer's Boy.
Campbell's Pleasures of Hope
Coleridge's Ancient Mariner.
Goldsmith's Deserted Village.
Goldsmith's Vicar of Wakefield.
Gray's Elegy in a Churchyard.
Keats' Eve of St. Agnes.
Milton's Allegro.
Poetry of Nature, by H. Weir.
Rogers' Pleasures of Memory.
Shakespeare's Songs and Sonnets.
Elizabethan Songs and Sonnets.
Tennyson's May Queen.
Wordsworth's Pastoral Poems.
CHREIMAN, *Physical Culture of Women,* 1s.
CLARK, A., *A Dark Place of the Earth,* 6s.
—— Mrs. K. M., *Southern Cross Fairy Tale,* 5s.
CLARKE, C. C., *Writers, and Letters,* 10s. 6d.
—— PERCY, *Three Diggers,* 6s.
—— *Valley Council;* from T. Bateman's Journal, 6s.
Classified Catalogue of English-printed Educational Works, 3rd edit. 6s.
Claude le Lorrain. See Great Artists.
CLOUGH, A. H., *Plutarch's Lives,* one vol. 18s.
COLERIDGE, C. R., *English Squire,* 6s.
—— S. T. See Choice Editions and Bayard Series.
COLLINGWOOD, H. See Low's Standard Books.
COLLINSON, Adm. SIR R., *H.M.S. Enterprise in Search of Franklin,* 14s.
CONDER, J., *Flowers of Japan; Decoration,* coloured Japanese Plates, 42s. nett.

CORREGGIO. See Great Artists.
COWLEY. See Bayard Series.
COX, DAVID. See Great Artists.
COZZENS, F., *American Yachts*, pfs. 21*l.*; art. pfs. 31*l.* 10*s*.
—— See also Low's Standard Books.
CRADDOCK. See Low's Standard Novels.
CREW, B. J., *Petroleum*, 21*s*.
CRISTIANI, R. S., *Soap and Candles*, 42*s*.
—— *Perfumery*, 25*s*.
CROKER, MRS. B. M. See Low's Standard Novels.
CROUCH, A. P., *Glimpses of Feverland* (West Africa), 6*s*.
—— *On a Surf-bound Coast*, 7*s*. 6*d*.; new edit. 5*s*.
CRUIKSHANK G. See Great Artists.
CUDWORTH, W., *Abraham Sharp*, 26*s*.
CUMBERLAND, STUART, *Thought-reader's Thoughts*, 10*s*. 6*d*.
—— See also Low's Standard Novels.
CUNDALL, F. See Great Artists.
—— J., *Shakespeare*, 3*s*. 6*d*., 5*s*. and 2*s*.
CURTIN, J., *Myths of the Russians*, 10*s*. 6*d*.
CURTIS, C. B., *Velazquez and Murillo*, with etchings, 31*s*. 6*d*. and 63*s*.
CUSHING, W., *Anonyms*, 2 vols. 52*s*. 6*d*.
—— *Initials and Pseudonyms*, 25*s*.; ser. II., 21*s*.
CUTCLIFFE, H. C., *Trout Fishing*, new edit. 3*s*. 6*d*.
DALY, MRS. D., *Digging, Squatting, &c., in N. S. Australia*, 12*s*.

D'ANVERS, N., *Architecture and Sculpture*, new edit. 5*s*.
—— *Elementary Art, Architecture, Sculpture, Painting*, new edit. 10*s*. 6*d*.
—— *Elementary History of Music*, 2*s*. 6*d*.
—— *Painting*, by F. Cundall, 6*s*.
DAUDET, A., *My Brother Jack*, 7*s*. 6*d*.; also 5*s*.
—— *Port Tarascon*, by H. James, 7*s*. 6*d*.; new edit. 5*s*.
DAVIES, C., *Modern Whist*, 4*s*.
DAVIS, C. T., *Bricks, Tiles, &c.*, new edit. 25*s*.
—— *Manufacture of Leather*, 52*s*. 6*d*.
—— *Manufacture of Paper*, 28*s*.
—— *Steam Boiler Incrustation*, 8*s*. 6*d*.
—— G. B., *International Law*, 10*s*. 6*d*.
DAWIDOWSKY, *Glue, Gelatine, &c.*, 12*s*. 6*d*.
Day of my Life, by an Eton boy, new edit. 2*s*. 6*d*.; also 1*s*.
DE JOINVILLE. See Bayard Series.
DE LEON, EDWIN, *Under the Stars and Under the Crescent*, 2 vols. 12*s*.; new edit. 6*s*.
DELLA ROBBIA. See Great Artists.
Denmark and Iceland. See Foreign Countries.
DENNETT, R. E., *Seven Years among the Fjort*, 7*s*. 6*d*.
DERRY (Bishop of). See Preachers.
DE WINT. See Great Artists.
DIGGLE, J. W., *Bishop Fraser's Lancashire Life*, new edit. 12*s*. 6*d*.; popular ed. 3*s*. 6*d*.
—— *Sermons for Daily Life*, 5*s*

DOBSON, AUSTIN, *Hogarth*, with a bibliography, &c., of prints, illust. 24s.; l. paper 52s. 6d.
—— See also Great Artists.
DODGE, MRS., *Hans Brinker, the Silver Skates*, new edit. 5s., 3s. 6d., 2s. 6d.; text only, 1s.
DONKIN, J. G., *Trooper and Redskin; N. W. mounted police, Canada*, 8s. 6d.
DONNELLY, IGNATIUS, *Atlantis, the Antediluvian World*, new edit. 12s. 6d.
—— *Cæsar's Column*, authorized edition, 3s. 6d.
—— *Doctor Huguet*, 3s. 6d.
—— *Great Cryptogram*, Bacon's Cipher in Shakespeare, 2 vols. 30s.
—— *Ragnarok : the Age of Fire and Gravel*, 12s. 6d.
DORÉ, GUSTAVE, *Life and Reminiscences*, by Blanche Roosevelt, fully illust. 24s.
DOS PASSOS, J. R., *Law of Stockbrokers and Stock Exchanges*, 35s.
DOUDNEY, SARAH, *Godiva Durleigh*, 3 vols. 31s. 6d.
DOUGALL, J. D., *Shooting Appliances, Practice, &c.*, 10s. 6d.; new edit. 7s. 6d.
DOUGHTY, H. M., *Friesland Meres and the Netherlands*, new edit. illust. 10s. 6d.
DOVETON, F. B., *Poems and Snatches of Songs*, 5s.; new edit. 3s. 6d.
DU CHAILLU, PAUL. See Low's Standard Books.
DUNCKLEY ("Verax.") See Prime Ministers.
DUNDERDALE, GEORGE, *Prairie and Bush*, 6s.
Dürer. See Great Artists.
DYKES, J. OSWALD. See Preachers.

Echoes from the Heart, 3s. 6d.
EDEN, C. H. See Foreign Countries.
EDMONDS, C., *Poetry of the Anti-Jacobin*, new edit. 7s. 6d. and 21s.
Educational Catalogue. See Classified Catalogue.
EDWARDS, *American Steam Engineer*, 12s. 6d.
—— *Modern Locomotive Engines*, 12s. 6d.
—— *Steam Engineer's Guide*, 12s. 6d.
—— H. SUTHERLAND. See Great Musicians.
—— M. B., *Dream of Millions, &c.*, 1s.
—— See Low's Standard Novels.
EGGLESTON, G. CARY, *Juggernaut*, 6s.
Egypt. See Foreign Countries.
Elizabethan Songs. See Choice Editions.
EMERSON, DR. P. H., *East Coast Yarns*, 1s.
—— *English Idylls*, new ed. 2s.
—— *Naturalistic Photography*, new edit. 5s.
—— *Pictures of East Anglian Life*; plates and vignettes, 105s. and 147s.
—— and GOODALL, *Life on the Norfolk Broads*, plates, 126s. and 210s.
—— *Wild Life on a Tidal Water*, copper plates, ord. edit. 25s.; édit. de luxe, 63s.
—— R. W., by G. W. COOKE, 8s. 6d.
—— *Birthday Book*, 3s. 6d.
—— *In Concord*, a memoir, 7s. 6d.
English Catalogue, 1863-71, 42s.; 1872-80, 42s.; 1881-9, 52s. 6d.; 5s. yearly.

English Catalogue, Index vol. 1837-56, 26*s*.; 1856-76, 42*s*.; 1874-80, 18*s*.
—— *Etchings*, vol. v. 45*s*.; vi., 25*s*.; vii., 25*s*.; viii., 42*s*.
English Philosophers, edited by E. B. Ivan Müller, M.A., 3*s*. 6*d*. each.
Bacon, by Fowler.
Hamilton, by Monck.
Hartley and James Mill, by Bower.
Shaftesbury & Hutcheson; Fowler.
Adam Smith, by J. A. Farrer.
ERCKMANN-CHATRIAN. See Low's Standard Books.
ERICHSON, *Life*, by W. C. Church, 2 vols. 24*s*.
ESMARCH, F., *Handbook of Surgery*, 24*s*.
Essays on English Writers. See Gentle Life Series.
EVANS, G. E., *Repentance of Magdalene Despar, &c.*, poems, 5*s*.
—— S. & F., *Upper Ten*, a story, 1*s*.
—— W. E., *Songs of the Birds*, n. ed. 6*s*.
EVELYN, J., *An Inca Queen*, 5*s*.
—— JOHN, *Life of Mrs. Godolphin*, 7*s*. 6*d*.
EVES, C. W., *West Indies*, n. ed. 7*s*. 6*d*.
FAIRBAIRN, A. M. See Preachers.
Familiar Words. See Gentle Life Series.
FARINI, G. A., *Kalahari Desert*, 21*s*.
FARRAR, C. S., *History of Sculpture, &c.*, 6*s*.
—— MAURICE, *Minnesota*, 6*s*.
FAURIEL, *Last Days of the Consulate*, 10*s*. 6*d*.
FAY, T., *Three Germanys*, 2 vols. 35*s*.

FEILDEN, H. ST. J., *Some Public Schools*, 2*s*. 6*d*.
—— Mrs., *My African Home*, 7*s*. 6*d*.
FENN, G. MANVILLE. See Low's Standard Books.
FENNELL, J. G., *Book of the Roach*, n. ed. 2*s*.
FFORDE, B., *Subaltern, Policeman, and the Little Girl*, 1*s*.
—— *Trotter, a Poona Mystery*, 1*s*.
FIELD, MAUNSELL B., *Memories*, 10*s*. 6*d*.
FIELDS, JAMES T., *Memoirs*, 12*s*. 6*d*.
—— *Yesterdays with Authors*, 16*s*.; also 10*s*. 6*d*.
Figure Painters of Holland. See Great Artists.
FINCK, HENRY T., *Pacific Coast Scenic Tour*, 10*s*. 6*d*.
FITCH, LUCY. See Nursing Record Series, 1*s*.
FITZGERALD. See Foreign Countries.
—— PERCY, *Book Fancier*, 5*s*. and 12*s*. 6*d*.
FITZPATRICK, T., *Autumn Cruise in the Ægean*, 10*s*. 6*d*
—— *Transatlantic Holiday*, 10*s*. 6*d*.
FLEMING, S., *England and Canada*, 6*s*.
Foreign Countries and British Colonies, descriptive handbooks edited by F. S. Pulling, M.A. Each volume is the work of a writer who has special acquaintance with the subject, 3*s*. 6*d*.
Australia, by Fitzgerald.
Austria-Hungary, by Kay.
Denmark and Iceland, by E. C. Ötré.
Egypt, by S. L. Poole.
France, by Miss Roberts.
Germany, by L. Sergeant.
Greece, by S. Baring Gould.

Foreign Countries, &c.—cont.
Japan, by Mossman.
Peru, by R. Markham.
Russia, by Morfill.
Spain, by Webster.
Sweden and Norway, by Woods.
West Indies, by C. H. Eden.
FOREMAN, J., *Philippine Islands*, 21s.
FOTHERINGHAM, L. M., *Nyassaland*, 7s. 6d.
FOWLER, *Japan, China, and India*, 10s. 6d.
FRA ANGELICO. See Great Artists.
FRA BARTOLOMMEO, ALBERTINELLI, and ANDREA DEL SARTO. See Great Artists.
FRANC, MAUD JEANNE, *Beatrice Melton*, 4s.
—— *Emily's Choice*, n. ed. 5s.
—— *Golden Gifts*, 4s.
—— *Hall's Vineyard*, 4s.
—— *Into the Light*, 4s.
—— *John's Wife*, 4s.
—— *Little Mercy; for better, for worse*, 4s.
—— *Marian, a Tale*, n. ed. 5s.
—— *Master of Ralston*, 4s.
—— *Minnie's Mission, a Temperance Tale*, 4s.
—— *No longer a Child*, 4s.
—— *Silken Cords and Iron Fetters, a Tale*, 4s.
—— *Two Sides to Every Question*, 4s.
—— *Vermont Vale*, 5s.
A plainer edition is published at 2s. 6d.
France. See Foreign Countries.
FRANCIS, F., *War, Waves, and Wanderings*, 2 vols. 24s.
—— See also Low's Standard Series.
Frank's Ranche; or, My Holiday in the Rockies, n. ed. 5s.

FRANKEL, JULIUS, *Starch Glucose, &c.*, 18s.
FRASER, BISHOP, *Lancashire Life*, n. ed. 12s. 6d.; popular ed. 3s. 6d.
FREEMAN, J., *Melbourne Life, lights and shadows*, 6s.
FRENCH, F., *Home Fairies and Heart Flowers*, illust. 24s.
French and English Birthday Book, by Kate D. Clark, 7s. 6d.
French Revolution, Letters from Paris, translated, 10s. 6d.
Fresh Woods and Pastures New, by the Author of "An Angler's Days," 5s., 1s. 6d., 1s.
FRIEZE, *Duprè, Florentine Sculptor*, 7s. 6d.
FRISWELL, J. H. See Gentle Life Series.
Froissart for Boys, by Lanier, new ed. 7s. 6d.
FROUDE, J. A. See Prime Ministers.
Gainsborough and Constable. See Great Artists.
GASPARIN, *Sunny Fields and Shady Woods*, 6s.
GEFFCKEN, *British Empire*, 7s. 6d.
Generation of Judges, n. e. 7s. 6d.
Gentle Life Series, edited by J. Hain Friswell, sm. 8vo. 6s. per vol.; calf extra, 10s. 6d. ea.; 16mo, 2s. 6d., except when price is given.
Gentle Life.
About in the World.
Like unto Christ.
Familiar Words, 6s.; also 3s. 6d.
Montaigne's Essays.
Sidney's Arcadia, 6s.
Gentle Life, second series.
Varia; readings, 10s. 6d.
Silent hour; essays.
Half-length Portraits.
Essays on English Writers.
Other People's Windows, 6s. & 2s. 6d.
A Man's Thoughts.

George Eliot, by G. W. Cooke, 10s. 6d.
Germany. See Foreign Countries.
GESSI, ROMOLO PASHA, *Seven Years in the Soudan*, 18s.
GHIBERTI & DONATELLO. See Great Artists.
GILES, E., *Australia Twice Traversed*, 1872-76, 2 vols. 30s.
GILL, J. See Low's Readers.
GILLESPIE, W. M., *Surveying*, n. ed. 21s.
Giotto, by Harry Quilter, illust. 15s.
—— See also Great Artists.
GIRDLESTONE, C., *Private Devotions*, 2s.
GLADSTONE. See Prime Ministers.
GLENELG, P., *Devil and the Doctor*, 1s.
GLOVER, R., *Light of the World*, n. ed., 2s. 6d.
GLÜCK. See Great Musicians.
Goethe's Faustus, in orig. rhyme, by Huth, 5s.
—— *Prosa*, by C. A. Buchheim (Low's German Series), 3s. 6d.
GOLDSMITH, O., *She Stoops to Conquer*, by Austin Dobson, illust. by E. A. Abbey, 84s.
—— See also Choice Editions.
GOOCH, FANNY C., *Mexicans*, 16s.
GOODALL, *Life and Landscape on the Norfolk Broads*, 126s. and 210s.
—— &EMERSON, *Pictures of East Anglian Life*, £5 5s. and £7 7s.
GOODMAN, E. J., *The Best Tour in Norway*, 6s.
—— N. & A., *Fen Skating*, 5s.
GOODYEAR, W. H., *Grammar of the Lotus, Ornament and Sun Worship*, 63s. nett.

GORDON, J. E. H., *Physical Treatise on Electricity and Magnetism*. 3rd ed. 2 vols. 42s.
—— *Electric Lighting*, 18s.
—— *School Electricity*, 5s.
—— Mrs. J. E. H., *Decorative Electricity*, illust. 12s.
GOWER, LORD RONALD, *Handbook to the Art Galleries of Belgium and Holland*, 5s.
—— *Northbrook Gallery*, 63s. and 105s.
—— *Portraits at Castle Howard*. 2 vols. 126s.
—— See also Great Artists.
GRAESSI, *Italian Dictionary*, 3s. 6d.; roan, 5s.
GRAY, T. See Choice Eds.
Great Artists, Biographies, illustrated, emblematical binding, 3s. 6d. per vol. except where the price is given.
Barbizon School, 2 vols.
Claude le Lorrain.
Correggio, 2s. 6d.
Cox and De Wint.
George Cruikshank.
Della Robbia and Cellini, 2s. 6d.
Albrecht Dürer.
Figure Paintings of Holland.
Fra Angelico, Masaccio, &c.
Fra Bartolommeo, &c.
Gainsborough and Constable.
Ghiberti and Donatello, 2s. 6d.
Giotto, by H. Quilter, 15s.
Hogarth, by A. Dobson.
Hans Holbein.
Landscape Painters of Holland.
Landseer.
Leonardo da Vinci.
Little Masters of Germany, by Scott; éd. de luxe, 10s. 6d.
Mantegna and Francia.
Meissonier, 2s. 6d.
Michelangelo.
Mulready.
Murillo, by Minor, 2s. 6d.
Overbeck.
Raphael.

Great Artists—continued.
Rembrandt.
Reynolds.
Romney and Lawrence, 2s. 6d.
Rubens, by Kett.
Tintoretto, by Osler.
Titian, by Heath.
Turner, by Monkhouse.
Vandyck and Hals.
Velasquez.
Vernet & Delaroche.
Watteau, by Mollett, 2s. 6d.
Wilkie, by Mollett.
Great Musicians, edited by F. Hueffer. A series of biographies, 3s. each :—
Bach, by Poole.
Beethoven.
*Berlioz.
Cherubini.
English Church Composers.
*Gluck.
Handel.
Haydn.
*Marcello.
Mendelssohn.
Mozart.
*Palestrina and the Roman School.
Purcell.
Rossini and Modern Italian School.
Schubert.
Schumann.
Richard Wagner.
Weber.
  * *Are not yet published.*
Greece. See Foreign Countries.
GRIEB, *German Dictionary*, n. ed. 2 vols. 21s.
GRIMM, H., *Literature*, 8s. 6d.
GROHMANN, *Camps in the Rockies*, 12s. 6d.
GROVES, J. PERCY. See Low's Standard Books.
GUIZOT, *History of England*, illust. 3 vols. re-issue at 10s. 6d. per vol.
—— *History of France*, illust. re-issue, 8 vols. 10s. 6d. each.
—— Abridged by G. Masson, 5s.
GUYON, MADAME, *Life*, 6s.

HADLEY, J., *Roman Law*, 7s. 6d.
Half-length Portraits. See Gentle Life Series.
HALFORD, F. M., *Dry Fly-fishing*, n. ed. 25s.
—— *Floating Flies*, 15s. & 30s.
HALL, *How to Live Long*, 2s.
HALSEY, F. A., *Slide Valve Gears*, 8s. 6d.
HAMILTON. See English Philosophers.
—— E. *Fly-fishing*, 6s. and 10s. 6d.
—— *Riverside Naturalist*, 14s.
HAMILTON'S *Mexican Handbook*, 8s. 6d.
HANDEL. See Great Musicians.
HANDS, T:, *Numerical Exercises in Chemistry*, 2s. 6d.; without ans. 2s.; ans. sep. 6d.
Handy Guide to Dry-fly Fishing, by Cotswold Isys, 1s.
Handy Guide Book to Japanese Islands, 6s. 6d.
HARDY, A. S., *Passe-rose*, 6s.
—— THOS. See Low's Standard Novels.
HARKUT, F., *Conspirator*, 6s.
HARLAND, MARION, *Home Kitchen*, 5s.
Harper's Young People, vols. I.—VII. 7s. 6d. each; gilt 8s.
HARRIES, A. See Nursing Record Series.
HARRIS, W. B., *Land of the African Sultan*, 10s. 6d.; l. p. 31s. 6d.
HARRISON, MARY, *Modern Cookery*, 6s.
—— *Skilful Cook*, n. ed. 5s.
—— MRS. B. *Old-fashioned Fairy Book*, 6s.
—— W., *London Houses*, Illust. n. edit. 1s. 6d., 6s. net; & 2s. 6d.

In all Departments of Literature. 13

HARTLEY and MILL. See English Philosophers.
HATTON, JOSEPH, *Journalistic London*, 12s. 6d.
—— See also Low's Standard Novels.
HAWEIS, H.R., *Broad Church*, 6s.
—— *Poets in the Pulpit*,'10s.6d. new edit. 6s.; also 3s. 6d.
—— Mrs., *Housekeeping*, 2s. 6d.
—— *Beautiful Houses*, 4s., new edit. 1s.
HAYDN. See Great Musicians.
HAZLITT, W., *Round Table*, 2s 6d.
HEAD, PERCY R. See Illus. Text Books and Great Artists.
HEARD, A.F., *Russian Church*, 16s.
HEARN, L., *Youma*, 5s.
HEATH, F. G., *Fern World*, 12s. 6d., new edit. 6s.
—— GERTRUDE, *Tell us Why*, 2s. 6d.
HELDMANN, B., *Mutiny of the "Leander,"* 7s. 6d. and 5s.
—— See also Low's Standard Books for Boys.
HENTY, G. A., *Hidden Foe*, 2 vols. 21s.
—— See also Low's Standard Books for Boys.
—— RICHMOND, *Australiana*, 5s.
HERBERT, T., *Salads and Sandwiches*, 6d.
HICKS, C. S., *Our Boys, and what to do with Them; Merchant Service*, 5s.
—— *Yachts, Boats, and Canoes*, 10s. 6d.
HIGGINSON, T. W., *Atlantic Essays*, 6s.
—— *History of the U.S.*, illust. 14s.

HILL, A. STAVELEY, *From Home to Home in N.-W. Canada*, 21s., new edit. 7s. 6d.
—— G. B., *Footsteps of Johnson*, 63s,; édition de luxe, 147s.
HINMAN, R., *Eclectic Physical Geography*, 5s.
Hints on proving Wills without Professional Assistance, n. ed. 1s.
HOEY, Mrs. CASHEL. See Low's Standard Novels.
HOFFER, *Caoutchouc & Gutta Percha*, 12s. 6d.
HOGARTH. See Gr. Artists.
HOLBEIN. See Great Artists.
HOLDER, CHARLES F., *Ivory King*, 8s. 6d.
—— *Living Lights*, 8s. 6d.
—— *Marvels of Animal Life*, 8s. 6d.
HOLM, SAXE, *Draxy Miller*, 2s. 6d. and 2s.
HOLMES, O. WENDELL, *Before the Curfew*, 5s.
—— *Over the Tea Cups*, 6s.
—— *Iron Gate, &c., Poems*, 6s.
—— *Last Leaf*, 42s.
—— *Mechanism in Thought and Morals*, 1s. 6d.
—— *Mortal Antipathy*, 8s. 6d., 2s. and 1s.
—— *Our Hundred Days in Europe*, new edit. 6s.; l. paper 15s.
—— *Poetical Works*, new edit., 2 vols. 10s. 6d.
—— *Works*, prose, 10 vols.; poetry, 4 vols.; 14 vols. 84s. Limited large paper edit., 14 vols. 294s. nett.
—— See also Low's Standard Novels and Rose Library.
HOLUB, E., *South Africa*, 2 vols. 42s.
HOPKINS, MANLEY, *Treatise on the Cardinal Numbers*, 2s. 6d.

Horace in Latin, with Smart's literal translation, 2s. 6d.; translation only, 1s. 6d.
HORETZKY, C., *Canada on the Pacific*, 5s.
How and where to Fish in Ireland, by H. Regan, 3s. 6d.
HOWARD, BLANCHE W., *Tony the Maid*, 3s. 6d.
—— See also Low's Standard Novels.
HOWELLS, W. D., *Suburban Sketches*, 7s. 6d.
—— *Undiscovered Country*, 3s. 6d. and 1s.
HOWORTH, H. H., *Glacial Nightmare*, 18s.
—— *Mammoth and the Flood*, 18s.
HUDSON, N. H., *Purple Land that England Lost; Banda Oriental* 2 vols. 21s.: 1 vol. 6s.
HUEFFER, E. See *Great Musicians*.
HUGHES, HUGH PRICE. See *Preachers*.
HUME, F., *Creature of the Night*, 1s.
Humorous Art at the Naval Exhibition, 1s.
HUMPHREYS, JENNET, *Some Little Britons in Brittany*, 2s. 6d.
Hundred Greatest Men, new edit. one vol. 21s.
HUNTINGDON, *The Squire's Nieces*, 2s. 6d. (Playtime Library.)
HYDE, *Hundred Years by Post*, 1s.
Hymnal Companion to the Book of Common Prayer, separate lists gratis.
Iceland. See Foreign Countries.
Illustrated Text-Books of Art-Education, edit. by E. J. Poynter, R.A., illust. 5s. each.
Architecture, Classic and Early Christian.

Illust. Text-Books—continued.
Architecture, Gothic and Renaissance.
German, Flemish, and Dutch Painting.
Painting, Classic and Italian.
Painting, English and American.
Sculpture, modern.
Sculpture, by G. Redford.
Spanish and French artists.
INDERWICK, F. A., *Interregnum*, 10s. 6d.
—— *Sidelights on the Stuarts*, new edit. 7s. 6d.
INGELOW, JEAN. See Low's Standard Novels.
INGLIS, *Our New Zealand Cousins*, 6s.
—— *Sport and Work on the Nepaul Frontier*, 21s.
—— *Tent Life in Tiger Land*, 18s.
IRVING, W., *Little Britain*, 10s. 6d. and 6s.
—— *Works*, "Geoffrey Crayon" edit. 27 vols. 16l. 16s.
JACKSON, J., *Handwriting in Relation to Hygiene*, 3d.
—— *New Style Vertical Writing Copy-Books*, Series I. 1—8, 2d. and 1d. each.
—— *New Code Copy-Books*, 22 Nos. 2d. each.
—— *Shorthand of Arithmetic*, Companion to all Arithmetics, 1s. 6d.
—— L., *Ten Centuries of European Progress*, with maps, 12s. 6d.
JAMES, CROAKE, *Law and Lawyers*, new edit. 7s. 6d.
—— HENRY. See Daudet, A.
JAMES and MOLE'S *French Dictionary*, 3s. 6d. cloth; roan, 5s.
JAMES, *German Dictionary*, 3s. 6d. cloth; roan 5s.
JANVIER, *Aztec Treasure House*, 7s. 6d.; new edit. 5s.

Japan. See Foreign Countries.
JEFFERIES, RICHARD, *Amaryllis at the Fair,* 7s. 6d.
—— *Bevis,* new edit. 5s.
JEPHSON, A. J. M., *Emin Pasha relief expedition,* 21s.
JERDON. See Low's Standard Series.
JOHNSTON, H. H., *The Congo,* 21s.
JOHNSTON-LAVIS, H. J., *South Italian Volcanoes,* 15s.
JOHNSTONE, D. L., *Land of the Mountain Kingdom,* new edit. 3s. 6d. and 2s. 6d.
JONES, MRS. HERBERT, *Sandringham, Past and Present,* illust., new edit. 8s. 6d.
JULIEN, F., *Conversational French Reader,* 2s. 6d.
—— *English Student's French Examiner,* 2s.
—— *First Lessons in Conversational French Grammar,* n. ed. 1s.
—— *French at Home and at School,* Book I. accidence, 2s.; key, 3s.
—— *Petites Leçons de Conversation et de Grammaire,* n. ed. 3s.
—— *Petites Leçons,* with phrases, 3s. 6d.
—— *Phrases of Daily Use,* separately, 6d.
KARR, H. W. SETON, *Shores and Alps of Alaska,* 16s.
KARSLAND, VEVA, *Women and their Work,* 1s.
KAY. See Foreign Countries.
KENNEDY, E. B., *Blacks and Bushrangers,* new edit. 5s., 3s. 6d. and 2s. 6d.
KERR, W. M., *Far Interior, the Cape, Zambesi, &c.,* 2 vols. 32s.
KERSHAW, S. W., *Protestants from France in their English Home,* 6s.
KETT, C. W., *Rubens,* 3s. 6d.

Khedives and Pashas, 7s. 6d.
KILNER, E. A., *Four Welsh Counties,* 5s.
King and Commons. See Cavalier in Bayard Series.
KINGSLEY, R. G., *Children of Westminster Abbey,* 5s.
KINGSTON. See Low's Standard Books.
KIPLING, RUDYARD, *Soldiers Three, &c.,* stories, 1s.
—— *Story of the Gadsbys,* new edit. 1s.
—— *In Black and White, &c.,* stories, 1s.
—— *Wee Willie Winkie, &c.,* stories, 1s.
—— *Under the Deodars, &c.,* stories, 1s.
—— *Phantom Rickshaw, &c.,* stories, 1s.
⁂ The six collections of stories may also be had in 2 vols. 3s. 6d. each.
—— *Stories,* Library Edition, 2 vols. 6s. each.
KIRKALDY, W. G., *David Kirkaldy's Mechanical Testing,* 84s.
KNIGHT, A. L., *In the Web of Destiny,* 7s. 6d.
—— E. F., *Cruise of the Falcon,* new edit. 3s. 6d.
—— E. J., *Albania and Montenegro,* 12s. 6d.
—— V. C., *Church Unity,* 5s.
KNOX, T. W., *Boy Travellers,* new edit. 5s.
KNOX-LITTLE, W. J., *Sermons,* 3s. 6d.
KUNHARDT, C. P., *Small Yachts,* new edit. 50s.
—— *Steam Yachts,* 16s.
KWONG, *English Phrases,* 21s.
LABOULLAYE, E., *Abdallah,* 2s. 6d.
LALANNE, *Etching,* 12s. 6d.

LAMB, CHAS., *Essays of Elia*, with designs by C. O. Murray, 6s.
LAMBERT, *Angling Literature*, 3s. 6d.
Landscape Painters of Holland. See Great Artists.
LANDSEER. See Great Artists.
LANGLEY, S. P., *New Astronomy*, 10s. 6d.
LANIER, S., *Boy's Froissart*, 7s. 6d.; *King Arthur*, 7s. 6d.; *Mabinogion*, 7s. 6d.; *Percy*, 7s. 6d.
LANSDELL, HENRY, *Through Siberia*, 1 v. 15s. and 10s. 6d.
—— *Russia in Central Asia*, 2 vols. 42s.
—— *Through Central Asia*, 12s.
LARDEN, W., *School Course on Heat*, n. ed. 5s.
LAURIE, A., *Secret of the Magian, the Mystery of Ecbatana*, illus. 6s. See also Low's Standard Books.
LAWRENCE, SERGEANT, *Autobiography*, 6s.
—— and ROMNEY. See Great Artists.
LAYARD, MRS., *West Indies*, 2s. 6d.
LEA, H. C., *Inquisition*, 3 vols. 42s.
LEARED, A., *Marocco*, n. ed. 16s.
LEAVITT, *New World Tragedies*, 7s. 6d.
LEFFINGWELL, W. B., *Shooting*, 18s.
—— *Wild Fowl Shooting*, 10s. 6d.
LEFROY, W., DEAN. See Preachers.
LELAND, C. G., *Algonquin Legends*, 8s.
LEMON, M., *Small House over the Water*, 6s.

Leo XIII. Life, 18s.
Leonardo da Vinci. See Great Artists.
—— *Literary Works*, by J. P. Richter, 2 vols. 252s.
LIEBER, *Telegraphic Cipher*, 42s. nett.
Like unto Christ. See Gentle Life Series.
LITTLE, ARCH. J., *Yang-tse Gorges*, n. ed., 10s. 6d.
Little Masters of Germany. See Great Artists.
LONGFELLOW, *Miles Standish*, illus. 21s.
—— *Maidenhood*, with col. pl. 2s. 6d.; gilt edges, 3s. 6d.
—— *Nuremberg*, photogr. illu. 31s. 6d.
—— *Song of Hiawatha*, illust. 21s.
LOOMIS, E., *Astronomy*, n. ed. 8s. 6d.
LORNE, MARQUIS OF, *Canada and Scotland*, 7s. 6d.
—— *Palmerston*. See Prime Ministers.
Louis, St. See Bayard Series.
Low's French Readers, edit. by C. F. Clifton, I. 3d., II. 3d., III. 6d.
—— *German Series*. See Goethe, Meissner, Sandars, and Schiller.
—— *London Charities*, annually, 1s. 6d.; sewed, 1s.
—— *Illustrated Germ. Primer*, 1s.
—— *Infant Primers*, I. illus. 3d.; II. illus. 6d. and 7d.
—— *Pocket Encyclopædia*, with plates, 3s. 6d.; roan, 4s. 6d.
—— *Readers*, I., 9d.; II., 10d.; III., 1s.; IV., 1s. 3d.; V., 1s. 4d.; VI., 1s. 6d.

Low's Select Parchment Series.
Aldrich (T. B.) Friar Jerome's Beautiful Book, 3s. 6d.
Lewis (Rev. Gerrard), Ballads of the Cid, 2s. 6d.
Whittier (J. G.) The King's Missive. 3s. 6d.

Low's Stand. Library of Travel (except where price is stated), per volume, 7s. 6d.
1. Butler, Great Lone Land; also 3s. 6d.
2. —— Wild North Land.
3. Stanley (H. M.) Coomassie, 3s. 6d.
4. —— How I Found Livingstone; also 3s. 6d.
5. —— Through the Dark Continent, 1 vol. illust., 12s. 6d.; also 3s. 6d.
8. MacGahan (J. A.) Oxus.
9. Spry, voyage, *Challenger.*
10. Burnaby's Asia Minor, 10s. 6d.
11. Schweinfurth's Heart of Africa, 2 vols. 15s.; also 3s. 6d. each.
12. Marshall (W.) Through America.
13. Lansdell (H). Through Siberia, 10s. 6d.
14. Coote, South by East, 10s. 6d.
15. Knight, Cruise of the *Falcon,* also 3s. 6d.
16. Thomson (Joseph) Through Masai Land.
19. Ashe (R. P.) Two Kings of Uganda, 3s. 6d.

Low's Standard Novels (except where price is stated), 6s.
Baker, John Westacott.
Black (W.) Craig Royston.
—— Daughter of Heth.
—— House Boat.
—— In Far Lochaber.
—— In Silk Attire.
—— Kilmeny.
—— Lady Siverdale's Sweetheart.
—— New Prince Fortunatus.
—— Penance of John Logan.
—— Stand Fast, Craig Royston!
—— Sunrise.
—— Three Feathers.

Low's Stand. Novels—continued
Blackmore (R. D.) Alice Lorraine.
—— Christowell.
—— Clara Vaughan.
—— Cradock Nowell.
—— Cripps the Carrier.
—— Ereme, or My Father's Sins.
—— Kit and Kitty.
—— Lorna Doone.
—— Mary Anerley.
—— Sir Thomas Upmore.
—— Springhaven.
Brémont, Gentleman Digger.
Brown (Robert) Jack Abbott's Log.
Bynner, Agnes Surriage.
—— Begum's Daughter.
Cable (G. W.) Bonaventure, 5s.
Coleridge (C. R.) English Squire.
Craddock, Despot of Broomsedge.
Croker (Mrs. B. M.) Some One Else.
Cumberland (Stuart) Vasty Deep.
De Leon, Under the Stars and Crescent.
Edwards (Miss Betham) Half-way.
Eggleston, Juggernaut.
French Heiress in her own Chateau.
Gilliat (E.) Story of the Dragonnades.
Hardy (A. S.) Passe-rose.
—— (Thos.) Far from the Madding.
—— Hand of Ethelberta.
—— Laodicean.
—— Mayor of Casterbridge.
—— Pair of Blue Eyes.
—— Return of the Native.
—— Trumpet-Major.
—— Two on a Tower.
Harkut, Conspirator.
Hatton (J.) Old House at Sandwich.
—— Three Recruits.
Hoey (Mrs. Cashel) Golden Sorrow.
—— Out of Court.
—— Stern Chase.
Howard (Blanche W.) Open Door.
Ingelow (Jean) Don John.
—— John Jerome, 5s.
—— Sarah de Berenger.
Lathrop, Newport, 5s.
Mac Donald (Geo.) Adela Cathcart.
—— Guild Court.

Low's Stand. Novels—continued.
Mac Donald (Geo.) Mary Marston.
—— Orts.
—— Stephen Archer, &c.
—— The Vicar's Daughter.
—— Weighed and Wanting.
Macmaster, Our Pleasant Vices.
Macquoid (Mrs.) Diane.
Musgrave (Mrs.) Miriam.
Osborn, Spell of Ashtaroth, 5s.
Prince Maskiloff.
Riddell (Mrs.) Alaric Spenceley.
—— Daisies and Buttercups.
—— Senior Partner.
—— Struggle for Fame.
Russell (W. Clark) Betwixt the Forelands.
—— Frozen Pirate.
—— Jack's Courtship.
—— John Holdsworth.
—— Little Loo.
—— My Watch Below.
—— Ocean Free Lance.
—— Sailor's Sweetheart.
—— Sea Queen.
—— Strange Voyage.
—— The Lady Maud.
—— Wreck of the *Grosvenor*.
Steuart, Kilgroom.
Stockton (F. R.) Ardis Claverden.
—— Bee-man of Orn, 5s.
—— Hundredth Man.
—— The late Mrs. Null.
Stoker, Snake's Pass.
Stowe (Mrs.) Old Town Folk.
—— Poganuc People.
Thomas, House on the Scar.
Thomson, Ulu, an African Romance.
Tourgee, Murvale Eastman.
Tytler (S.) Duchess Frances.
Vane, From the Dead.
Wallace (Lew.) Ben Hur.
Warner, Little Journey in the World.
Woolson (Constance Fenimore) Anne.
—— East Angles.
—— For the Major, 5s.
—— Jupiter Lights.

See also Sea Stories.

Low's Stand. Novels, new issue at short intervals, 2s. 6d. and 2s.
Blackmore, Alice Lorraine.
—— Christowell.
—— Clara Vaughan.
—— Cripps the Carrier.
—— Kit and Kitty.
—— Lorna Doone.
—— Mary Anerley.
—— Tommy Upmore.
Cable, Bonaventure.
Croker, Some One Else.
Cumberland, Vasty Deep.
De Leon, Under the Stars.
Edwards, Half-way.
Hardy, Laodicean.
—— Madding Crowd.
—— Mayor of Casterbridge.
—— Trumpet-Major,
—— Two on a Tower.
Hatton, Old House at Sandwich.
—— Three Recruits.
Hoey, Golden Sorrow.
—— Out of Court.
—— Stern Chase.
Holmes, Guardian Angel.
Ingelow, John Jerome.
—— Sarah de Berenger.
Mac Donald, Adela Cathcart.
—— Guild Court.
—— Stephen Archer.
—— Vicar's Daughter.
Oliphant, Innocent.
Riddell, Daisies and Buttercups.
—— Senior Partner.
Stockton, Bee-man of Orn, 5s.
—— Dusantes.
—— Mrs. Leeks and Mrs. Aleshine.
Stowe, Dred.
—— Old Town Folk.
—— Poganuc People.
Thomson, Ulu.
Walford, Her Great Idea, &c., Stories.

Low's German Series, a graduated course. See "German."

Low's Readers. See English Reader and French Reader.

Low's Standard Books for Boys, with numerous illustrations, 2s. 6d. each; gilt edges, 3s. 6d.

Low's Stand. Books for Boys—continued.

Adventures in New Guinea: the Narrative of Louis Tregance.
Biart (Lucien) Adventures of a Young Naturalist.
—— My Rambles in the New World.
Boussenard, Crusoes of Guiana.
—— Gold Seekers, a sequel to the above.
Butler (Col. Sir Wm., K.C.B.) Red Cloud, the Solitary Sioux: a Tale of the Great Prairie.
Cahun (Leon) Adventures of Captain Mago.
—— Blue Banner.
Célière, Startling Exploits of the Doctor.
Chaillu (Paul du) Wild Life under the Equator.
Collingwood (Harry) Under the Meteor Flag.
—— Voyage of the *Aurora*.
Cozzens (S.W.) Marvellous Country.
Dodge (Mrs.) Hans Brinker; or, The Silver Skates.
Du Chaillu (Paul) Stories of the Gorilla Country.
Erckmann - Chatrian, Brothers Rantzau.
Fenn (G. Manville) Off to the Wilds.
—— Silver Cañon.
Groves (Percy) Charmouth Grange; a Tale of the 17th Century.
Heldmann (B.) Mutiny on Board the Ship *Leander*.
Henty (G. A.) Cornet of Horse: a Tale of Marlborough's Wars.
—— Jack Archer; a Tale of the Crimea.
—— Winning his Spurs: a Tale of the Crusades.
Johnstone (D. Lawson) Mountain Kingdom.
Kennedy (E. B.) Blacks and Bushrangers in Queensland.
Kingston (W. H. G.) Ben Burton; or, Born and Bred at Sea.
—— Captain Mugford; or, Our Salt and Fresh Water Tutors.
—— Dick Cheveley.
—— Heir of Kilfinnan.

Low's Stand. Books for Boys—continued.

Kingston (W. H. G.) Snowshoes and Canoes.
—— Two Supercargoes.
—— With Axe and Rifle on the Western Prairies.
Laurie (A.) Conquest of the Moon.
—— New York to Brest in Seven Hours.
MacGregor (John) A Thousand Miles in the *Rob Roy* Canoe on Rivers and Lakes of Europe.
Maclean (H. E.) Maid of the Ship *Golden Age*.
Meunier, Great Hunting Grounds of the World.
Muller, Noble Words and Deeds.
Perelaer, The Three Deserters; or, Ran Away from the Dutch.
Reed (Talbot Baines) Sir Ludar: a Tale of the Days of the Good Queen Bess.
Rousselet (Louis) Drummer-boy: a Story of the Time of Washington.
—— King of the Tigers.
—— Serpent Charmer.
—— Son of the Constable of France.
Russell (W. Clark) Frozen Pirates.
Stanley, My Kalulu—Prince, King and Slave.
Winder (F. H.) Lost in Africa.

Low's Standard Series of Books by popular writers, cloth gilt, 2s.; gilt edges, 2s. 6d. each.

Alcott (L. M.) A Rose in Bloom.
—— An Old-Fashioned Girl.
—— Aunt Jo's Scrap Bag.
—— Eight Cousins, illust.
—— Jack and Jill.
—— Jimmy's Cruise.
—— Little Men.
—— Little Women and Little Women Wedded.
—— Lulu's Library, illust.
—— Shawl Straps.
—— Silver Pitchers.
—— Spinning-Wheel Stories.
—— Under the Lilacs, illust.
—— Work and Beginning Again, ill.

A Select List of Books

Low's Stand. Series—continued.
Alden (W. L.) Jimmy Brown, illust.
—— Trying to Find Europe.
Bunyan (John) Pilgrim's Progress, (extra volume), gilt, 2s.
De Witt (Madame) An Only Sister.
Francis (Francis) Eric and Ethel, illust.
Holm (Saxe) Draxy Miller's Dowry.
Jerdon (Gert.) Keyhole Country, illust.
Robinson (Phil) In My Indian Garden.
—— Under the Punkah.
Roe (E. P.) Nature's Serial Story.
Saintine, Picciola.
Samuels, Forecastle to Cabin, illust.
Sandeau (Jules) Seagull Rock.
Stowe (Mrs.) Dred.
—— Ghost in the Mill, &c.
—— My Wife and I.
—— We and our Neighbours.
See also Low's Standard Series.
Tooley (Mrs.) Life of Harriet Beecher Stowe.
Warner (C. Dudley) In the Wilderness.
—— My Summer in a Garden.
Whitney (Mrs.) A Summer in Leslie Goldthwaite's Life.
—— Faith Gartney's Girlhood.
—— Hitherto.
—— Real Folks.
—— The Gayworthys.
—— We Girls.
—— The Other Girls: a Sequel.
*** *A new illustrated list of books for boys and girls, with portraits of celebrated authors, sent post free on application.*

LOWELL, J. R., *Among my Books*, Series I. and II., 7s. 6d. each.
—— *My Study Windows*, n. ed. 1s.
—— *Vision of Sir Launfal*, illus. 63s.
MACDONALD, A., *Our Sceptred Isle*, 3s. 6d.
—— D., *Oceania*, 6s.

MACDONALD, GEO., *Castle Warlock, a Homely Romance*, 3 vols. 31s. 6d.
—— See also Low's Standard Novels.
—— SIR JOHN A., *Life*.
MACDOWALL, ALEX. B., *Curve Pictures of London*, 1s.
MACGAHAN, J. A., *Oxus*, 7s. 6d.
MACGOUN, *Commercial Correspondence*, 5s.
MACGREGOR, J., *Rob Roy in the Baltic*, n. ed. 3s. 6d. and 2s. 6d.
—— *Rob Roy Canoe*, new edit., 3s. 6d. and 2s. 6d.
—— *Yawl Rob Roy*, new edit., 3s. 6d. and 2s. 6d.
MACKENNA, *Brave Men in Action*, 10s. 6d.
MACKENZIE, SIR MORELL, *Fatal Illness of Frederick the Noble*, 2s. 6d.
MACKINNON and SHADBOLT, *South African Campaign*, 50s.
MACLAREN, A. See Preachers.
MACLEAN, H. E. See Low's Standard Books.
MACMASTER. See Low's Standard Novels.
MACMURDO, E., *History of Portugal*, 21s.; II. 21s.; III. 21s.
MAHAN, A. T., *Influence of Sea Power on History*, 18s.
Maid of Florence, 10s. 6d.
MAIN, MRS., *High Life*, 10s. 6d.
—— See also Burnaby, Mrs.
MALAN, A. N., *Cobbler of Cornikeranium*, 5s.
—— C. F. DE M., *Eric and Connie's Cruise*, 5s.
Man's Thoughts. See Gentle Life Series.
MANLEY, J. J., *Fish and Fishing*, 6s.

MANTEGNA and FRANCIA.
See Great Artists.
MARCH, F. A., *Comparative Anglo-Saxon Grammar*, 12s.
—— *Anglo-Saxon Reader*, 7s. 6d.
MARKHAM, ADM., *Naval Career*, 14s.
—— *Whaling Cruise*, new edit. 7s. 6d.
—— C. R., *Peru*. See Foreign Countries.
—— *Fighting Veres*, 18s.
—— *War Between Peru and Chili*, 10s. 6d.
MARSH, G. P., *Lectures on the English Language*, 18s.
—— *Origin and History of the English Language*, 18s.
MARSHALL, W. G., *Through America*, new edit. 7s. 6d.
MARSTON, E., *How Stanley wrote " In Darkest Africa,"* 1s.
—— See also Amateur Angler, Frank's Ranche, and Fresh Woods.
—— W., *Eminent Actors*, n. ed. 6s.
MARTIN, J. W., *Float Fishing and Spinning*, new edit. 2s.
Massage. See Nursing Record Series.
MATTHEWS, J. W., *Incwadi Yami*, 14s.
MAURY, M. F., *Life*, 12s. 6d.
—— *Physical Geography and Meteorology of the Sea*, new ed. 6s.
MEISSNER, A. L., *Children's Own German Book* (Low's Series), 1s. 6d.
—— *First German Reader* (Low's Series), 1s. 6d.
—— *Second German Reader* (Low's Series), 1s. 6d.
MEISSONIER. See Great Artists.

MELBOURNE, LORD. See Prime Ministers.
MELIO, G. L., *Swedish Drill*, 1s. 6d.
MENDELSSOHN *Family*, 1729-1847, Letters and Journals, 2 vols. 30s.; new edit. 30s.
—— See also Great Musicians.
MERRIFIELD, J., *Nautical Astronomy*, 7s. 6d.
MERRYLEES, J., *Carlsbad*, 7s. 6d. and 9s.
MESNEY, W., *Tungking*, 3s. 6d.
Metal Workers' Recipes and Processes, by W. T. Brannt, 12s. 6d.
MEUNIER, V. See Low's Standard Books.
Michelangelo. See Great Artists.
MILFORD, P. *Ned Stafford's Experiences*, 5s.
MILL, JAMES. See English Philosophers.
MILLS, J., *Alternative Elementary Chemistry*, 1s. 6d.
—— *Chemistry Based on the Science and Art Syllabus*, 2s. 6d.
—— *Elementary Chemistry*, answers, 2 vols. 1s. each.
MILTON'S *Allegro*. See Choice Editions.
MITCHELL, D. G. (Ik. Marvel) *English Lands, Letters and Kings*, 2 vols. 6s. each.
—— *Writings*, new edit. per vol. 5s.
MITFORD, J., *Letters*, 3s. 6d.
—— MISS, *Our Village*, illust. 5s.
Modern Etchings, 63s. & 31s. 6d.
MOLLETT, J. W., *Dictionary of Words in Art and Archæology*, illust. 15s.
—— *Etched Examples*, 31s. 6d. and 63s.
—— See also Great Artists.

MONCK. See English Philosophers.
MONEY, E., *The Truth About America*, 5s.; new edit. 2s. 6d.
MONKHOUSE. See G. Artists.
Montaigne's Essays, revised by J. Hain Friswell, 2s. 6d.
—— See Gentle Life Series.
MOORE, J. M., *New Zealand for Emigrant, Invalid, and Tourist*, 5s.
MORFILL, W. R., *Russia*, 3s. 6d.
MORLEY, HENRY, *English Literature in the Reign of Victoria*, 2s. 6d.
—— *Five Centuries of English Literature*, 2s.
MORSE, E. S., *Japanese Homes*, new edit. 10s. 6d.
MORTEN, *Hospital Life*, 1s.
MORTIMER, J., *Chess Player's Pocket-Book*, new edit. 1s.
MORWOOD, V.S., *Our Gipsies*, 18s.
MOSS, F. J., *Great South Sea*, 8s. 6d.
MOSSMAN, S., *Japan*, 3s. 6d.
MOTTI, PIETRO, *Elementary Russian Grammar*, 2s. 6d.
—— *Russian Conversation Grammar*, 5s.; Key, 2s.
MOULE, H. C. G., *Sermons*, 3s. 6d.
MOXLEY, *West India Sanatorium, and Barbados*, 3s. 6d.
MOXON, W., *Pilocereus Senilis*, 3s. 6d.
MOZART, 3s. Gr. Musicians.
MULLER, E. See Low's Standard Books.
MULLIN, J. P., *Moulding and Pattern Making*, 12s. 6d.
MULREADY, 3s. 6d. Great Artists.
MURILLO. See Great Artists.

MUSGRAVE, MRS. See Low's Standard Novels.
—— *Savage London*, n. e. 3s. 6d.
My Comforter, &c., Religious Poems, 2s. 6d.
Napoleon I. See Bayard Series.
Napoleon I. and Marie Louise, 7s. 6d.
NELSON, WOLFRED, *Panama*, 6s.
Nelson's Words and Deeds, 3s. 6d.
NETHERCOTE, *Pytchley Hunt*, 8s. 6d.
New Democracy, 1s.
New Zealand, chromos, by Barrand, 168s.
NICHOLSON, *British Association Work and Workers*, 1s.
Nineteenth Century, a Monthly Review, 2s. 6d. per No.
NISBET, HUME, *Life and Nature Studies*, 6s.
NIXON, *Story of the Transvaal*, 12s. 6d.
Nordenskiöld's Voyage, trans. 21s.
NORDHOFF, C., *California*, new edit. 12s. 6d.
NORRIS, RACHEL, *Nursing Notes*, 2s.
NORTH, W., *Roman Fever*, 25s.
Northern Fairy Tales, 5s
NORTON, C. L., *Florida*, 5s.
NORWAY, G., *How Martin Drake Found his Father* illus. 5s.
NUGENT'S *French Dictionary*, new edit. 3s.
Nuggets of the Gouph, 3s.
Nursing Record Series, text books and manuals. Edited by Charles F. Rideal.
1. Lectures to Nurses on Antiseptics in Surgery. By E. Stanmore Bishop. With coloured plates, 2s.

Nursing Record Series—contin.
2. Nursing Notes. Medical and Surgical information. For Hospital Nurses, &c. With illustrations and a glossary of terms. By Rachel Norris (née Williams), late Acting Superintendent of Royal Victoria Military Hospital at Suez, 2s.
3. Practical Electro-Therapeutics. By Arthur Harries, M.D., and H. Newman Lawrence. With photographs and diagrams, 1s. 6d.
4. Massage for Beginners. Simple and easy directions for learning and remembering the different movements. By Lucy Fitch, 1s.

O'BRIEN, *Fifty Years of Concession to Ireland*, vol. i. 16s.; vol. ii. 16s.
—— *Irish Land Question*, 2s.
OGDEN, JAMES, *Fly-tying*, 2s. 6d.
O'GRADY, *Bardic Literature of Ireland*, 1s.
—— *History of Ireland*, vol. i. 7s. 6d.; ii. 7s. 6d.
Old Masters in Photo. 73s. 6d.
Orient Line Guide, new edit. 2s. 6d.
ORLEBAR, *Sancta Christina*, 5s.
Other People's Windows. See Gentle Life Series.
OTTÉ, *Denmark and Iceland*, 3s. 6d. Foreign Countries.
Our Little Ones in Heaven, 5s.
Out of School at Eton, 2s. 6d.
OVERBECK. See Great Artists.
OWEN, DOUGLAS, *Marine Insurance*, 15s.
Oxford Days, by a M.A., 2s. 6d.
PALGRAVE, *Chairman's Handbook*, new edit. 2s.
—— *Oliver Cromwell*, 10s. 6d.

PALLISER, *China Collector's Companion*, 5s.
—— *History of Lace*, n. ed. 21s.
PANTON, *Homes of Taste*, 2s. 6d.
PARKE, *Emin Pasha Relief Expedition*, 21s.
PARKER, E. H., *Chinese Account of the Opium War*, 1s. 6d.
PARSONS, J., *Principles of Partnership*, 31s. 6d.
—— T. P., *Marine Insurance*, 2 vols. 63s.
PEACH, *Annals of Swainswick*, 10s. 6d.
Peel. See Prime Ministers.
PELLESCHI, G., *Gran Chaco*, 8s. 6d.
PENNELL, H. C., *Fishing Tackle*, 2s.
—— *Sporting Fish*, 15s. & 30s.
Penny Postage Jubilee, 1s.
PERRY, NORA, *Another Flock of Girls*, illus. by Birch & Copeland, 7s. 6d.
Peru, 3s. 6d. Foreign Countries.
PHELPS, E. S., *Struggle for Immortality*, 5s.
—— SAMUEL, *Life*, by W. M. Phelps and Forbes-Robertson, 12s.
PHILLIMORE, C. M., *Italian Literature*, new. edit. 3s. 6d.
PHILLIPPS, W. M., *English Elegies*, 5s.
PHILLIPS, L. P., *Dictionary of Biographical Reference*, new. edit. 25s.
—— W., *Law of Insurance*, 2 vols. 73s. 6d.
PHILPOT, H. J., *Diabetes Mellitus*, 5s.
—— *Diet Tables*, 1s. each.
Picture Gallery of British Art. I. to VI. 18s. each.
—— *Modern Art*, 3 vols. 31s. 6d. each.

PINTO, *How I Crossed Africa*, 2 vols. 42s.
Playtime Library. See Humphrey and Huntingdon.
Pleasant History of Reynard the Fox, trans. by T. Roscoe, illus. 7s. 6d.
POCOCK, R., *Gravesend Historian*, 5s.
POE, by E. C. Stedman, 3s. 6d.
—— *Raven*, ill. by G. Doré, 63s.
Poems of the Inner Life, 5s.
Poetry of Nature. See Choice Editions.
Poetry of the Anti-Jacobin, 7s. 6d. and 21s.
POOLE, *Somerset Customs and Legends*, 5s.
—— S. LANE, *Egypt*, 3s. 6d. Foreign Countries.
POPE, *Select Poetical Works*, (Bernhard Tauchnitz Collection), 2s.
PORCHER, A., *Juvenile French Plays*, 1s.
Portraits of Racehorses, 4 vols. 126s.
POSSELT, *Structure of Fibres*, 63s.
—— *Textile Design*, illust. 28s.
POYNTER. See Illustrated Text Books.
Preachers of the Age, 3s. 6d. ea.
Living Theology, by His Grace the Archbishop of Canterbury.
The Conquering Christ, by Rev. A. Maclaren.
Verbum Crucis, by the Bishop of Derry.
Ethical Christianity, by H. P. Hughes.
Sermons, by Canon W. J. Knox-Little.
Light and Peace, by H. R. Reynolds.
Faith and Duty, by A. M. Fairbairn.
Plain Words on Great Themes, by J. O. Dykes.
Sermons, by the Bishop of Ripon,

Preachers of the Age—continued.
Sermons, by Rev. C. H. Spurgeon.
Agoniæ Christi, by Dean Lefroy, of Norwich.
Sermons, by H. C. G. Moule, M.A.
Volumes will follow in quick succession by other well-known men.

Prime Ministers, a series of political biographies, edited by Stuart J. Reid, 3s. 6d. each.
1. Earl of Beaconsfield, by J. Anthony Froude.
2. Viscount Melbourne, by Henry Dunckley ("*Verax*").
3. Sir Robert Peel, by Justin McCarthy.
4. Viscount Palmerston, by the Marquis of Lorne.
5. Earl Russell, by Stuart J. Reid.
6. Right Hon. W. E. Gladstone, by G. W. E. Russell.
7. Earl of Aberdeen, by Sir Arthur Gordon.
8. Marquis of Salisbury, by H. D. Traill.
9. Earl of Derby, by George Saintsbury.
⁎⁎⁎ An edition, limited to 250 copies, is issued on hand-made paper, medium 8vo, bound in half vellum, cloth sides, gilt top. Price for the 9 vols. 4l. 4s. nett.

Prince Maskiloff. See Low's Standard Novels.
Prince of Nursery Playmates, new edit. 2s. 6d.
PRITT, T. N., *Country Trout Flies*, 10s. 6d.
Reynolds. See Great Artists.
Purcell. See Great Musicians.
QUILTER, H., *Giotto, Life, &c.* 15s.
RAMBAUD, *History of Russia*, new edit., 3 vols. 21s.
RAPHAEL. See Great Artists.
REDFORD, *Sculpture*. See Illustrated Text-books.
REDGRAVE, *Engl. Painters*, 10s. 6d. and 12s.

REED, Sir E. J., *Modern Ships of War*, 10s. 6d.
—— T. B., *Roger Ingleton, Minor*, 5s.
—— *Sir Ludar*. See Low's Standard Books.
REID, Mayne, Capt., *Stories of Strange Adventures*, illust. 5s.
—— Stuart J. See Prime Ministers.
—— T. Wemyss, *Land of the Bey*, 10s. 6d.
Remarkable Bindings in British Museum, 168s.; 94s. 6d.; 73s. 6d. and 63s.
REMBRANDT. See Great Artists.
Reminiscences of a Boyhood, 6s.
REMUSAT, *Memoirs*, Vols. I. and II. new ed. 16s. each.
—— *Select Letters*, 16s.
REYNOLDS. See Gr. Artists.
—— Henry R., *Light & Peace, &c. Sermons*, 3s. 6d.
RICHARDS, J. W., *Aluminium*, new edit. 21s.
RICHARDSON, *Choice of Books*, 3s. 6d.
RICHTER, J. P., *Italian Art*, 42s.
—— See also Great Artists.
RIDDELL. See Low's Standard Novels.
RIDEAL, *Women of the Time*, 14s.
RIFFAULT, *Colours for Painting*, 31s. 6d.
RIIS, *How the Other Half Lives*, 10s. 6d.
RIPON, Bp. of. See Preachers.
ROBERTS, Miss, *France*. See Foreign Countries.
—— W., *English Bookselling*, earlier history, 7s. 6d.
ROBIDA, A., *Toilette*, coloured, 7s. 6d.

ROBINSON, "*Romeo*" *Coates*, 7s. 6d.
—— *Noah's Ark*, n. ed. 3s. 6d.
—— *Sinners & Saints*, 10s. 6d.
—— See also Low's Standard Series.
—— *Wealth and its Sources*, 5s.
—— W. C., *Law of Patents*, 3 vols. 105s.
ROCHEFOUCAULD. See Bayard Series.
ROCKSTRO, *History of Music*, new ed. 14s.
RODRIGUES, *Panama Canal*, 5s.
ROE, E. P. See Low's Standard Series.
ROGERS, S. See Choice Editions.
ROLFE, *Pompeii*, 7s. 6d.
Romantic Stories of the Legal Profession, 7s. 6d.
ROMNEY. See Great Artists.
ROOSEVELT, Blanche R. *Home Life of Longfellow*, 7s. 6d.
ROSE, J., *Mechanical Drawing*, 16s.
—— *Practical Machinist*, new ed. 12s. 6d.
—— *Key to Engines*, 8s. 6d.
—— *Modern Steam Engines*, 31s. 6d.
—— *Steam Boilers*, 12s. 6d.
Rose Library. Popular Literature of all countries, per vol. 1s., unless the price is given.
Alcott (L. M.) Eight Cousins, 2s.; cloth, 3s. 6d.
—— Jack and Jill, 2s.; cloth, 5s.
—— Jimmy's cruise in the *Pinafore*, 2s.; cloth, 3s. 6d.
—— Little Women.
—— Little Women Wedded; Nos. 4 and 5 in 1 vol. cloth, 3s. 6d.
—— Little Men, 2s.; cloth gilt, 3s. 6d.

Rose Library—continued.
Alcott (L. M.) Old-fashioned Girls, 2s.; cloth, 3s. 6d.
—— Rose in Bloom, 2s.; cl. 3s. 6d.
—— Silver Pitchers.
—— Under the Lilacs, 2s.; cloth, 3s. 6d.
—— Work, A Story of Experience, 2 vols. in 1, cloth, 3s. 6d.
Stowe (Mrs.) Pearl of Orr's Island.
—— Minister's Wooing.
—— We and Our Neighbours, 2s.
—— My Wife and I, 2s.
Dodge (Mrs.) Hans Brinker, or, The Silver Skates, 1s.; cloth, 5s.; 3s. 6d.; 2s. 6d.
Lowell (J. R.) My Study Windows.
Holmes (Oliver Wendell) Guardian Angel, cloth, 2s.
Warner (C. D.) My Summer in a Garden, cloth, 2s.
Stowe (Mrs.) Dred, 2s.; cloth gilt, 3s. 6d.
Carleton (W.) City Ballads, 2 vols. in 1, cloth gilt, 2s. 6d.
—— Legends, 2 vols. in 1, cloth gilt, 2s. 6d.
—— Farm Ballads, 6d. and 9d.; 3 vols. in 1, cloth gilt, 3s. 6d.
—— Farm Festivals, 3 vols. in 1, cloth gilt, 3s. 6d.
—— Farm Legends, 3 vols. in 1, cloth gilt, 3s. 6d.
Clients of Dr. Bernagius, 2 vols.
Howells (W. D.) Undiscovered Country.
Clay (C. M.) Baby Rue.
—— Story of Helen Troy.
Whitney (Mrs.) Hitherto, 2 vols. cloth, 3s. 6d.
Fawcett (E.) Gentleman of Leisure.
Butler, Nothing to Wear.
ROSS, MARS, *Cantabria*, 21s.
ROSSINI, &c., See Great Musicians.
Rothschilds, by J. Reeves, 7s. 6d.
Roughing it after Gold, by Rux, new edit. 1s.
ROUSSELET. See Low's Standard Books.

ROWBOTHAM, F. J., *Prairie Land*, 5s.
Royal Naval Exhibition, a souvenir, illus. 1s.
RUBENS. See Great Artists.
RUGGLES, H. J., *Shakespeare's Method*, 7s. 6d.
RUSSELL, G. W. E., *Gladstone*. See Prime Ministers.
—— W. CLARK, *Mrs. Dines' Jewels*, 2s. 6d.
—— *Nelson's Words and Deeds*, 3s. 6d.
—— *Sailor's Language*, illus. 3s. 6d.
—— See also Low's Standard Novels and Sea Stories.
—— W. HOWARD, *Prince of Wales' Tour*, illust. 52s. 6d. and 84s.
Russia. See Foreign Countries.
Saints and their Symbols, 3s. 6d.
SAINTSBURY, G., *Earl of Derby.* See Prime Ministers.
SAINTINE, *Picciola*, 2s. 6d. and 2s. See Low's Standard Series.
SALISBURY, LORD. See Prime Ministers.
SAMUELS. See Low's Standard Series.
SANDARS, *German Primer*, 1s.
SANDEAU, *Seagull Rock*, 2s. and 2s. 6d. Low's Standard Series.
SANDLANDS, *How to Develop Vocal Power*, 1s.
SAUER, *European Commerce*, 5s.
—— *Italian Grammar* (Key, 2s.), 5s.
—— *Spanish Dialogues*, 2s. 6d.
—— *Spanish Grammar* (Key, 2s.), 5s.
—— *Spanish Reader*, new edit. 3s. 6d.
SAUNDERS, J., *Jaspar Deane*, 10s. 6d.

SCHAACK, M. J., *Anarchy*, 16s.
SCHAUERMANN, *Ornament for technical schools*, 10s. 6d.
SCHERER, *Essays in English Literature*, by G. Saintsbury, 6s.
SCHERR, *English Literature*, history, 8s. 6d.
SCHILLER'S *Prosa*, selections by Buchheim. Low's Series 2s. 6d.
SCHUBERT. See Great Musicians.
SCHUMANN. See Great Musicians.
SCHWEINFURTH. See Low's Standard Library.
Scientific Education of Dogs, 6s.
SCOTT, LEADER, *Renaissance of Art in Italy*, 31s. 6d.
—— See also Illust. Text-books.
—— SIR GILBERT, *Autobiography*, 18s.
—— W. B. See Great Artists.
SELMA, ROBERT, *Poems*, 5s.
SERGEANT, L. See Foreign Countries.
Shadow of the Rock, 2s. 6d.
SHAFTESBURY. See English Philosophers.
SHAKESPEARE, ed. by R. G. White, 3 vols. 36s.; édit. de luxe, 63s.
—— *Annals; Life & Work*, 2s.
—— *Hamlet*, 1603, also 1604, 7s. 6d.
—— *Hamlet*, by Karl Elze, 12s. 6d.
—— *Heroines*, by living painters, 105s.; artists' proofs, 630s.
—— *Macbeth*, with etchings, 105s. and 52s. 6d.
—— *Songs and Sonnets*. See Choice Editions.
—— *Taming of the Shrew*, adapted for drawing-room, paper wrapper, 1s.

SHEPHERD, *British School of Painting*, 2nd edit. 5s.; 3rd edit. sewed, 1s.
SHERIDAN, *Rivals*, col. plates, 52s. 6d. nett; art. pr. 105s. nett.
SHIELDS, G. O., *Big Game of North America*, 21s.
—— *Cruisings in the Cascades*, 10s. 6d.
SHOCK, W. H., *Steam Boilers*, 73s. 6d.
SIDNEY. See Gentle Life Series.
Silent Hour. See Gentle Life Series.
SIMKIN, *Our Armies*, plates in imitation of water-colour (5 parts at 1s.), 6s.
SIMSON, *Ecuador and the Putumayor*, 8s. 6d.
SKOTTOWE, *Hanoverian Kings*, new edit. 3s. 6d.
SLOANE, T. O., *Home Experiments*, 6s.
SMITH, HAMILTON, and LEGROS' *French Dictionary*, 2 vols. 16s., 21s., and 22s.
SMITH, EDWARD, *Cobbett*, 2 vols. 24s.
—— G., *Assyria*, 18s.
—— *Chaldean Account of Genesis*, new edit. by Sayce, 18s.
—— GERARD. See Illustrated Text Books.
—— T. ROGER. See Illustrated Text Books.
Socrates. See Bayard Series.
SOMERSET, *Our Village Life*, 5s.
Spain. See Foreign Countries.
SPAYTH, *Draught Player*, new edit. 12s. 6d.
SPIERS, *French Dictionary*, 2 vols. 18s., half bound, 2 vols., 21s.
SPRY. See Low's Stand. Library.

SPURGEON, C. H. See Preachers.

STANLEY, H. M., *Congo*, 2 vols. 42s. and 21s.
—— *In Darkest Africa*, 2 vols., 42s.
—— *Emin's Rescue*, 1s.
—— See also Low's Standard Library and Low's Standard Books.

START, *Exercises in Mensuration*, 8d.

STEPHENS, F. G., *Celebrated Flemish and French Pictures*, with notes, 28s.
—— See also Great Artists.

STERNE. See Bayard Series.

STERRY, J. Ashby, *Cucumber Chronicles*, 5s.

STEUART, J. A., *Letters to Living Authors*, new edit. 2s. 6d.; édit. de luxe, 10s. 6d.
—— See also Low's Standard Novels.

STEVENS, J. W., *Practical Workings of the Leather Manufacture*, illust. 18s.
—— T., *Around the World on a Bicycle*, over 100 illust. 16s.; part II. 16s.

STEWART, Dugald, *Outlines of Moral Philosophy*, 3s. 6d.

STOCKTON, F. R., *Casting Away of Mrs. Lecks*, 1s.
—— *The Dusantes*, a sequel, 1s.
—— *Merry Chanter*, 2s. 6d.
—— *Personally Conducted*, illust. by Joseph Pennell, 7s. 6d.
—— *Rudder Grangers Abroad*, 2s. 6d.
—— *Squirrel Inn*, illust. 6s.
—— *Story of Viteau*, illust. 5s. new edit. 3s. 6d.
—— *Three Burglars*, 1s. & 2s.
—— See also Low's Standard Novels.

STORER, F. H., *Agriculture*, 2 vols., 25s.

STOWE, Edwin. See Great Artists.
—— Mrs., *Flowers and Fruit from Her Writings*, 3s. 6d.
—— *Life . . . her own Words . . . Letters and Original Composition*, 15s.
—— *Life*, told for boys and girls, by S. A. Tooley, 5s., new edit. 2s. 6d. and 2s.
—— *Little Foxes*, cheap edit. 1s.; 4s. 6d.
—— *Minister's Wooing*, 1s.
—— *Pearl of Orr's Island*, 3s. 6d. and 1s.
—— *Uncle Tom's Cabin*, with 126 new illust. 2 vols. 18s.
—— See also Low's Standard Novels and Low's Standard Series.

STRACHAN, J., *New Guinea*, 12s.

STRANAHAN, *French Painting*, 21s.

STRICKLAND, F., *Engadine*, new edit. 5s.

STUTFIELD, *El Maghreb*, ride through Morocco, 8s. 6d.

SUMNER, C., *Memoir*, new edit. 2 vols. 36s.

Sweden and Norway. See Foreign Countries.

Sylvanus Redivivus, 10s. 6d.

SZCZEPANSKI, *Technical Literature*, a directory, 2s

TAINE, H. A., *Origines*, I. Ancient Régime, French Revolution, 3 vols.; Modern Régime, vol. I. 16s.

TAYLOR, H., *English Constitution*, 18s.
—— R. L., *Analysis Tables*, 1s.
—— *Chemistry*, 1s. 6d.

Techno-Chemical Receipt Book, 10s. 6d.

In all Departments of Literature. 29

TENNYSON. See Choice Editions.
Ten Years of a Sailor's Life, 7s. 6d.
THAUSING, Malt and Beer, 45s.
THEAKSTON, British Angling Flies, 5s.
Thomas à Kempis Birthday-Book, 3s. 6d.
—— Daily Text-Book, 2s. 6d.
—— See also Gentle Life Series.
THOMAS, BERTHA, House on the Scar, Tale of South Devon, 6s.
THOMSON, JOSEPH. See Low's Standard Library and Low's Standard Novels.
—— W., Algebra, 5s.; without Answers, 4s. 6d.; Key, 1s. 6d.
THORNTON, W. PUGIN, Heads, and what they tell us, 1s.
THORODSEN, J. P., Lad and Lass, 6s.
TICKNOR, G., Memoir, new edit., 2 vols. 21s.
TILESTON, MARY W., Daily Strength, 4s. 6d.
TINTORETTO. See Great Artists.
TITIAN. See Great Artists.
TODD, Life, by J. E. Todd, 12s.
TOURGEE. See Low's Standard Novels.
TOY, C. H., Judaism, 14s.
Tracks in Norway, 2s., n. ed. 1s.
TRAILL. See Prime Ministers.
Transactions of the Hong Kong Medical Society, vol. I. 12s. 6d.
TROMHOLT, Aurora Borealis, 2 vols., 30s.
TUCKER, Eastern Europe, 15s.
TUCKERMAN, B., English Fiction, 8s. 6d.
—— Lafayette, 2 vols. 12s.
TURNER, J. M. W. See Gr. Artists.

TYSON, Arctic Adventures, 25s.
TYTLER, SARAH. See Low's Standard Novels.
—— M. C., American Literature, vols. I. and II. 24s.
UPTON, H., Dairy Farming, 2s.
Valley Council, by P. Clarke, 6s.
VANDYCK and HALS. See Great Artists.
VANE, DENZIL, Lynn's Court Mystery, 1s.
—— See also Low's Standard Novels.
Vane, Young Sir Harry, 18s.
VELAZQUEZ. See Gr. Artists.
—— and MURILLO, by C. B. Curtis, with etchings, 31s. 6d. and 63s.
VERE, SIR F., Fighting Veres, 18s.
VERNE, J., Works by. See page 31.
Vernet and Delaroche. See Great Artists.
VERSCHUUR, G., At the Antipodes, 7s. 6d.
VIGNY, Cinq Mars, with etchings, 2 vols. 30s.
VINCENT, F., Through and through the Tropics, 10s. 6d.
—— MRS. H., 40,000 Miles over Land and Water, 2 vols. 21s.; also 3s. 6d.
VIOLLET-LE-DUC, Architecture, 2 vols. 31s. 6d. each.
WAGNER. See Gr. Musicians.
WALERY, Our Celebrities, vol. II. part i., 30s.
WALFORD, MRS. L. B. See Low's Standard Novels.
WALL, Tombs of the Kings of England, 21s.
WALLACE, L., Ben Hur, 2s. 6d.
—— Boyhood of Christ, 15s.
—— See also Low's Stand. Novs.

WALLACE, R., *Rural Economy of Australia and New Zealand*, illust. 21s. nett.

WALLER, C. H., *Names on the Gates of Pearl*, 3s. 6d.

—— *Silver Sockets*, 6s.

WALTON, *Angler*, Lea and Dove edit. by R. B. Marston, with photos., 210s. and 105s.

—— *Wallet-book*, 21s. & 42s.

—— T. H., *Coal-mining*, 25s.

WARNER, C. D., *Their Pilgrimage*, illust, by O. S. Reinhard, 7s. 6d.

—— See also LOW's Standard Novels and Low's Standard Series.

WARREN, W. F., *Paradise Found, Cradle of the Human Race*, illust. 12s. 6d.

WASHBURNE, *Recollections* (Siege of Paris, &c.), 2 vols. 36s.

WATTEAU. See Great Artists.

WEBER. See Great Musicians.

WEBSTER, *Spain*. See Foreign Countries and British Colonies.

WELLINGTON. See Bayard Series.

WELLS, H. P., *Salmon Fisherman*, 6s.

—— *Fly-rods and Tackle*, 10s. 6d.

—— J. W., *Brazil*, 2 vols. 32s.

WENZEL, *Chemical Products of the German Empire*, 25s.

West Indies. See Foreign Countries.

WESTGARTH, *Australasian Progress*, 12s.

WESTOBY, *Postage Stamps; a descriptive Catalogue*, 6s.

WHITE, RHODA E., *From Infancy to Womanhood*, 10s. 6d.

—— R. GRANT, *England without and within*, new ed. 10s. 6d.

—— *Every-day English*, 10s. 6d.

WHITE, R. GRANT, *Studies in Shakespeare*, 10s. 6d.

—— *Words and their Uses*, new edit. 5s.

—— W., *Our English Homer, Shakespeare and his Plays*, 6s.

WHITNEY, MRS. See LOW's Standard Series.

WHITTIER, *St. Gregory's Guest*, 5s.

—— *Text and Verse for Every Day in the Year*, selections, 1s. 6d.

WHYTE, *Asia to Europe*, 12s.

WIKOFF, *Four Civilizations*, 6s.

WILKES, G., *Shakespeare*, 16s.

WILKIE. See Great Artists.

WILLS, *Persia as it is*, 8s. 6d.

WILSON, *Health for the People*, 7s. 6d.

WINDER, *Lost in Africa.* See Low's Standard Books.

WINSOR, J., *Columbus*, 21s.

—— *History of America*, 8 vols. per vol. 30s. and 63s.

WITTHAUS, *Chemistry*, 16s.

WOOD, *Sweden and Norway.* See Foreign Countries.

WOLLYS, *Vegetable Kingdom*, 5s.

WOOLSEY, *Communism and Socialism*, 7s. 6d.

—— *International Law*, 6th ed. 18s.

—— *Political Science*, 2 vols. 30s.

WOOLSON, C. FENIMORE. See Low's Standard Novels.

WORDSWORTH. See Choice Editions.

Wreck of the "Grosvenor," 6d.

WRIGHT, H., *Friendship of God*, 6s.

—— T., *Town of Cowper*, 6s.

WRIGLEY, *Algiers Illust.* 45s

Written to Order, 6s.

www.ingramcontent.com/pod-product-compliance
Lightning Source LLC
Chambersburg PA
CBHW031417230426
43668CB00007B/343